# ARAM
# KHACHATURYAN

ARAM ILYCH KHACHATURYAN

# ARAM KHACHATURYAN

*Victor Yuzefovich*

Translators

**Nicholas Kournokoff**
*and*
**Vladimir Bobrov**

*Sphinx Press, Inc.*
*New York*

**Library of Congress Cataloging-in-Publication Data**

IUzefovich, Viktor Aronovich.
  Aram Ilych Khachaturyan

  1. Khachaturian, Aram Il'ich, 1903–1978.
2. Composers—Armenian S.S.R.—Biography. I. Title.
ML410.K39I95 1985      780'.92'4 [B]        85-18265
ISBN 0-8236-8658-2

The publisher wishes to thank Mr. Anatoli Kandalintsev of Novosti for suggesting the publication of this book and for his assistance, which was essential for its successful completion.

Manufactured in the United States of America

# Contents

# Introduction

*I highly value and passionately love the art of Aram Ilych Khachaturyan. He has brought Armenian music world fame. His compositions have made this music dear and understandable to the peoples of the whole world. . . .*

PANCHO VLADIGEROV

*For the young and ambitious musicians of Asia who strive to write music with European means of expression, the work and achievements of Aram Khachaturyan are like a beacon. In his music he expresses serene optimism and faith in humanity.*

NARAYANA MENON

*We Brazilians show a clear preference for Soviet composers and among them—Khachaturyan, as one of the most eminent. He is probably the only modern composer known to the broad public, from common working people to intellectuals.*

CLAUDIO SANTORO

*I am happy at this opportunity to convey my most sincere congratulations to an esteemed composer whose works I often performed to the general delight of myself and the public.*

HERBERT VON KARAJAN

*He "plowed up" new, hitherto untouched layers of the musical folklore of the Caucasus and, using the traditions of folk and professional music, created works of inimitable originality, thoroughly modern and permeated with the traits of genuine innovation. Today it is difficult to imagine Soviet and world musical culture without Khachaturyan.*

DMITRI SHOSTAKOVICH

*We have, long and rightly, been placing Aram Ilych Khachaturyan's works among the classics of Soviet music. For many years he has been ranking as an outstanding master, a creator of twentieth-century music who has made a priceless contribution to the treasury of modern art. And now, half a century after his first works appeared, we can say with certainty: His is living music, music that has thrilled several generations, music that will always be with us.*

TIKHON KHRENNIKOV

*Khachaturyan's music has always had a voice of its own, a voice clearly distinguishable in the great chorus of the twentieth century.*

RODION SHCHEDRIN

*Whatever Khachaturyan discovered has acquired meaning not only for himself. Continuing the experience of his great predecessors—the older generation of Transcaucasian composers—he opened a window into the wide world of musical culture for the music of the Soviet East. At the same time he started a new trend in Soviet music by giving invaluable aid in developing younger composers who started out much later.*

KARA KARAEV

. . . All these and much more is what this book is about. It was conceived together with Khachaturyan. For almost two years—alas, his last—I had the good fortune to associate with him, to have long talks and take down his answers to my questions. When our talks were broken off so abruptly by his death, I resolved to write a book that would be as close as possible to what Aram Ilych wanted . . . a book about his life, his meditations about his work, and his most important compositions, a book about the powerful influence exerted by Soviet reality on his artistic development, a book containing recollections of his meetings with writers, actors, and musicians. This is a documented narrative based on articles Khachaturyan wrote for the press, his many interviews and letters (taken from government archives and personal collections), impressions of Khachaturyan by outstanding musicians who knew him well, fragments of my talks with him, and, of course, his music.

I should like to express my sincere gratitude for valuable assistance to the staffs of archives in Moscow, Leningrad, and Erevan, to all who helped create this book by sharing with me the letters in their possession, and their recollections of Khachaturyan.

Armenia. You have just arrived, never having been here before. It is late, you are tired and fall asleep immediately. Next morning to your surprise you feel as though you are flying, borne so high that the horizon seems endless. This is how birds see the earth, this is how that wonderful Armenian painter, Martiros Saryan, must often have seen it. You are astonished by the brightness of the sun, no, not the sun itself, but the transparency of the light that seems to fill the whole world. Everything sparkles, shimmers, and rejoices, and this rejoicing sweeps you along with it.

What is this magic that has raised you to such heights, creating an entirely new impression of the world? It is delight at the beauty of this flourishing land called Armenia. It lays spread out before you, cradled by the snow-capped mountains, looking like a carpet woven of pure colors by light itself. You seem to be all eyes, but it is not so. Listen, in your ears you will hear music, the music of Aram Khachaturyan. You hear it because it is a hymn to this beautiful world. You hear it because, to quote an American critic, "If light, pure light were to be melted down into sound, the music it produced would be the music of Aram Khachaturyan."

VICTOR YUZEFOVICH

# *Childhood and Youth*

*We will most likely arrive at the culture of communism in an historically short time. Why do I think so? Because of the experience of building national cultures in the Soviet Union.*

*Never before has life been so stirringly beautiful, so interesting, so rich in historically significant events, as in our epoch, the epoch of building communism. Never before have artists been faced with such fascinating tasks, never have they had such enormous reading, viewing and listening audiences.*

*I believe an artist is truly innovative when he finds his own way of expressing his time, finds precise and convincing forms for expressing the new content.*

*—Aram Khachaturyan*

*Was it possible for mother,*
*and for me, a child,*
*to see*
*That from birth*
*He wore a bracelet,*
*of poetry?*

OVANES SHIRAZ

Aram Ilych Khachaturyan was born June 6, 1903, near Tiflis, Georgia, as Tbilisi was then called. From the backwoods of tsarist Russia he came to Moscow to study, to absorb culture at a time when the Communist Party was working to help the formerly oppressed peoples shed their economic and cultural backwardness. When the first five year plan was adopted in 1929, he became a student at the Moscow Conservatory, crowning his own "five year plan" with his First Symphony.

Like all great artists Khachaturyan lived at the crossroads of the two mainstreams of his society. All his work was dedicated to communist ideals. His music became a historical fact, thanks to the implementation of Lenin's national policy. Khachaturyan was a product of the times, of the epoch, and of his socialist country, a fact in which he took pride. So rapid was his rise to the heights of professionalism and musical maturity that he won recognition as a shining star of Soviet culture, indeed, a star of all twentieth-century progressive culture before World War Two. His compositions came pouring out as though from a horn of plenty: the Piano Concerto, *Poem to Stalin,* the ballet *Happiness,* the Violin Concerto, and music for the theatrical productions *The Widow of Valencia* and *Masquerade.*

When war broke out and the country bristled with antitank

barriers, Khachaturyan's music, so familiar, now seemed grimmer and more compact, and it conveyed deeper philosophical insight. That was when he created his Second Symphony, known also as the *Bell* Symphony.

Then, in a burst of energy, came the ballet *Spartacus.*

Aram Khachaturyan was born the year the Wright brothers made their historical flight. He lived to witness the beginning of the space age and was a friend of Yuri Gagarin, the world's first astronaut.

Khachaturyan was born in Kodjori, a suburb of Tiflis that was later to become part of the city proper. He always had the warmest recollections of his native town. He revisited Tbilisi many times, walking the old streets and finding the houses where he had lived with his parents at different times. The population of this city now numbers more than a million, about ten times more than in Khachaturyan's childhood. But Tiflis had always been the industrial and cultural center of the Transcaucasus, and more important, a city with international traditions. Georgians, Armenians, and Azerbaijanians lived side by side, all feeling at home. Khachatur Abovyan, the writer and educator, outstanding representative of Armenian culture and founder of the new national literature and new literary language, lived there too. It was the home also of Gabriel Sundukyan, the writer and playwright after whom Armenia's foremost drama theater is named, and author of the finest poetic interpretation of the Armenian ballad "David Sasunsky." One of Armenia's best known poets, Ovanes Tumanyan, lived there too. The operas *Anush*, by Armen Tigranyan, and *Almast*, by Alexander Spendiarov, are based on his poems.

The colorful scenes of old Tiflis, now practically non-existent, were etched deeply in Khachaturyan's memory: the houses with verandas hanging precariously over the Kura river and seeming to race one another up Mt. David. The hustle and bustle of the narrow streets with their small stores, jewelers, and coffee shops. Then, of course, there was the market with its green-striped watermelons, succulent melons, grapes, peaches,

4

nuts, dark-purple eggplants, blood-red pomegranates, and greens of every variety. Doors rarely were closed in Tiflis; life teemed in the streets and small yards. Many spoke of it as a city always open to the sun. Although life was not easy for most of the people, they never lost their gaiety; like children they loved life and infected everyone with their carefree optimism.

Young Khachaturyan saw characters and scenes in Tiflis like those depicted in the works of Niko Pirosmani, Georgia's outstanding self-taught painter: a bearded janitor wearing a badge on his cap; a restaurant owner with impressive whiskers, holding a skewer of aromatic shashlik; a peasant on an oxcart bringing barrels of wine from Kahetia; a water carrier with a huge goatskin of water on his shoulders; a doctor holding an umbrella, riding his donkey at a leisurely pace on his way to a patient; a proud horseman in national garb sitting astride his prancing steed; a *kinto** in billowing pantaloons; and young ladies showing off the latest in fashions and hairdos. A truly unique and inimitable city with a symphony of color and aromas all its own. But it was the city's sounds that Khachaturyan best remembered.

"Tbilisi, they say, is a city that sings. This is really so," Aram Ilych remarked.

I always call it a surprising city of sounds, where life—and this is true of the present to a certain extent—was so much more open in the days of my youth than in our northern cities like Moscow and Leningrad. The sounds came at you from all sides; the city was saturated with music. The sounds of the *tara* and *kemancha*, the *zurna* and *duduk*,† monophonic Armenian songs and polyphonic Georgian folk songs, small groups of musicians playing folk instruments, the street calls of the quince vendors—such were the sounds of my childhood. . . .
I can still see the fruit vendor carrying his *tabahi*—a huge wooden tray resting on his head on a towel twisted into a ring.

*Kinto*—a street peddler, merrymaker, streetsinger of sorts; a happy-go-lucky, carefree person.
†Transcaucasian folk instruments: The *Tara* and *kemancha* are string instruments, the *zurna* and *duduk*, wind instruments.

He goes from yard to yard, singing melodic couplets which by themselves would be excellent material for a composer. Add to this the numerous family occasions where everyone sings, and the sad events which bring together many people and where there is also singing. And finally the folk singing and dancing, the traditions that greatly influenced me.

Khachaturyan's parents had a hard time making ends meet. They came from Aza Gothana, a mountain village in the Nahichevan region. Until recently, their dilapidated little shack was still standing next to the old church.

"It was there I saw the land of my forefathers," Aram Khachaturyan wrote.

The sky is bluer there and the door to our house creaked so pathetically.

Our family had a great yearning for culture and art, but the ever-present lack of money kept these desires within narrow bounds. Our parents found it a strain to give their sons even an elementary education and make something of them. . . .

My father, Ilya [Egiya] Khachaturyan, a Tbilisi bookbinder, brought up four sons. Three of us dedicated our lives to art. The eldest, Suren, became a director of the Moscow Art Theater. The second, Levon, was a well-known singer on the radio. I, the youngest member of the family, devoted myself to composing music.

Khachaturyan's father, Egiya, left for Tiflis at the age of thirteen to make a life for himself. Aram left home when he was eighteen and headed for Moscow to become a musician. Social conditions at the end of the 1870s and immediately after the revolution were quite different, of course. The people with whom father and son associated in their day were different, too, nor can there be any comparison between their natural talents. They were very much alike in character, however. Nina Musanyan, a friend of Aram's during his years at the Conservatory, says of his father, "Though no longer young, the moment you met him he gave you the impression of a very warmhearted and very active person. He was clearly exceptional; Aram had obviously inherited many of his traits."

Aram Ilych thought so too.

Father and I were known for our tireless energy, determination and thirst for knowledge, though expressed in different ways and directed toward different goals.

Father came to Tiflis wearing bast sandals and with just a few coppers in his pocket, but with the most radiant hopes in his heart. . . . An illiterate peasant from an isolated village, he not only became an expert bookbinder in a short time but also made a name for himself among the Tiflis bookbinders and attracted many customers, particularly Russians. Here he also learned to read and write a little Armenian; he was familiar with Russian type, too, because he dealt with Russian books; he could even scribble his name in Russian.

At the beginning of the nineties Father was able to purchase his employer's shop, for the business had gone to pieces, the old man now being unable to manage it.

Thinking of my father, I can say that he was truly talented. . . . Besides his great energy and amazing industriousness, he had a nimble mind, a sharp eye for reality, and a good sense of humor. . . .

Father had an exceptionally vivid personality. Despite an explosive temperament, he was kind and cooled off quickly. He would never hold a grudge against anyone for long. I remember he was terrified of the police; this was strange, for he had lived by honest labor all his life. . . .

There were many books in the home of this modest bookbinder—the classics in the Armenian language, also newspapers and magazines. Despite his great yearning for culture and knowledge he had far too little education for me to say that I was surrounded with books in my childhood. Later, however, I was lucky, for Soviet power gave me everything—an education, culture, and encouragement in my boldest plans.

Khachaturyan's father had a natural gift for music; he knew many Armenian and Azerbaijan folk songs and liked to sing at home with the rest of the family in the evening. He was particularly fond of a song by the folk bard Jivani, "The Storm, Like the Winter, Will Come and Go." Though he lived in Tiflis for some time, he never forgot the Armenian peasant songs which Aram, living in the city, could hear only from his parents. People who speak of the folklore that influenced Khachatur-yan's work often forget this fact.

Aram always spoke very warmly of his mother. His first composition for cello and piano, "Song of the Wandering Ashug" (1925), written while he was still a student, was dedicated to her.

There was nothing about my mother—Kumash Sarkisovna—to distinguish her from the environment in which I grew up. She was a wonderful woman, completely devoted to her home, her children, and husband. My love and respect for her grew as I matured. Mother died at an old age. Unfortunately, she lost her eyesight early in life. This darkened her life and those of her children. . . .

Father did not help much in our upbringing. The shop kept him busy; we saw him only in the evening. It was all Mother's doing. She was strict to a point, but gentle, soft-spoken, and fair.

She was religious and regularly attended the Armenian church near our home. On Sundays she would take me with her dressed in my best suit. I cannot say I liked going to church, where I had to stand for long spells hemmed in by skirts.

Now that I am well along in years, I can say in all certainty that I got my love of music from my mother. She sang Armenian folk songs very expressively, with great feeling. They left a deep impression on me.

It is interesting that my mother, from whom I heard so many Armenian and Azerbaijan folk songs in my childhood, especially liked to sing when she was alone. Could it be that I inherited from her my dislike, or, more precisely, my complete inability to compose in the presence of others, even my immediate family?

Khachaturyan's musical consciousness developed passively at first, mostly through the sounds he heard about him. He tried to absorb everything and realized only much later how varied were Tbilisi's tonal effects. The closely interlaced traditions of Georgian, Armenian, and Azerbaijan cultures, though each preserved its singular traits, provided the soil from which emerged an absolutely distinctive culture, which scholars of Transcaucasian art usually refer to as the Tiflis culture.

"In those days, life in Tiflis . . . had a distinctive aura all its own, so much so that it could hardly be ascribed to a single nationality. It was Tiflis; and that explained everything," wrote Alexander Kamensky, the art critic. This aptly describes the musical atmosphere surrounding Khachaturyan in his youth. As he said, "Along with the wonderful folk melodies, my still undeveloped ear obediently took in the cheap, shallow songs, the songs which the *kintos* sang in the streets, and the tunes from the music halls, to say nothing of the dance melodies that set my teeth on edge. . . ."

And still, Khachaturyan was instinctively drawn to the folk musicians; his natural artistic intuition did not deceive him as to the purity of their art.

> Before I started school, spending my days out in the streets with the other boys of my age, I loved to listen for hours on end to the itinerant musicians, the *ashugs* and *sazandars*.* Their songs and legends acclaimed freedom, brotherhood, love, and courage, and exposed evil, violence, and injustice. For this they were called in the East "the artistic conscience of the people." In the simple but inspired improvisations of these poets and musicians I heard echoes of the folk songs my mother used to sing. But when sung by the ashugs these seemingly familiar melodies struck me as being much richer, more beautiful, enchanting one with their free, colorful interpretation and the magic of the rhythm found only in folk art. Greedily I absorbed this art, although there was a good deal that I did not understand at the time.

But Aram did not confine his interests to music alone. A lively and energetic boy, he was never still for a moment, now running to the circus with his brother Levon, now going to the small movie house nearby, or just chasing around with his friends through the maze of side streets and yards, fighting or wrestling and coming home with a black eye. He also played

*Ashugs* were Armenian bards or minstrels. *Sazandars* were performers who played the *sazeh*, a pizzicato folk instrument; the term was applied also to musicians who played other folk instruments.

Caucasian *lakhti*, a game requiring agility and even courage. Did Khachaturyan ever lose his youthful zest? Did his "shiners" influence his development as an individual?

I do not think they helped my formation as an individual. However, childhood years are, after all, childhood years and children's temperaments and interests differ. As a boy I was crazy about soccer and was known among my friends as a good forward. I won international acclaim as a soccer player long before I became known as a musician. Foreign troops were stationed in Tbilisi when I was still a boy. Soviet power was established there only in 1921. I remember once going to see a match between the English and the Indians. One of the men on the Indian team didn't show up. I do not recall just how they learned about me, but I was asked to "defend the flag" of India; in three or four minutes I scored a goal against the English.

Many years later I played billiards with no less enthusiasm, particularly while living in the old apartment house of the Composers Union on Miussi Street in Moscow.

A zest in the broader sense has always been a feature of my creative work. I believe a composer when writing should be in a state bordering on the ecstatic. You must give yourself completely to your work."

In time the boy became a teenager, then a young man. Little by little, music became his world; passive interest gave way to attempts at composing. Neither his lessons at school—he was first sent to a private boarding school, and later his father's friends got him into the School of Commerce, where the majority of the children were from well-to-do homes—nor the rowdy children's games were able to take his mind off music.

As a child I loved to sing and beat out rhythms with my hands. My love of music often interfered with my lessons. There were times when instead of studying I would sing my favorite melodies for hours on end.

Up in the attic I would take a copper pan and zealously beat out rhythms that had impressed me, trying out different variations and combinations. This early musical activity afforded me great pleasure but nearly drove my parents to distraction. "What shall I do with that crazy improvisor?" my father would exclaim after hours of my drumming in the attic. Nevertheless, he did buy me a cheap, beat-up old piano that should have gone as firewood. I quickly learned to pick out folk and dance tunes by ear and would blissfully bang them out with one or two fingers. . . .

Finding the right keys to produce the familiar melody was a helter-skelter process at first. Later came clumsy attempts at some sort of harmony and at connecting the melody in the right hand with the chords in the left. These, if you like, were my first steps at composing. . . .

Though utterly ignorant of the most elementary musical theory, I did manage to play popular songs and dances, adding some simple improvisations of my own.

Possibly it was this absolute freedom in little Aram's musical consciousness, the absence of any encumbering standards, that contributed to the formation of his tireless creative imagination.

His boyhood friends were quick to perceive his abilities. "I knew Aram Khachaturyan back in the days when we went to school together," recalls Martin Mazmanyan.

His brother Levon and I were in the same class in the Armenian Seminary in Tbilisi. I would go to the Khachaturyan home almost every day. Levon and I would do our homework together, then we would play the piano and sing. Aram played very well by ear. He would pick out the harmony to any melody and promptly accompany us. His whole family was very musical, but we always particularly admired his talent.

Nevertheless, his interest in music met with little understanding. His parents were skeptical, his school teachers unperceptive.

Musicians were not respected among us. When I was living in Moscow my father, who loved folk music, learned that I planned to enroll at the Gnessin School of Music. "Do you plan to become a *sazandar*?" he asked with bitter irony. Adults believed that music was no profession for a man. Father wanted me to be an engineer or doctor, anything but a musician.

Here is how Khachaturyan recalls Musheg Agayan, his singing teacher in the boarding school: "We had singing lessons once a week in our school under Musheg Lazarevich Agayan. . . . We would learn Russian, Armenian, and Georgian folk songs, which we sang with great pleasure while our teacher accompanied us on an old piano."

The School of Commerce had an amateur brass band, and Aram became a member.

I learned to play the instruments rather quickly, but I soon tired of marches and dance music. Despondent over the monotonous and simple scores I had to play [Aram played third tenor horn], I started improvising counterpoint and rhythmic structure on what we were playing. "Young man, if you persist in your impertinence with such zeal I shall chase you out," said the conductor on noticing my experiments. So I had to tone down my enthusiasm and continue my variations more carefully, trying not to irritate our conductor's not too fine ear.

In an early autobiography, Khachaturyan recalled that in that brass band "I paid more attention to organizing groups of brass. I also composed marches and waltzes for the band but someone else had to take down the notes."

Besides being a colorful city, Tbilisi boasted the best cultural and musical activities in the Transcaucasus. Khachaturyan, however, was influenced almost exclusively by folk music. One of the determining factors here was the family's social and cultural level. But the professionally performed music from the classical repertoire that he did absorb in those years left a deep impression. That was true of the Armenian choral music included in the repertoire of the chorus led by the composer Spiridon Melikyan, in which Aram's brother Levon sang.

Khachaturyan's only visit to the local opera was also unforgettable.

I bought a ticket with my meager savings. *Abesalom and Eteri*, by the classic Georgian composer, Zakhariya Paliashvili, was being shown that evening. The opera had just been staged, and this was one of its first performances. I was only sixteen at the time.

I can't find words to describe the strong artistic impact and excitement that gripped me from the opening bars of the orchestral introduction, when the curtain parted and the opera began. . . .

It is difficult for me to say today what astounded me most then—the brilliant opera, with its heroic and romantic plot in which both of the leading characters perish; the fabulous sets and costumes, or the wonderful mass scenes and dances. Most likely it was everything I saw and heard, which is how it should be in an opera.

The intonations and rhythms of Georgian folk music, familiar since childhood, transformed and developed by the hand of the master, now seemed to me to find a new, exciting, and wonderful embodiment. I remember also that someone pointed to a man sitting nearby, saying "That's the author." That was my first encounter with great music, my first glimpse of a living composer.

It was then, in the spring of 1919, that I discovered the boundless expanses of truly great art.

The idea of studying music had now taken complete command of me.

More and more Khachaturyan dreamt of studying music, although many years were to pass before the dream came true—turbulent years for his parents and for all of Tbilisi.

The First World War, which had broken out in 1914, brought great hardships to the Khachaturyan family. People needed neither books nor bookbinders. One by one, the older sons left home: Suren had left for Moscow back in 1908, and now Vaginak left for Ekaterinodar (now Krasnodar). Nineteen-fifteen, the year of the tragic Armenian genocide at the hands of the Osman Empire, when hundreds of thousands of innocent men, women, and children were brutally massacred, now obsessed all Armenians.

In the spring of 1915, driven by panic and fright, mother and father with their two younger sons abandoned the house and shop, and set out on the long trek to Ekaterinodar in the Kuban, where Vaginak lived. Those were terrible days of danger, of moral and physical strain. We walked almost the whole way on foot, even down the Georgian Military Highway, carrying our meager belongings on our backs.

Luckily, the Turkish hangmen did not make it to Tiflis. That same autumn we returned home.

The economic crisis and destruction, the revolutionary days of 1917, the establishment of Soviet power in Georgia, the counterrevolution, domination by the Menshevik government and foreign armies—German, English, American, and French, with soldiers from all over the world, even India, roaming the streets of Tiflis, and the hunger, when for weeks on end there was nothing but bread and water—all this left its imprint on Aram's mind. He recalled that no suffering or privations could dampen his parents' optimism.

Soviet power was finally established in Georgia on February 25, 1921. The Mensheviks fled and the foreign armies were driven out. A new era now began in the history of the Transcaucasus. A few months earlier, on November 29, 1920, Armenia was proclaimed a Soviet republic.

"With all my being I felt the birth of the new world that broke into my life so turbulently," Aram recalled.

A propaganda train was organized in the summer of 1921 with Armenian art workers living in Georgia. I was invited to take part and readily agreed. Our group traveled from Tbilisi to Erevan, visiting towns and villages in Armenia to explain the great ideas of the revolution, hand out leaflets and pamphlets, and hold meetings and combination lecture-concerts.

One old freight car, with a piano standing by the open door, was used as a stage. When our train would stop at a station siding I would start to play rousing marches while others of our team would call the people to the train. We would start a meeting, with singing and music, after which leaflets would be handed out. I still remember the genuine delight of the mixed crowd."

The train finally reached Erevan. What were Khachaturyan's first impressions of the city? About a century and a half ago, Alexander Pushkin, traveling on horseback through Armenia, asked, "What's new in Erevan?" "The plague," came the frightful answer. In the early 1920s this ancient city, once known as Erebuni, the capital of Urartu, was still a dirty provincial town with no more than sixty thousand inhabitants. The dominating colors were black, for most of the houses were built of the local black *tufa* stone, and yellow, the color of the unpaved streets. The clock tower over the commandant's office, one of the few large buildings, rarely showed the correct time, for the hands were often moved by the many crows who liked to perch on them. Time seemed to stand still there.

The city's true rebirth was to start a few years later, when outstanding representatives of Armenian science and culture took up residence there: the writer Alexander Shirvanzade, from Paris; the composer Alexander Spendiarov, from the Crimea; the conductor Konstantin Saradjev, from Moscow; the painter Martiros Saryan, from Rostov; the film director Amo Bek-Nazarov, from Tbilisi. Erevan would soon have a conservatory, a symphony orchestra, and an opera house.

Aram was delighted by this trip, from which he brought back so many impressions—his first sight of Armenia and its surroundings that charmed him so, the hundreds of people he met there, and, most important, the fervid optimism so characteristic of those first postrevolutionary years.

Could Aram have imagined then, as he shared his impressions of the trip with his family and friends, that he would soon embark on a much longer trip?

His brother Suren returned from Moscow in July 1921. Fourteen years older then Aram, he was a graduate of Moscow University's history and philology department. He was versatile and well read, with a good knowledge of Russian, Armenian, and foreign classics. But even in his student days he had been most interested in the stage. He had met such outstanding personalities of the Moscow Art Theater as Konstantin Stanislavsky, Vladimir Nemirovich-Danchenko, and Leopold Sulerzhitsky. Suren Khachaturov (the name he used in Moscow) became assistant stage director and, later, head of the arts and sets department of this celebrated company, not of the Art Theater itself, but of its newly formed Studio One. There he collaborated closely with Leopold Sulerzhitsky, Evgeny Vakhtangov, and Mikhail Chekhov, the founders of this studio.

Besides his work for Studio One, Suren was also employed in the Commission on Culture and Enlightenment of the Moscow Soviet and the theatrical department of the People's Commissariat of Public Instruction. He also organized national theatrical studios in Moscow. One such studio, the Armenian, which had given its first performance in 1919, was sorely in need of actors, a national repertory, national folklore material, and broad contacts with Armenian intellectuals in the Transcaucasus. It was to help meet these needs that Suren came to Tbilisi, with a mandate signed by Anatoly Lunacharsky—People's Commissar of Public Instruction.

Energetic like his father, Suren stirred up a flurry of activity in Tbilisi and in Erevan, which he visited subsequently. He was enthusiastic about the idea of a new Armenian theater, insisting that it must have a broad repertory. In his diligent search for young people of talent, he was able to infuse them with his love of the theater. He persuaded several persons outstanding in Armenian culture, among them the poet Ovanes Tumanyan and the writer Derenik Demirchyan, to sit on his commission in Tbilisi.

The next step was back to Moscow, for the cultural soil in Armenia and even in Tiflis was not fertile enough to foster the growth of young actors. It was no simple matter to get the future studio members to the capital, for there was destruction everywhere and transportation was almost totally paralyzed.

Khachaturyan remembered how Suren looked: "handsome, very smart, and elegant in his own way. He was respectful with our parents and watched his younger brothers with apparent interest."

Levon had a good baritone, and Suren decided to take him to Moscow. "The boys follow me around as though I were their father, eating me up with their eyes, pouncing on my every word, waiting to hear if I will take them," wrote Suren in a letter to his wife from Tbilisi. "I really love them, for in them I perceive the genius and spirit of my people."

"Suren suggested that I, too, go with him to Moscow, promising to help and encourage me," Khachaturyan recalled. " 'You're no commercial consultant,' he said, 'you had better turn to art.' "

It took their train twenty-four days to reach Moscow. They traveled in two freight cars fitted out with plank beds. All around them the civil war was raging. Their cars were shunted off onto sidings at every whistlestop. No one knew how long they would have to wait before continuing on their way to the capital. On one such stop, in the village of Baladjara, all the theater people crowded around and heartily greeted a man unknown to Khachaturyan. This was Martiros Saryan, who was taking his family in an identical freight car in the opposite direction, to Erevan, to help build a new cultural life in Soviet Armenia.

"I hadn't heard of Saryan at the time, although he was quite well known. But then, whom did I know except our few friends in Tiflis?"

Years later Khachaturyan and Saryan often recalled that chance meeting on the road.

In all the villages where the train stopped, the future studio members would improvise concerts, gathering large, eager crowds. Led by Martin Mazmanyan, who had the choral class at the studio, the young people would sing Armenian and Russian songs. Khachaturyan wrote that

> during these concerts I played the piano, accompanied the singers and dancers, and conducted the chorus, boldly playing polkas, waltzes, and mazurkas. . . . The food I had taken from home lasted only three days and we had very little money. So whatever we received for those concerts, a loaf of bread or a basket of vegetables, was very welcome.

It is difficult to say just what Aram could have played on the piano in those days. He recalls, not without irony:

My trip with the propaganda train, my ability to pick out melodies, and my inclination to improvise were a big help in my concert activity. Later I learned that it was this that attracted Ashkhen Mamikonyan's attention. While still on the road to Moscow she advised me to study music seriously.

Mamikonyan, who taught rhythm and singing in Suren Khachaturov's Armenian studio, was exceptionally talented. She was in her last year at the Institute of Rhythmic Education, learning the then very popular Jacques Dalcroz system. Earlier she had also studied under Mikhail Gnessin, to whom she would soon send Aram Khachaturyan.

# Understanding Life, People, and Art

*Music had such power over me that I was ready to
overcome any osbstacles for its sake.*

ARAM KHACHATURYAN

Khachaturyan's rise to fame began as he, a provincial young
man just starting to master the ABCs of music, found himself
in the vortex of the musical and theatrical life of Moscow. The
cultural revolution was just starting in the country, and huge
new audiences were getting their first taste of art and beginning
to influence it. Moscow, a huge city so totally different from
Tiflis, swamped Aram with vivid impressions. He moved in with
his brother Suren, who lived on a small sidestreet in the center
of the city. It seemed that anyone who was anybody frequented
that house; the debates and discussions of those to be found
there revolved around art. Luckily, Aram knew enough Russian
not to be confused by similar-sounding words that had entirely
different meanings in Armenian.

Every day Aram came to know his brother better and to
respect him more.

My older brother was a great authority for me. I realized that
considering our family background he had made great intellectual progress. Everything he said, every word of advice, carried
great weight with me.

He was my teacher in the fullest and most human sense of
the word. He taught me about life, taught me to understand
and love art, and also to think and act independently. A tireless
seeker and courageous advocate of new trends, his way of thinking invariably served me as a moral ideal.

18

The everyday, the ordinary, did not seem to suit my brother. Invariably brimming over with enthusiasm and inspiration, possessed of a free and fiery imagination, a probing mind and a pure and kind heart—all these treasured human qualities were happily joined in him. With his drama studio Suren started a wonderful movement that brought new life to the theatrical culture of Soviet Armenia.

Since he was the first to ignite the flame that illuminated our entire national artistic life, our writers, painters, actors, directors, musicians, and sculptors focused their attention on his activities.

An associate of the great director Konstantin Stanislavsky, Suren Khachaturov's ideas and convictions on art were progressive. Dreaming of a new Armenian theater, he wrote:

Our future theater must be founded on a heroic-romantic repertory, a world repertory. It is time we rejected our purely traditional subjects with all their negative and positive sides . . . we must give the peasants and workers access to the treasures of world culture.

In those days not everyone in Armenia shared his views. But they were important not only for the Armenian theater, but for the theater in general. They played a decisive role also in forming the views of young Aram, particularly his views on the relationship between the artist and the people, always an acute problem, especially so at a time when millions were gaining access to art. As he wrote,

Performances, concerts, heated discussions on the ways music, poetry, the theater, and the future cinema should develop—all of this was new, interesting, and fascinating, although not always understandable.

I cannot say now whether I fully realized what was going on around me then. I do know, however, that I matured as a person and a citizen under the direct influence of the intensive artistic life around me in Moscow.

The Bolshoi and Maly Theaters, the Moscow Art Theater,

the theaters of Meyerhold and Tairov, and performances by numerous small studios made Moscow at the start of the twenties truly a theatrical Mecca.

One of Khachaturyan's most vivid impressions came from the inimitable work of Mikhail Chekhov, an actor at the Art Theater's Studio One. Mikhail, Anton Chekhov's nephew, was a bright star on the theatrical horizon in a period in which there was no shortage of stars. "I saw Mikhail Chekhov in all his roles several times," recalled Khachaturyan,

> and his inexhaustible imagination, his excellent transformations, his emotional versatility, and his endless ability to vary the pattern of the role, to invent ever new suggested circumstances, as Stanislavsky termed it, never failed to amaze me. I always tell my students that one can watch and listen without end to a true work of art. Mikhail Chekhov was just such a work.

Suren's interests were not restricted to the theater. He understood the beautiful in all its forms, was deeply moved by music, and knew how to listen to it. He loved to sing, played the mandolin and piano, and was always ready to improvise. From Tiflis Suren wrote to his wife:

> There are such musical works here by our countless talented composers that were I to bring all of them to Moscow I would eclipse that entire Orient about which persons like Ippolitov-Ivanov speak and write so much. I collect and buy music, even music that has not yet been published and is still with the authors in manuscript.

What enthusiasm there is in those words! what interesting material for reflection regarding the import for Aram of his talks with his brother about the future of national art, and about Oriental and quasi-Oriental music.*

*Before leaving home for Moscow, Suren accidentally broke a mirror, which augured bad luck. His life, which had begun so brilliantly, ended tragically. One of his friends wrote that he burned with enthusiasm for the theater and was consumed by that fire. Suren died of tuberculosis at the age of forty-five. He no longer had his studio, which he had been forced to leave after a conflict with studio members. He died fully aware that his creative potential and his talent were not enough to found the theater of his dreams.

Suren and his wife, the painter Sarah Dunaeva, were like father and mother to Aram. "I was nineteen years old, full of energy, hope, and good intentions. I wanted to study, but how, where, and what? That I didn't know," Khachaturyan reminisced.

> In that difficult, changing period of my life, my brother Suren guided me wisely and carefully in my education. He did everything to introduce me into an atmosphere of work where there would be nothing drab, none of the mediocrity of thoughtless existence.
>
> To this day, whenever I think of my brother I am proud and happy for my good luck in associating with such a gifted person. No matter where I happened to be in later years, no matter how interesting the people I met or how strong the impressions of my whole life—the image of my brother remains for me the most vivid and significant. . . .

On his brother's advice Aram began studying biology in Moscow University's science department.

> I cannot say that biology accorded with my vocation in the slightest degree. What, after all, did I know about biology? I must admit it was difficult for me to get used to the subjects I had to study, to the laboratory work and to dissecting frogs. I did not flee the university as Hector Berlioz fled the anatomy theater in his time. But as in his case, musical interests gradually gained over all others.

Nevertheless, Khachaturyan remained in the university for three years, studying chemistry, plant morphology, osteology, and anatomy. He was eager to read and learn as much as possible. There were many interesting books in Suren's home, from Dumas's *The Count of Monte Cristo* to Russian and world classics.

> I remember that I started reading voraciously at an early age. The plot was not the only thing that interested me: I had to find out how the story was constructed, where the exposition lay, where the intrigue started, where the reminiscences and recap-

itulations were placed. This analytical reading remained with me in later years. Possibly it slowed down my acquaintance with the treasures of world literature, but it unquestionably broadened my knowledge and helped me greatly in my future work.

Though young Khachaturyan had not yet begun studying music, he seized every opportunity to play the piano and to improvise for his student friends, who liked to hear him play Armenian folk songs. For Aram the piano in Suren's home was beautiful compared with the dilapidated instrument he had used in the attic of his home in Tiflis. At times Aram would even venture to improvise for Suren's guests, invariably drawing favorable comments on his talent.

He was enraptured by his first encounter with the world of classical European music. Beethoven's Ninth Symphony was played at the first concert he attended in the Grand Hall of the Conservatory.

It shook me to the depths. The impressions of that concert have remained etched in my memory for all time.

I shall never forget the thunderous impact of that evening, one of the strongest artistic experiences of my whole life. I shan't say anything about the music and of this, the first symphony orchestra I had ever heard. I was astonished by the very atmosphere of the concert, the excitement in the huge hall, the rapt attention of the audience. . . .

I recall that I watched as avidly as I listened. I was especially interested in observing each instrument, each group of instruments in the orchestra. Though familiar with the brasses from my days with the School of Commerce amateur orchestra in Tiflis, I knew little or nothing about the strings. . . .

The conductor on that memorable evening was Alexander Hessin. Besides Beethoven's Ninth the program included Rachmaninov's Second Piano Concerto, played by Konstantin Igumnov. For Khachaturyan that, too, was a great experience.

The enormous gulf between the ideas about music which he had brought with him from Tiflis and the brilliant heights of professional musical art that opened up before him in Moscow might have frightened him away from any daring attempts to conquer those heights. Besides, his brother had not shown much faith in his abilities.

> It was only in 1929, when prominent musicians were congratulating me after the premiere in the Small Hall of the Conservatory of my song-poem "In Honor of the Ashugs," that Suren said: "You know Aram, I think I was mistaken; I believe you really can become a composer. . . ."

Luckily, Aram survived the early tests of character and dedication that fate had in store for him. "Aptitude, that is, a good ear, is not enough to study music, and difficulties awaited me at every turn. But my desire to study music was strong. Music already had such a hold on me that I was prepared to overcome all obstacles for its sake."

In the autumn of 1922 Aram crossed the threshold of a small, old house in one of Moscow's sidestreets. This was the Gnessin Music School. Eager to give the people musical knowledge, the Gnessin sisters—Elena, Evgeniya, and Maria—had founded a school in Moscow in 1895 which was destined to play an important role in Russia's musical education. It later came to be called the Gnessin Music and Pedagogical Institute, where other members of the family—Olga, Elizaveta, and Mikhail—also worked, where many outstanding musicians taught, and where, in time, Khachaturyan himself would teach.

> I faced the admissions committee without even the most elementary knowledge of theory. To show my voice and ear, I glibly sang a heart-rending romance, something on the order of "Break the Glass, There Is No More Wine," causing members of the committee to smile. . . .

Aram also played several dance tunes on the piano. "I remember that I easily passed the tests for ear, rhythm, and musical memory, though this was the first time I ever had to do anything like it."

The committee decided unanimously to enroll Aram Khachaturyan in the Gnessin Music School. He was twenty years old then, older than the other students.

A great deal has been written about the Gnessin family and their contribution to the development of professional musical teaching, and I doubt if I have anything new to add. You will find former students of the Gnessin School all over the Soviet Union. Is there any other institution which has had one and the same person at its head for seventy years? I know of only one such person—Elena Fabianovna Gnessin, fanatically devoted to musical education and an unusually kind person, always ready to help her former students no matter how much time had passed since they had studied under her. When I started teaching at the Gnessin School, I would visit Elena Fabianovna every Wednesday at her apartment in the school building. What affectionate interest she would show in my work and in the difficulties I faced!

In the 1920s the Gnessin School was considered the best Moscow school preparing students for the Moscow Conservatory. The teachers were excellent, and there was never a shortage of young talent. Young people were attracted by the general atmosphere of the school, by the relations between teachers and students and among the students themselves. Though the Gnessins were strict and their demands high, their concern for the students was touching; they knew everyone by name and, together with the other teachers, took part in student get-togethers, skits, and charades, inventing clever musical parodies. The students received more than a professional musical training; their human qualities were cultivated here, preparing them for their task of bringing musical culture to the masses.

It was too late to begin studying the piano at twenty, and the beginning cello class, taught by Sergei Bychkov, was short of students, so Khachaturyan was enrolled in it. Professor Andrei Borisyak, under whom Khachaturyan studied cello in his second year, was an experienced teacher, well-known and highly respected among musicians, who had himself studied under the famous Pablo Casals. Though Khachaturyan did not become a cellist, he retained the warmest recollections of his studies with his first professor.

> Thanks to him I learned not only what the cello was, I also discovered the boundless possibilities of a string quartet. This proved invaluable in my future work as a composer. An excellent musician and wonderful person, Borisyak was not without a touch of the romantic. Regretfully, I was too young to have attended his concerts although I knew that he was an outstanding cellist, with advanced views about art.
>
> I should like to emphasize the importance for both composer and conductor of knowing the specific features of every instrument in the orchestra. When, on tour in this country or abroad, I approach a musician during a break in rehearsals and ask him to play some passage from my work in a certain way, I can feel his respect for me growing. From an abstract composer—Aram Khachaturyan, a name he has heard—I become something very concrete, for he sees I am familiar with his instrument.
>
> I recall how, during rehearsals of my First Symphony, the conductor, Oigen Senkar, asked the musicians to play a certain passage with three trombones—the first and third trombones hold the note while the second slides up for a moment and returns. This slide did not come through well and Senkar said: "Second trombone—solo!" Everything immediately slipped into place. For me this was a lesson about the importance of even the most minor, seemingly inconsequential, remarks by the author on the score.

Those were difficult years for Khachaturyan. His studies took up a good deal of time and energy. He had to work hard on theory while practicing the cello; at twenty this was far more difficult than in childhood. His hands were not as flexible as in those years, and his fingers seemed made of wood. His progress, however, was apparent. In two years he was already playing Mikhail Gnessin's far-from-simple cello piece, "Song of the Wandering Knight," and very expressively too, as Gnessin himself recalls. Aram's fellow student, today a well-known composer and songwriter, Sigismund Katz, recalls that at a soiree given by the school he and Khachaturyan played Grieg's Sonata in A Major for Cello and Piano:

> As we were playing, the student who was turning the pages dropped the piano music on the floor. Left without notes, I started improvising something indistinct while Aram calmly played something on his own. When the music was back in place he continued playing unperturbed, but this was now the music of Grieg. Together, we finally finished the first movement of the Sonata.

After the concert he said smilingly, "You see, it's a good thing that we are composers to some extent at least. We were able to compose ad libitum, without stopping. Otherwise the pause would have been too long."

Need it be said that it took quite some time to learn to compose more seriously than just to fill in a pause? But how does a cellist become a composer?

The prominent Soviet musician and member of the Komitas Quartet, Mikhail Teryan, recalls:

> All the members of our quartet were friendly with Aram and could not but notice that he rather envied us. He suddenly started practicing the cello with such diligence that he hurt his hand. I remember during Mikhail Gnessin's class in harmony, Aram, quite downhearted, complained that he could not move the fingers of his left hand. He would not accept at the time what I deemed the wise advice of Mikhail Gnessin to drop the cello and take up composing. Aram and I recalled that incident many times in later years and laughingly agreed that it helped him become a composer and the world to discover Aram Khachaturyan.

It was at this time, in 1925, that Mikhail Gnessin started an experimental class in composing that was also open to instrumentalists. As Khachaturyan told it:

> One day Gnessin told us to compose counterpoint on an 8- to

12-bar theme. I brought him forty-two bars. He liked my work and I was among the first whom he invited to study composition. I owe it to him that my budding inclinations as a composer were heard and encouraged.

Gnessin recalls:

He once showed me a fragment—just a few bars—from a small composition for cello. After working on different types of exercises he soon proved his aptitude for composition. By about the end of his second year his work was so outstanding that the question arose of making it public. Several compositions that soon brought him recognition were written while he was a student of our music school.

A student of Rimsky-Korsakov and Lyadov, ardent patriot of the traditions of Russian classics, Mikhail Gnessin gave forty-five years of his life to teaching several generations of composers at the Moscow and Leningrad conservatories. Tikhon Khrennikov, Vadim Salmanov, Boris Kliusner, Albert Leman, and Sigismund Katz—the last-named has already been mentioned—were among his students.

"Gnessin was an outstanding pedagogue and composer, and undeservedly forgotten in our day," mourned Khachaturyan. He especially prized his teacher's ability to recognize young talent and spoke of his sensitive feeling for the individuality of each student's work.

Gnessin gave us an excellent knowledge of Russian musical culture. The author's idea, he said, should be the cornerstone of a composition. He taught us to love our folk music and developed our taste for harmony. He was able to excite the imagination of us future composers by suggesting we write several different accompaniments to a given melody.

Gnessin played an inestimable role in the development of the Armenian school of composing. Besides Aram Khachaturyan, he taught Aro Stepanyan, Sergei Barhudaryan, and Ashunavan Ter-Gevondyan. Armenian musicians who studied under Gnessin could not remain indifferent to his interest in the East and Eastern culture. From 1910 to 1920 Gnessin traveled extensively through the East, visiting Palestine and the Transcaucasian and Central Asian republics. He collected many folk melodies, including Jewish ones, which he later used in his compositions based on folk themes. Mikhail Gnessin wrote:

> Though not yet aware of his deep feelings for the national forms of music, Khachaturyan most likely benefited from the fact that the teacher, in his own compositions—which Khachaturyan heard often, some while they were still being written—displayed a similar treatment of Jewish themes. Khachaturyan himself agreed that these works of mine were of basic importance in the formation of his harmonic style. However, the seeds of independent musical thinking were apparent in Khachaturyan's work from the very outset; one could sense in them an entirely different, youthful, modern pulsation of life.

In his recollections of Mikhail Gnessin, Aram Khachaturyan underscored that his teacher paid attention least of all to technique and details of musical form and instrumentation. From the very outset Gnessin would ease the student into the creative process, without demanding a preliminary and complete knowledge of theory.

This method was obviously the only acceptable one in the experimental class of such a school. Yet for Khachaturyan's future as a composer it had both desirable and undesirable effects. Undesirable, in that the method prevented him from getting what he most needed, schooling. On the other side, being "trusted" to compose freely before completing classes in theory, harmony and counterpoint, as the rules of the Conservatory required, contributed to Khachaturyan's confidence in himself. From this viewpoint, it would seem that Gnessin's method was intended specially for Khachaturyan. For someone who had improvised on a copper pan in his childhood and who later asked friends to write down his compositions for brass band, it was unthinkable to wait until he had completed the entire academic course of the Conservatory before starting to compose.

Gnessin was against imitation in art—against imitation of highly regarded artists, against blind application of academic rules. He wrote in his *Elementary Course in Practical Composition,* a highly original textbook,

> I believe that every young musician, every one of our students, should be regarded as a recognized, well-known composer of the future, and that we must see in his shortcomings the elements of his fruition, the hidden roots of a new plant. *Undoubtedly, in this respect, the teacher must possess considerable perspicacity.* What may (under favorable conditions) become understandable and attractive even to an unprepared audience at some future time must be detected and understood by the teacher immediately or soon after becoming acquainted with the student.

The formation of Aram Khachaturyan as an artist and an individual from those "hidden roots"—which soon were to produce such mighty stems—is the best proof that Mikhail Gnessin's teaching method was correct. Khachaturyan himself held Gnessin in high regard:

> Well educated, intelligent and perceptive, Mikhail Fabianovich contributed greatly to my artistic development.
>
> I am grateful to him for having helped me preserve and develop the national element in my work. I was interested in Scriabin at the time. Gnessin convinced me that only deeply national art, and not imitative art, could be appreciated by the public.
>
> Mikhail Gnessin would assign us an ordinary theme on which to compose variations. Once he suggested that we try Grieg's "Solvejg's Song." Everyone worked diligently to preserve the character of Grieg's music. I composed two variations—Intermezzo and Dance, built on specific Oriental rhythms. After hearing my variations Gnessin said, "I don't know who imitates whom, but Khachaturyan imitates himself. . . ."

His friends and teachers agree that the originality of Khachaturyan's work was apparent from his very first compositions.

Another event that played an important role in his life while still at the Gnessin School was his meeting with Reinhold Gliere.

> I first heard of Reinhold Gliere in 1923 from Mikhail and Elena Gnessin. They were good friends of his and called him "Goldy." Elena Fabianovna introduced me to him as a young cellist who "sinned" by composing—at that time I improvised a good deal. I attended Gliere's class for a year. He often held his classes at home, on Petrovka Boulevard. I remember his neglected apartment and large household, even such details as the floors, which creaked. I always had the impression that being busy with his students, he continually put aside his own composing; it bothered me that I took up so much of his time.

Gliere's composing and teaching overlapped, of course. As a teacher he was demanding and strict but very tactful with his students. If anyone brought poor work to class, Gliere would ask the other students to comment on it, as though wishing not to become involved. Usually this had a very appreciable pedagogical effect. At that time, as well as many years later, when Khachaturyan himself was teaching, Gliere's method, which assumed that the budding composer was doing serious and independent work, was a great help to Aram.

> Once, while arranging a trio according to an exercise in Conusse's textbook, which called for the use of two French horns, I gave the upper and lower voices to the horns and the middle part to the bassoon. On checking my work, Gliere did not notice the conditions of the exercise and remarked that it would have been better to have used three French horns.
>
> I did not correct his oversight, but when he suggested that I take a look at a similar trio in the score of Wagner's *The Valkyrie,* I told him I could not buy the score because it was too expensive. "That does not interest me," I heard him say. "When you need a score sell your trousers or ask me for the money but be sure you buy it." I don't recall whether or not I managed to acquire Wagner's score, but I took my teacher's advice and studied hard.

On one occasion Khachaturyan ventured to show Gliere his *Poem for Piano,* a composition Khachaturyan cherished.

Gliere listened carefully to the music, then said approximately the following: "If you study theory, harmony, musical forms, and instrumentation and are very diligent, you could become a composer." Much later, thinking over his words, I understood what he had in mind. In those years music attracted many people poorly equipped to become composers; some of them tried far too actively to assert themselves in their chosen field.

His association with Gliere (which continued for decades) and his intimate acquaintance with Gliere's work were important for Khachaturyan because, apart from other considerations, Gliere was the first of the Moscow composers to extend a helping hand to the professional music schools in the republics of the Soviet East, which were just then being established. He studied Eastern music in depth and deliberated at length on how to synthesize it with traditional European music, saying: "Face the real East, which will enrich modern music . . . with its original melodic patterns and unusual variety of refined rhythms." A second intuition was to prove as important for Khachaturyan's maturing musical awareness as for Gliere himself: "A new and fresh spring, the spontaneous folk art of the East, will undoubtedly irrigate the fevered soil of European art."

Fate indeed had placed Aram Khachaturyan in the hands of just the teachers he needed to help him crystallize his aims and tasks as a composer. And as matters turned out, Gliere was true to his word—his 1927 opera, *Shakhsenem,* based on Azerbaijan national music, was an important landmark in Soviet music.

Khachaturyan's first compositions brought him academic success. In addition to the aforementioned "Song of the Wandering Ashugs" for cello and piano and his "Poem" for piano, there were the Dance for Violin and Piano of 1926 and the Waltz-Caprice for Piano of the same year. They were far from accomplished pieces, but they did reveal Khachaturyan's individual qualities as a composer—his lively feeling for Armenian folk music, his improvisatory skill, his colorful and pungent harmonies. Subsequently they would also win public acclaim.

Khachaturyan recalled some of his earliest compositions:

While still a student at the Gnessin School, I was vacationing in Kislovodsk, where I became friends with Avetik Gabrielyan, first violinist of the Komitas Quartet. After watching him practice for some time, I decided to write a virtuoso piece for him, and did. Three years after the Dance for Violin and Piano, I wrote my second violin piece, "In Honor of the Ashugs." I have already mentioned that it was this that helped me change Suren's skeptical view of my future as a composer. Among those who congratulated me after Gabrielyan's performance of the piece were Conservatory professors Abraham Yampolsky and Lev Zeitlin. Zeitlin, so lively and expansive, asked me where I had learned the possibilities of the violin so well.

In those years Khachaturyan had to earn a living besides studying music. He worked at different jobs, hauling heavy crates in the wine cellars of the Moscow Armenvino plant and singing in the Armenian church choir.

Although I grew up in the South, I had never touched a drop of anything except dry wine until 1939 and even that, very moderately, like my father. It was only after the Moscow premiere of my ballet *Happiness* that I first tasted cognac. In that sense the wine cellars did not interest me. I was young and healthy, I needed money like all the other students, and I thought at that time that they paid well here— one and a half rubles a day. After working there for a while I was able to buy myself a pair of trousers for the first time. Could it have been those very trousers, which I flaunted so proudly, that Gliere noticed as a potential means of purchasing the score of *The Valkyrie*? However, loading crates was no work for a cellist. Once I cut my finger so badly on a broken bottle that I almost had to say goodbye to my musical career. This was before fortune led me to become a composer. . . .

Another source of my modest income in those days was singing in the Armenian church choir. The choir was led by Martin Mazmanyan—the same teacher from Suren's studio who had led our singing on the way from Tbilisi to Moscow. My brother Levon also sang in the choir. He studied voice professionally under Professor Tutunik. The church paid much more than the wine cellars—ten rubles for every performance. Too bad the service was held only once a week, on Sundays.

Martin Mazmanyan, the composer, one of the oldest figures in Armenian musical culture, recalls that Aram was exceptionally musical—like his father, mother, and brother Levon. As he wrote,

> I led the church choir back in Tbilisi, where I studied in the same seminary as his brothers. Levon was our soloist. Our choir performed the liturgy every Sunday. Aram would come often and listen. Later, in Moscow, when I had organized the chorus in the Armenian drama studio, we also sang Makar Ekmalyan's liturgy in the Armenian church. Aram knew the entire score and sang the tenor part very well. His voice was good though not strong.

Aram Khachaturyan also sang at some of the concerts given by the Armenian choir. He took part in the concert on January 14, 1924, where the entire program consisted of works by Komitas. The Moscow public that filled the Hall of the Armenia House of Culture was delighted with the masterpieces "Krunk," "Kali Erg," "Garuna," and "Antuni." Several songs were repeated as encores. Among the celebrities in the audience were Alexander Spendiarov, Konstantin Saradjev, Alexander Alexandrov, Konstantin Igumnov, and the poet Egishe Charentz.

As Khachaturyan recalled:

> I was always nervous on the day of a choir premiere. I was enthralled by the noble beauty of Armenian hymns. Of course, I did not become religious, but I think that were I a believer, after seeing the way the service in the Armenian church in Moscow was staged, I would quickly have become an atheist. . . .

Luckily, as soon as Aram had acquired the most elementary skills in solfeggio and theory, Elena Gnessin helped him find work tutoring lagging students for examinations. The wine cellars and Armenian church choir were forgotten. Also easing his financial situation was the favorable action on his request for an Armenian State Scholarship. He had written to the Association of Transcaucasian Students in Moscow:

Being a professional musician I am forced to do work that is harmful to my basic studies, for the sake of which I am in Moscow and for which I have a calling. The enclosed opinions of me as a musician bear me out.

In my work, my thoughts, and my desires I am wholly bound to Armenia by blood ties. I intend to work only in Armenia after completing my studies. . . .

With this letter were included notes from Mikhail and Elena Gnessin attesting to the fact that Aram Khachaturyan "possessed excellent musical talents, excelled in two specialties . . . and held out great hopes that he would become a prominent figure in music."

It must be assumed that Khachaturyan's intentions to work in Armenia were quite sincere. He was then completely engrossed in the study of Armenian art, thanks to his work in the House of Culture of Soviet Armenia.

Khachaturyan spoke many times of the importance of this period in the formation of his creative work. He was taken on at the House on the recommendation of Suren Khachaturov and immediately felt himself immersed in Armenian culture. Persons prominent in Armenian literature, science, and the arts gathered there regularly for concerts in which the works of Armenian composers were performed by Armenians.

Sociable and active by nature, Khachaturyan took part in almost all the social functions at the Armenian House of Culture. He started by teaching music in the kindergarten and Armenian school, where he eagerly worked with the children, writing simple songs and dances for them. Here he acquired his teaching abilities, which proved so helpful later on. Years later, writing on the education of the growing generation, Khachaturyan noted that he had seen for himself what an important place music played in the life of a child:

While a student I taught music in a kindergarten where I organized various orchestras. Our fame spread throughout Moscow and we were soon invited to perform in other kindergartens. I wrote music for children's performances, invented musical games accompanied with improvisation. The children listened to my music with great interest. They really understood what I was trying to say. Working with children was a great help, for it excited my imagination, inducing me to find exact colors and precise means of expression.*

As eloquent proof of this there are two notebooks that Khachaturyan composed years later, his *Children's Album* for piano (the first notebook in 1947, the second in 1965). Young pianists find the familiar figures in them easy to understand; at the same time, these figures are truly artistic images.

In the Armenian House of Culture Aram Khachaturyan read Armenian classical poetry and drama and found new friends. He met the poet Egish Charentz, the composer Alexander Spendiarov, the painter Martiros Saryan, the conductor Konstantin Saradjev, and the theater director Ruben Simonov. His association with Spendiarov left strong artistic impressions. As a musician, Spendiarov stood at the fount of renewal of the Armenian national school of composing. In a broader sense he heralded, together with Uzeir Gajibekov in Azerbaijan and Zakharia Paliashvili in Georgia, the renewal of all the music of the Transcaucasus. His best-known works—*Erevan Sketches* for symphony orchestra and the opera *Almast,* both based on the heritage of national music—show how fruitful a creative approach to folklore can be.

"All of Spendiarov, all his creative genius, is contained in the *Erevan Sketches*," wrote Aram Khachaturyan.

He recreates Armenian folk melodies with surprising simplicity and almost ethnographic accuracy, though with truly creative freedom. His means are sparing in the extreme; nothing excessive. Lightness, transparency and a surprising wealth of colors. . . . Actually, Armenian composers of the preceding period did not

*As music instructor in a kindergarten, Khachaturyan traveled to Erevan at the time to find talented children and check the work of Armenian music teachers. In one kindergarten in Erevan he discovered an exceptionally talented boy for whom he predicted a wonderful musical career. This was Arno Babajanyan, today an outstanding Soviet composer.

venture beyond the vocal school. Spendiarov opened the way to the development of national symphonic music in its fullest sense; it was a veritable revolution. Armenian music was immediately raised to a new level. It was then that the roads of our musical art were determined for many decades to come.

In 1924, responding to an appeal from Armenia, Spendiarov moved to Erevan, where he plunged wholeheartedly into the work of building a new culture. He was active in the conservatory and symphony orchestra which he helped found, and also organized research work and publishing in the field of music. He was often in Moscow and invariably visited the Armenian House of Culture. As Khachaturyan recalled,

The general atmosphere in Armenia House was exceptionally creative. . . . Alexander Spendiarov was exceedingly interested in the younger generation and was invariably caught up by their enthusiasm. I recall how eagerly he took part in our interesting creative activities. I was composing music then for the productions of the House drama studio, which Ruben Simonov directed. Spendiarov would attend our rehearsals and give me professional advice as the story unfolded.

We discussed many topics but mostly what was so near and dear to both of us—music. . . . He spoke most warmly about his favorite work, the opera *Almast*. He could already picture his heroine, what she looked like, her gestures, and her way of walking. He dreamed of the day he would hear the opera performed on stage. Regrettably, he died before completing it.

Once, walking down Arbat Street, Khachaturyan and Spendiarov met Zakharia Paliashvili, whose music had had such an impact on Aram in Tbilisi. Until that time, he had seen the composer only from a distance, at the theater. Now Spendiarov introduced them to each other.

Although almost half a century has passed since that memorable day, I can still see Spendiarov and Paliashvili smiling, embracing, and kissing. You should have seen them! They seemed to radiate joy. Every word, every gesture of theirs seemed to bespeak their deep, mutual respect. . . . I often recall that scene . . . and never tire of describing how two great representatives of these neighboring peoples liked and respected each other.

Spendiarov called Aram Khachaturyan a "mighty rock," predicting that his talent would blossom profusely. It is regrettable that he did not live to see his words come true. He presented his young colleague the score of his *Erevan Sketches*, bearing a warm inscription, and helped him publish his first works—the "Poem for Piano" and the song-poem "In Honor of the Ashugs."

I gratefully remember Spendiarov's regard for me, a budding composer. It was always with trepidation that I would bring my first compositions to him for judgment. But his thoughtful, serious approach to my work, his attention and involvement, inspired and encouraged me. A strict but well-disposed critic, he would note the good and the bad, missing nothing. Meeting him was one of the decisive turning points in my life.

Another important event in Khachaturyan's life was his meeting with the *ashug* ensemble led by Shara Talyan in Armenia House. The group sang rousing and lyrical sagas, as well as humorous and passionate Armenian love songs. The son of Jamani, a well-known Armenian *ashug*, Shara Talyan had been taught to revere folk art since childhood. As a vocalist he enjoyed truly national popularity, both as an opera singer and a performer of Armenian songs. As Khachaturyan recalled,

He was the first to sing the role of the shepherd Saro in Tigranyan's opera *Anush*. He was probably the best interpreter of that role I have ever heard. Everyone in Erevan knew him. Walking down the street, he would be followed by a crowd of boys gaily shouting, "Hello, Saro." I was closely acquainted with Shara Talyan; his wife, who sang and played the *kemancha*; and his brother, who played several instruments. My song-poem "In Honor of the Ashugs" was a gift as it were, to this talented group, whose performances I shall never forget.

The performances of the drama studio in Armenia House,

for which he wrote music, were a good school for Khachaturyan. It staged classic Armenian plays such as Akop Paronyan's comedies *Uncle Bagdasar* and *The Oriental Dentist* (1927, 1928), and Gabriel Sundukyan's *Hatabala* and *The Ravaged Hearth* (1928, 1935). The first three plays were staged by Ruben Simonov and Iosef Rappoport, the last by Simonov alone.

Equally important for Khachaturyan were the works of the classic Armenian composers—Komitas, the brothers Spiridon, Romanos Melikyan, and Kara-Murza—and the works of the modern Armenians. Access to them was facilitated by his work as representative, in Armenia House, of the Armenian People's Commissariat of Public Instruction in the sphere of music publication.

Though greatly interested in Armenian art and wholly dedicated to its needs, Khachaturyan did not shun non-Armenian cultures, especially Russian culture. National chauvinism was alien to him; he never held one culture, even the Armenian, above others. In those years Khachaturyan heard a great deal of classical music, paid tribute to Scriabin, and was specially attracted to the French Impressionists. Many years later the accomplished Azerbaijan composer, Kara Karaev, wrote that where Ravel was concerned Khachaturyan had been primarily interested in his attitude to Spanish folk music, which, it is generally agreed, was strongly influenced by Arabic music:

> The improvisational manner of playing preserved to this day in the Spanish flamenco, the frenzy of the opening steps, the colors—all these qualities that distinguish Ravel's works, were not invented by him. He sensed them in Spanish folk music. This ability to take from the treasures of folk music precisely what you need, what accords with your personality was, in turn, grasped by Khachaturyan.

Aram spent many an evening in the home of Elena Bekman-Shcherbina, a well-known pianist and teacher at the Gnessin School and at Moscow Conservatory. Many young musicians gathered here, playing and listening to new music. An excellent interpreter of Chopin, Scriabin, Debussy, and Ravel, Bekman-

Shcherbina also took a lively interest in the works of contemporary composers.

Khachaturyan naturally had interests apart from music. One was the poet Vladimir Mayakovsky. Aram heard him reading his poetry in Moscow's Polytechnical Museum.

> It was difficult for me to accept Mayakovsky at first, but in time I came to like his work more and more. Looking back at my younger days, however, I cannot say that one or another poet touched my heart more than any other. At that time I was already well acquainted with Russian and Armenian poetry; I had read a good deal of Pushkin, Lermontov, Nekrasov, Tiutchev, Esenin, Svetlov, Avetik Isaakyan, and Egishe Charentz. I had read and reread the works of Sayat-Nova. I was fascinated by the passion, intensity, and force of his poetry, and his vivid, rounded imagery. I had read his poetry in Valery Briusov's wonderful translations from Armenian, which enable the Russian reader to penetrate into the refined poetic world of Sayat-Nova.

To the end of his days Khachaturyan retained his love for the works of this wonderful Armenian poet.

On graduating from the Gnessin School in the spring of 1929, Aram Khachaturyan could justly say: "I studied the algebra of music—solfeggio, theory, harmony—and did a good deal of composing." Although he had not yet absorbed everything there was to know about the difficult profession of music, and although years of persevering work still lay ahead, Khachaturyan swept aside all doubts about his future and chose to be a composer.

Autumn 1929 came, bringing the tense period of examinations for admission to the Moscow Conservatory. On the board of examiners, together with other Conservatory professors and teachers, were Reinhold Gliere and Nikolai Zhilyev—at one time Sergei Taneyev's favorite student, a close friend of Alexander Scriabin, and a highly popular professor. Khachaturyan passed the exams and was enrolled.

Khachaturyan was assigned to Mikhail Gnessin's class. However, because Gnessin was to leave the Conservatory in 1931, Khachaturyan transferred to Nikolai Myaskovsky's class in his second year. He studied instrumentation under Sergei Vasilenko and Nikolai Ivanov-Radkevitch, polyphony under Heinrich Litinsky, and analysis of musical forms under Dmitri Kabalevsky, who was younger than Khachaturyan. It was clear from the very beginning that Khachaturyan was gifted and independent in his work, qualities that had been apparent while he was still at the Gnessin School. All who remember him as a student agree on this.

"My studies under well-known teachers played a decisive role in my ideological and artistic growth," Khachaturyan recalled. The pedagogues at the Conservatory in those days were outstanding—a brilliant constellation of professors. Piano classes were conducted by Alexander Goldenweiser, Samuel Feinberg, Heinrich Neuhaus, and Konstantin Igumnov; orchestration, by Abram Yampolsky, Lev Tseitlin, Anatoly Brandukov, and Semyon Kozolupov. Composition was taught by Gliere, Myaskovsky, and Zhilyev—all of them not only highly respected musicians but to the students embodying a living bond with the past. Gliere had studied under Taneyev and Arensky; Lyadov and Rimsky-Korsakov had taught Myaskovsky, and Zhilyev had studied under Taneyev. This afforded the younger generation the invaluable opportunity of absorbing the best traditions of Russian classical music at first hand.

The older generation of musicians took a warm interest in Khachaturyan. Heinrich Litinsky, just three years older than his student, recalls that soon after meeting Khachaturyan he realized the need for a special approach. "Many years later I happened to hold gold nuggets in my hands that had not yet been touched by jewelers. They were black, unpolished, and did not shine. That is what Khachaturyan was like in those days." Mikhail Gnessin had almost the same impression: "As a musician Aram Khachaturyan was so like an unpolished precious stone in those days that it was difficult to evaluate him." Litinsky went on to say,

Strict style is the alpha and omega of polyphony. But I saw that rigid conformity with the canons was alien to Khachaturyan's nature. At that time I decided to start my classes with free style, referring to examples in strict style when necessary. My judgment was correct—Khachaturyan did not develop a penchant for polyphony. This experiment served me subsequently when I was working with a group of Armenian composers of the younger generation—Edward Mirzoyan, Arno Babajanyan, Alexander Arutiunayan, and others.

From the minutes of meetings of the Conservatory composers' research department we learn what his teachers thought of Khachaturyan. They spoke of his earnest and independent work. "Very active. Has made excellent progress," Professor Sergei Vasilenko wrote of Khachaturyan in his second year. "Arranged ten songs (worthy of attention), wrote two mass songs, started orchestrating a suite on Armenian themes," we read in the minutes signed by Gnessin.

In the early 1930s Khachaturyan lived in a small dormitory room on Arbat Street.

The student ration was pretty meager but that didn't bother me. I would gulp down a piece of dry bread soaked in sweetened hot water and rush off to the Conservatory. . . . I was lucky with my teachers. There was, first of all, my unforgettable teacher, Nikolai Yakovlevich Myaskovsky, whose life and work are inseparable from the history of Soviet music.

Aram Khachaturyan was familiar with Myaskovsky's music before meeting him, and dreamed of attending his classes, as did other budding composers. "For us young composers, his name was surrounded by something of a halo." Though he dreamed, he never really believed the dream would come true. But a recommendation from Vladimir Derjanovsky, a prominent music critic and friend of Sergei Prokofiev, helped. "One winter day in 1929, when I had been in the hospital for some time, my friends brought me news that did me more good than all the medicines—I had been assigned to Nikolai Myaskovsky's class."

Nikolai Myaskovsky's significance in Russian musical culture can be equated only with Rimsky-Korsakov's importance as head of the Petersburg School at the turn of the century, and with Sergei Taneyev's as head of the Moscow school. Besides composing in their own right, they educated an entire generation of composers over a period of many years. Myaskovsky taught at the Moscow Conservatory for almost thirty years—from 1921 to the end of his days in 1950. He founded his own school, which carried on the best traditions of the Russian classics.

It was no accident that Myaskovsky's classes came to be known as a laboratory of Soviet music. Among those who studied here were Nikolai Mossolov, Vissarion Shebalin, Vano Muradeli, Gherman Galinin, Dmitri Kabalevsky, Nikolai Pieko, Boris Tchaikovsky, and many others whose works are widely known.

> Myaskovsky was a real patriarch of Russian music of the first half of the twentieth century. All the composers, irrespective of position or prominence, respected him and sought his advice. He enjoyed a very special authority which we all acknowledged. Even Prokofiev, who rarely recognized any authority, held Myaskovsky in high esteem and listened attentively to his opinions and advice.

Myaskovsky's culture, his rare tact, the impression of deep and noble beauty he projected, the contrast between his seemingly calm movements and the quick, penetrating glance of his bright intelligent eyes were etched in Khachaturyan's memory in later years.

Khachaturyan eventually became well acquainted with his teacher and often visited his apartment in one of Moscow's typical old neighborhoods, not far from where Sergei Taneyev once lived and worked. But he entered Myaskovsky's Conservatory class with apprehension, as the famous composer gave the initial impression of being morose and rather severe. Nonetheless, Myaskovsky's exceptional knowledge of classical and modern music, as well as the relaxed and informal atmosphere at his lessons, attracted young people to his classes. All the students were usually present and took a lively part in discussing one another's work. "From the very beginning," remembered Khachaturyan,

> I was carried away by the unusual atmosphere. There was nothing ordinary or repetitious in his lessons. On coming into his class we seemed to step into a world where all the intricacies and beauty of our art were opened up to us, that art which we loved so blindly. Nikolai Myaskovsky taught us music and the cultural standards of composing, at the same time weaving in many other aspects of classical and modern art.

An exceptionally gifted pedagogue, Myaskovsky never tired of teaching; on the contrary, he loved it and was drawn to young people. A student would bring one of his new works. Myaskovsky would listen carefully, say a few words, and then refer to one or another classical example. "He would express an idea," wrote Khachaturyan,

> then get up and go to the music shelf, quickly find the notes he wanted and say: "Schumann's coda is like this, while Liszt's is entirely different, look. . . ." There were many different examples—a form or parts of a form, polyphonic methods, the tonal quality of the orchestra, harmony, how the material unfolds, types of codas, cadences, etc.

Myaskovsky's purpose was twofold—to bolster the student's confidence by the weight of an accepted example, and to show how important a good knowledge of the classical heritage was for the future composer. Most often the music taken from the shelf would be Glinka, Tchaikovsky, Rimsky-Korsakov, Borodin, or Taneyev. "I remember," wrote Khachaturyan, "what a delight it was to hear Nikolai Yakovlevich recalling his meetings with Rimsky-Korsakov and Lyadov. The great composers seemed so much closer to us; each of the students felt himself to be part of a common effort with them."

Apparently aware of the students' frank delight in his knowledge and memory, Myaskovsky would say with a smile that it was necessary to know musical literature well, if only to avoid composing out of ignorance what had already been written. His gentle sense of humor, his patience with people and often with their shortcomings, would soon dispel the student's first impressions of him as a severe professor.

> We would come to Myaskovsky as to a religious rite, wondering what he would say, and would he like our music. By his very existence Nikolai Yakovlevich created a very special aura in class. His exacting demands were softened by his indulgence, for not all the students were equally gifted, and their scores not always skillfully written.
>
> I remember very well how he would appraise a composition. It was extremely important for him to understand the student's conception, and that is how he would usually start his analysis. He respected the student's idea, though he may not always have agreed with it. He had no time for "smooth, facile," clever music written by rote and devoid of fresh ideas. Even in the shortest compositions he would first look for expressions of the student's individuality.

Could this be the secret of his immediate interest in Khachaturyan? Aram never produced "smooth" music or composed by rote. Even in his conservatory years his individuality stood out.

Myaskovsky's talent as a pedagogue lay in the fact that, as Khachaturyan said, "he never sought to override or change the live feeling of national music as spontaneity which I had absorbed with my mother's milk."*

In Myaskovsky's class Khachaturyan found the same uncompromising atmosphere so familiar to him from his association with Gliere. Myaskovsky insisted that his students "think

---

*Approximately the same thought is to be found in what Nikolai Rimsky-Korsakov said to his student, Alexander Spendiarov, many years before Myaskovsky. "You are an Easterner by birth, you have the East in your blood, as they say. And because of it, in music, in this field, you may be able to produce something real, truly valuable. With me it is different. My East is in my head, it is contemplative."

big." Aram Ilych recalled that neither household difficulties nor personal affairs could excuse a student for not having done his homework.

> I told him I was having emotional problems. Myaskovsky smiled suddenly and said: "Well, take advantage of them. Write music. The worst thing you could do is be inactive. It is possible to think of music always and everywhere." Years later I found an entry in his diary saying that only he who creates tirelessly may be considered an artist. "Otherwise," he wrote, "the brain gets rusty." I have never forgotten those words and I never tire of repeating them to my students and young colleagues.

It would be wrong to assume that Khachaturyan's artistic growth in the Conservatory was all smooth sailing. Like all young composers he had his difficulties, and his exacting teacher was not always satisfied with his work. His irresistible urge to find new forms often would clash with classical standards and traditions. His natural gift for the melodic persistently demanded a corresponding craftsmanship in developing his material.

In analyzing a student's work, Myaskovsky would draw a clear line between specific national features and obvious musical shortcomings which had little to do with the Eastern folk idiom.

> Take my passion for whole and half intervals for which the critics and Conservatory teachers would turn on me (except Myaskovsky, of course). They have been a part of me since my childhood, when I used to hear trios of folk instruments—the *tara, kemancha,* and tambourine. I delighted in them, taking the piercing sounds of the intervals as perfect consonances.
> 
> Myaskovsky did not like my intervals too much. But since he understood my natural inclination for them, he did not attempt to suppress my individuality. "It is interesting to work with a student," he would say, "when you know what he wants. I cannot decide for the student. What he hears is what is important."

However, if Myaskovsky believed that Khachaturyan's passion for these intervals, chords, and tonalities was quite natural for one raised in the traditions of Eastern folk music, he refused to accept the "laziness" and inactivity of the bass voices in his works. Aram Ilych recalled this more than once with gratitude.

> Myaskovsky helped me greatly when I was learning to work with material; he taught me to elaborate a theme. Because of my Eastern ear, I had an inclination for immobile basses and organ points. Nikolai Yakovlevich helped me to shake this off. He pointed out that a mobile bass "moves" all music.
>
> Tactfully, without listening, he made me aware of the need to view the "problem of the basses" differently. I may not always be successful in this, but I am always aware of it.
>
> It is my opinion, incidentally, that Myaskovsky's basses are excessively mobile at times; I once dared to tell him so, referring to a specific example. I was more surprised than flattered to see that he was considering my advice.

Recalling Myaskovsky's classes, Khachaturyan stressed his rare ability "to speak simply, convincingly, and concretely to young composers on such vital matters as the ideological direction art should pursue and the balance between content and form."

This same thought is found in the reminiscences of Khachaturyan's wife, Nina Makarova, also a student of Myaskovsky. At her first lesson with Nikolai Yakovlevich she had just finished playing a piano sonata she had written, when she heard him ask what seemed an unexpected question: "And what is the idea in this composition?" "It was then I first realized that besides philosophical and literary ideas there are also musical ideas which one must know how to state and verify."

Khachaturyan wrote his recollections of Myaskovsky when he himself was already teaching. His thoughts and judgments about his teacher were based on his own pedagogical experience and principles acquired under Myaskovsky's direct influence. Khachaturyan often wondered if Myaskovsky had his own complete pedagogical system. "More likely," he opined, "he had definite general principles that he followed."

His basic principle was to prepare a musician who was not

only a technically well-equipped professional, but who also possessed very definite views on life and art. When I asked Aram Ilych what his most vivid recollections of his student days were, he replied:

> Myaskovsky's classes. I consider myself very lucky to have studied under Myaskovsky for so many years. He was much more to me than a teacher in composition. He not only taught me all there is to know about our profession, not only helped form my taste in art and helped me to understand music from the "inside," as it were—he also influenced my world view, and my ideas on life and art.

While still a Conservatory student Khachaturyan wrote more than fifty works. The best—"In Honor of the Ashugs" for violin and piano (1929), Trio for Clarinet, Violin, and Piano (1932), Dance Suite for Symphony Orchestra (1933), and the First Symphony (1934)—attracted the attention of the music world. The composer's natural gifts—and he could already be called a composer—his diligence and persistence, were apparent. "Besides working on his compositions," wrote Myaskovsky, "Khachaturyan attended almost all my classes in composition and took an active part in discussing the work of other students."

Boris Haikin, the celebrated opera and symphony conductor recalls,

> In 1930, when the radio was just becoming popular and crystal sets were still in use, a young boy made me a huge box with tubes sticking out of it. I remember putting my ear to this box and suddenly hearing astonishing music. It was announced that the composer was Aram Khachaturyan. I had already heard a march of his. This early work was highly original. I kept his name in mind from then on and sought opportunities to meet this very original artist.

In time Haikin conducted many of Khachaturyan's works and was the first interpreter of his Second Symphony.

Not everything Khachaturyan wrote in his student years has

survived. But then, the composer, himself not always satisfied, was well aware that not all his early works were up to par, and so did not make some of them public. Among these was his Suite for Viola and Piano, performed in his first year at the Conservatory. Parts of the suite were performed at a private concert on June 11, 1930.

Khachaturyan recalled that "several times Vadim Borisovsky, that wonderful viola player, urged me to compose for the viola. But my Sonata for Unaccompanied Viola appeared only after his death."

Khachaturyan commenced work on a string quartet but completed only one movement—a double fugue. His violin sonata, two movements of which were often played during his recitals in the 1930s, remained only half finished. His cycle of piano fugues, composed in 1928, before he entered the Conservatory, also seemed destined to be forgotten.

> I always had trouble squeezing my imagination into the framework of established standards. And there were more of them in fugues, I think, than in sonatas. It is no accident that the piano fugues which I wrote on Mikhail Gnessin's advice à la Bach lay hidden until 1970. They turned out to be absolutely unlike Bach. I remember Prokofiev saying that he did not think fugues should be written in our times. "Everything that could be done in this field has been done by Bach," he said. I felt he was wrong; hadn't Dmitri Shostakovich composed a wonderful cycle of piano fugues and preludes? Nevertheless, I was not ready to make my fugues public.

Khachaturyan did not like to return to his old compositions, to alter them on his own initiative. His fugues were possibly the only exception. Ballet was another matter, for new productions required new arrangements, and composers were often excessively compliant.

Talking with Khachaturyan one day, I quoted Olivier Messiaen: "What has once been written is complete forever. Any changes I could make in later years would be written in a different style." Khachaturyan reflected a moment. "I cannot agree with my esteemed French colleague," he said. "Of course a composer's style may become richer and acquire new traits, but it does not disappear, it does not change radically if he has any style at all." Here Khachaturyan instanced his cycle of fugues:

> For example, take my seven fugues, which I have decided to revise, adding recitatives and publishing them under the date 1928–1970—so frightening for editors. Now, have I remained the same in 1970 as I was in 1928? I hope not. Have I become entirely different as far as my style is concerned? I am certain that I have not. There is probably a certain creative logic in that.

Evaluating Khachaturyan's early compositions, the scholar Georgi Hubov wrote that

> they attracted by their spontaneous, forceful imagination and temperament, despite a somewhat blatant tonal palette. . . . One can sense the naïve, though understandable desire in a beginning composer to show at once everything he had learned and absorbed. Experience had not yet taught him to select and synthesize.

Of all his works written in those years, the best is the Trio for Clarinet, Violin, and Piano, composed in 1932. Sergei Prokofiev heard it soon after and was attracted by its independent tonal qualities, its rich melody and surprisingly relaxed manner of musical self-expression, and its sincere warmth. Prokofiev recommended that the Trio be published, and it appeared almost simultaneously in Moscow and Paris. Today, half a century later, the music is still delightfully fresh. The vivid emotional contrasts, the engaging boldness of the dance . . . an unexpected wave of sorrow . . . and again the even more reckless, unrestrained dance are striking, as is the composer's skill, hidden under a cloak of improvisational exposition. The instrumentation of the Trio is original, the violin, clarinet, and piano imitating the *duduk, kemancha,* and *dool,** folk instruments so

---

*The *dool* is an Armenian folk instrument, a two-headed drum played with sticks or with the hands.

dear to Khachaturyan's heart. The violin-clarinet combination was repeated in many of the composer's later works. For instance, a violin and clarinet duet introduces the cadenza in the first movement of the Violin Concerto. In the reprise of the same movement the clarinet is secondary, accompanied by the violin. We find the same duet in the second and third movements of the Violin Concerto and in the Concerto-Rhapsody for Violin. "Even before Prokofiev had heard the Trio," Khachaturyan recalled, "Samuel Feinberg came up to me in the Conservatory and said: 'How can you keep such a composition hidden away?'"

Many years later, in 1960, Khachaturyan was elected an Honorary member of the St. Cecilia Academy of Music in Rome.

At the concert following the presentation of diplomas, a pleasant surprise awaited me. Students of the Academy, founded in the sixteenth century by Palestrina, played the Trio of my student days. I found the young musicians after their brilliant rendition, thanked them, and told them that I had written that music when I was approximately their age and a student at the Moscow Conservatory. The well-known Italian composer, Professor Goffredo Petrassi, present during this conversation, said, "The Moscow Conservatory can be proud of such a student."

Khachaturyan's first major work was his Dance Suite, a true hymn to the dance, so congenial to his temperament and talent. Parts of the suite were played in the Grand Hall of the Conservatory on June 22, 1933, with Nikolai Anosov conducting. The following season, however, Alexander Gauk, the eminent Soviet conductor, took an interest in it and conducted the entire work. For many years after, Gauk and Khachaturyan were bound by ties of friendship and collaboration.

The notebook of Dmitri Kabalevsky, who was present at the first performance of the Dance Suite, contains an interesting entry:

June 22. A symphony concert devoted to works by students of the Moscow Conservatory. Khachaturyan, three movements from his Dance Suite. A devilishly gifted person. A mature composition (even in this form, which allows for many improvements). Very temperamental, rich in full-blooded, healthy emotions, beautifully arranged, a truly Soviet composer. The fabric a bit overcrowded with detail.

Kabalevsky explains this, saying that in those years "a great deal of formless music was being written, void of genuinely vital force or deep emotions or, more important, of a joyful perception of life." He reminds us that Khachaturyan's music appeared before Myaskovsky had composed his Fifteenth and Sixteenth symphonies, Shostakovich his Fifth, and Prokofiev his opera *Semyon Kotko,* justly concluding that the young Armenian composer's Dance Suite was a suitable continuation of the trend started by Shostakovich's First Symphony and Myaskovsky's Sixth. It was, at the same time, one of the harbingers of the coming achievements of Soviet music.

In order to objectively appraise the Dance Suite today, to understand its significance within the context of Soviet music in the first half of the 1930s, we must try to forget the listening experience of the 1970s and 1980s, and especially the later evolution of Khachaturyan's work. For Khachaturyan, the Dance Suite was his first attempt—as he termed it—to "symphonize" Armenian, Azerbaijan, Georgian, and Uzbek national music. "I cannot judge to what extent I was successful in symphonizing this material, that is, to subordinate it to the principle of contrasting, dialectical development. But that was my goal," said Khachaturyan.

Was he successful? Not quite. "When Myaskovsky was studying my suite he remarked that my themes did not develop, that they were merely enriched by new harmonic and orchestral colors. The insufficient mobility of the bass was another shortcoming, in his opinion."

Be that as it may, the passionate and ardent Dance Suite is a vehicle not only for the very manifest expressions of Khachaturyan's great talent, but his equally obvious ability to portray the exciting atmosphere of the life around him.

"Superb abilities, a great and vivid temperament matched

by excellent harmonic taste, an extraordinary melodic gift of national [Armenian] character, a rich palette," reads a character reference written by Nikolai Myaskovsky soon after Khachaturyan's graduation from the Conservatory. "A striving for technical inventiveness, original language, and manner of exposition. An ability to use forms of grand scope. Has free command of orchestral (excellent sense of orchestral coloring), chamber, piano, and vocal music (both lyrical and choral)."

Back in his student years Khachaturyan was already giving serious thought to the nature of the composing profession, its goals, the tasks facing the young Soviet art, and the specific character of the national element in music.

"What does national harmony signify? Who can say that national music should develop along this or that line?" Khachaturyan asked in 1933 during a discussion of a concert given by Moscow Conservatory student composers. "Why can't we use French harmony? It is absolutely impossible to be completely original in composition. If a composer is fresh and original in musical qualities, forms, and contrapuntal structure, let him use French harmony." That was probably Khachaturyan's response to those who accused him of imitating the Impressionists.

His identity as a composer was formed in the years when a difficult struggle was going on in Soviet music between different trends in art, a struggle of ideas accompanied by a fervent search for the true meaning of art. The situation was defined by a confrontation between the Russian Association of Proletarian Musicians (RAPM) and the Association of Modern Music (AMM). Khachaturyan had a vivid recollection of those days when, as he said,

The tone was set by RAPM. . . . The leaders of this association apparently had noble aims—to help build a revolutionary musical culture, to attract the interest of the broad masses, to give them compositions inspired by revolutionary themes. In practice, however, RAPM's activities, more administrative than creative, were harmful to artistic development. I remember stormy meetings when RAPM leaders would belabor all who thought differently, and indiscriminately praise its members, mainly for choosing themes connected with a rather primitive interpretation of revolutionary and democratic concepts.

They had their own very confused ideas of what music should be like in a communist society and attempted to force them upon the music world. Some were talented composers who wrote excellent works. But the minute they faced the public, an unbelievable muddle would start, with everything turned upside down. Even Lenin said that the Proletcult workers were muddled in their thinking. . . . God save us from attempts to bottle up musical creativeness, to confine it within an artificial framework. History has shown that nothing good will come of it.

Nevertheless, I cannot completely ignore some of RAPM's good initiatives in introducing greater democracy into many musical establishments, nor can I deny the fact that several talented composers emerged from this group who in time earned a prominent place in our musical world. These were Alexander Davidenko, Nikolai Chemberji, Boris Shekhter, and Victor Bely.

Khachaturyan's opinion of RAPM is easy to understand. As an artist with highly democratic views, he could not but share the desire to create music understandable to the masses, whom life itself, and the great cultural achievements taking place throughout the country, had pulled into the orbit of art. He understood and sympathized with an article Boris Asafiev wrote in 1924 under the heading "Hurry, Composers," in which he appealed to his colleagues to unite. Aram Khachaturyan was aware that many representatives of RAPM were not yet ready professionally to write music worthy of the new audiences nor to deal with the great themes dictated by life itself. He was aware that a narrow approach to classical music and to many aspects of contemporary art was objectively harmful to the entire musical process and held back its progressive development.

On the other hand, Khachaturyan certainly was not satisfied with the Association of Modern Music—particularly the isolation of composers' work from the vital problems of the day, a certain aloofness and political indifference. Nevertheless, he held such AMM members as Vissarion Shebalin and Yuri Shaporin, to say nothing of Nikolai Myaskovsky, in high esteem.

It was just this dual evaluation of the RAPM and AMM platform that brought Khachaturyan to the Production collective of Moscow Conservatory student-composers, or Procoll as it was called. Its membership included Victor Bely, Nikolai Chemberji, Marian Koval, Vladimir Fere, Sergei Ryauzov, and Boris Shekhter, among others. From the day it was founded in 1925 it was headed by Alexander Davidenko. The members would regularly gather at the Conservatory to discuss new works and criticize them mercilessly. Their aim was to achieve close links between music, the revolutionary times, and the broad democratic audience. Davidenko dreamed of big compositions produced by the collective efforts of young composers, all rich with universally important ideas. One such work, an oratorio, *The Road of October,* by Davidenko, Bely, Shekhter, Koval, Zara Levin, and others, composed for the tenth anniversary of the 1917 Revolution, was written before Khachaturyan joined the group. Davidenko planned for another work to be written three years later, in 1930. It was to be an opera, with the 1905 Russian Revolution for its subject. Parts of the libretto had already been distributed among the composers; some of the scenes were ready, but the authors were not satisfied with the fruits of their collective efforts and it was never completed. The minutes of Procoll meetings convey the atmosphere reigning in that corporation of musicians. The minutes were taken down and preserved for us by Sergei Ryauzov.

*February 1, 1930.* Aram Khachaturyan, just made a member, shows his colleagues his "March No. 1" for brass band [the same March that caught Boris Haikin's attention]. The March is approved by his colleagues. Fere notes the good contrapuntal continuity of different themes. Davidenko is laconic as usual—"too much splendor," he says.*

*Sergei Ryauzov recalls, "Immediately after hearing Khachaturyan's March for brass band, Procoll members sensed the music's freshness and originality, and to a certain extent, the composer's spontaneous technique, particularly the skill of the polyphonic supporting voices, the colorful arrangement, and spicy harmony. Khachaturyan's music was already easily recognizable, a quality that Dmitri Shostakovich subsequently noted."

*April 26, 1930.* We hear Khachaturyan's song-poem "In Honor of the Ashugs," "Song of the Black Sea Fleet" (performed by the composer), and harmonizing on "Javus Idin"—a Turkish folk melody. Fabius Vitachek: "A vivid and fresh piece—the first." Boris Shekhter: "Khachaturyan Frenchifies the arrangement of the Turkish song and his Ashugs." Davidenko: "In emotion, assertiveness, and musical freshness Khachaturyan is closer to Procoll than others. Similar elements are heard in his choral songs, which he himself considers poor. . . . The French influence is debatable. Joyful impression."

*June 10, 1930.* Khachaturyan plays his Scenes on the Barricades, written for the opera *The Year 1905*, a joint effort. Shekhter: "This is Khachaturyan's first attempt at reflecting the revolutionary theme in his work. And he feels this on the emotional plane. There is no insincerity here. . . ." Davidenko: "This is a striking example of an intellectual fellow traveler approaching the proletariat. But can find no simple solution to the problem. Khachaturyan wants to convey hidden emotional ideas and not simple thoughts. That was the road Shekhter followed. I believe there is a shade of insincerity in the pathos." Khachaturyan: "I don't like the music myself, but I believe the idea is correct."

*August 7, 1930.* After hearing the Circus and Quartet of Policemen—scenes written for the same opera by Zinovi Kompaneyets and Sergei Ryauzov, Khachaturyan said: "The barrenness of the methods applied by Kompaneyets is quite appropriate, but in the Quartet of Policemen it should be spiced up a bit, filtered through his own ego. It's a good scene."

Judging by these short quotations from the minutes, the Procoll meetings encouraged sincere discussion of the problems of musical art by long-standing members and newcomers alike. The younger members, Khachaturyan for one, allowed themselves the luxury of not always agreeing with the veterans on methods of reflecting life and revolutionary events in music. Then as in later years, Khachaturyan always opposed a direct, frontal approach to the idea of what the artist's mission is in life and the tasks of Soviet composers. As a young man he was already able to defend his viewpoint convincingly. Music did not exist for him that was not "spiced up," that was not "filtered through the ego," i.e., through the artist's very soul.

> I am against working collectively. Twice I have been convinced that this method is not for me. The first time was when Dmitri Shostakovich and I attempted to collaborate on a national anthem—there was a contest for a new anthem at the time. We worked together for several evenings, checking what each had written separately and finally putting all the individual variations together. Nothing came of it, however. The second time was a family affair. My wife Nina Makarova and I wrote the music to the play *Zoya,* produced by the Soviet Army Theater in Moscow, and based on a poem by Margarita Aliger. Although the music was accepted and the play was staged, our collaboration almost led to a divorce.

Nevertheless, when he was a member of Procoll, Khachaturyan did not hold such categorical views of collective creative work. On the contrary, he was among those who advocated continuing work on the opera *The Year 1905* and starting work on another collective opera, to be called *The Law of the Taiga.* Among other works he played for his colleagues, besides his popular songs and marches, was the Sonata Allegro for Violin and Piano, written for the play *A Question of Honor,* staged by the Moscow Art Theater—Studio Two, earlier known as the Moscow Art Theater—Studio One. Procoll thus transcended the limitations of RAPM. This may be seen also from some of the works of Victor Bely, Boris Shekhter, and Nikolai Chemberji.

In 1931–1932 the idea of creating a single association of composers came under consideration. After publication on April 23, 1932, of a resolution by the Communist Party Central Committee on "Restructuring Literary and Artistic Organizations," RAPM and similar literary and art groupings were dissolved. That same year branches of the composers union were formed in Moscow, Leningrad, and several other cities. They later merged to form the Union of Soviet Composers.

The student years were coming to an end. Khachaturyan would continue as a postgraduate with Nikolai Myaskovsky for two more years. But since it was the graduation thesis that entitled one to call oneself a professional composer, Khachaturyan decided to write a symphony.

"My youthful efforts and creative quest were crowned by the First Symphony," he recalled many years later. This was one of the first symphonies in the history of Armenian music.

The spontaneity of Transcaucasian folk music was the source that gave his music life from the very start of his career. In every new work he reached farther down into the wellsprings of folk music, compressed over the centuries, to express the most universal thoughts and feelings; he learned to select from the rich treasure chest of folklore its most characteristic features, learned to speak clearly and freely in the musical language of his people. In this respect the First Symphony denoted a significant achievement for the composer. It captivated audiences by the range of its emotional imagery and lavish melodiousness, its amazing embodiment of Armenian folk songs and dances. He dedicated this work to the fifteenth anniversary of the establishment of Soviet Power in Armenia, saying:

> For me the Symphony will always be identified with the image of my country, for it is the story of the Armenian people's historical past, so charged with the struggle for national independence. It is the story of the people's present—filled with the joy of creative endeavor.

At his final examination, June 11, 1934, the First Symphony was played in an arrangement for two pianos by Lev Stepanov and Nina Musinyan. "I shall never forget our rehearsals with Aram Ilych," Nina Musinyan recalls. "He sang, conducted, and spoke as excitedly as if his symphonic offspring had already been accepted."

The Moscow Conservatory qualifying committee, which included Nikolai Myaskovsky, Reinhold Gliere, Vissarion Shebalin, Heinrich Litinsky, and Nikolai Zhilyev, unanimously agreed that Khachaturyan's work deserved the grade "excellent." His name was engraved in gold letters on the Moscow Conservatory Honor Board, where it can be seen to this day.

The premiere of the First Symphony soon followed. The chief conductor of the Moscow Philharmonic Symphony Orchestra, Oigen Senkar, was interested in it and conducted its premier performance in the Grand Hall of the Conservatory on April 23, 1935.

"For me," wrote Khachaturyan, "the premiere of the First was an unforgettable experience. The atmosphere was one of pomp and ceremony. Both the audience and the critics greeted my first symphonic work with exceptional warmth." At the beginning of the following season Senkar conducted the Symphony twice more (October 22 and 24, 1935), and on April 23, 1936, a year after its premiere, it was performed in Leningrad on the program of Fritz Shtidri, chief conductor of the Leningrad Philharmonic. This marked the beginning of regular performances of Khachaturyan's new works in Leningrad.

Dmitri Shostakovich attended Khachaturyan's debut in Leningrad. The professional friendship between these two composers, of which more later, played an exceptionally important part in Khachaturyan's life.

The music of the First Symphony was vividly descriptive, captivating in the spontaneity of its folk music improvisatory feel and the author's original expressiveness. However, it had not been easy to write. None of his earlier works had taken so much of his energy nor given him so much trouble, especially with regard to the musical form. As the composer recalled,

> The strict sonata–symphonic form was truly a Procrustean bed for me. I felt confined; my wild imagination kept breaking its norms no matter how hard I tried to conform to them at first. Subsequently, however, I never regretted that I had chosen a rather unusual form for the first movement, for it fully coincided with the content I wished to put into the music.

Actually, the form of the first movement was quite innovative. And Khachaturyan returned many times to his sonata–symphonic allegro "model," perfecting and modifying it. It is noteworthy that already in the First Symphony he planned to blend the improvisations of Eastern folk music with the traditional European symphonic form.

The classical canons of the sonata form imply a contention of two contrasting subjects in an elaborated exposition and a recurrence of these two themes in the recapitulation. This schema could never have supported the profound development of the European symphony that took place in the eighteenth, nineteenth, and twentieth centuries had it not been continually stretched or even violated by composers. Aram Khachaturyan was among those "daring" composers. In the exposition of the first movement of his First Symphony we hear two themes whose intonational kernels can easily be traced in the intro-duction-prologue. In the exposition he promptly begins to vary and elaborate them. In the recapitulation we again hear the material further developed. As for the two elaborated parts, their themes do not clash; this is, rather, a comparison. The modifying and developing is thus a continuous process throughout the first movement. This is set off only by the pro-logue and epilogue, built on the music of *ashug* improvisation, i.e., the original tale of the country's historic past as told by a bard. The Armenian music critic Margarita Rukhyan interprets the form of the symphony's first movement as a comparison of the singing of two *ashugs*. "The contest of two *ashugs,* voicing two philosophies, two temperaments, contains the nucleus of the development of the elaboration which acquires an original trend thanks to a third party—the people, who judge this con-test." Such was Khachaturyan's new interpretation of sonatas. And that is why the First Symphony was so important for the development of all of Armenian music, and not only Armenian; it was possibly no less important than the more mature Second Symphony.

It is not really important that Khachaturyan did not argue with the critics, who pointed out that the music was not balanced in all the movements, that some of the episodes were overex-tended and ambiguous, or that the Finale did not summarize, as required by the symphonic genre. Neither was it accidental that before the performance of the symphony in the autumn of 1935 Khachaturyan made several minor changes in the score. Despite this, he always loved his First.

"The symphony—that is my face," he wrote in 1935. In time, however, he did regret that he had not been more resolute in ignoring the canons of classical forms in his score.

When he started conducting in the 1950s, Khachaturyan often performed his First Symphony, both at home and abroad. On the eve of his visit to Erevan for the celebration of his sixtieth birthday, he said:

> I want to play the First Symphony. I have not presented it in Armenia. I believe that all of me, and not only me, has come from the First Symphony.
>
> Parts of the First are intuitive, but I did succeed in posing the main problems in this composition.

The young composer could not have been expected to resolve these problems. Not only because he had started studying music only ten years earlier, but because attainment of the heights of the symphonic genre was still a thing of the future for Soviet music. Aram Khachaturyan's First Symphony appeared and was heard at a time when song-symphonies were still fresh in the minds of the public, when music critics insisted that only such symphonies could allow composers to mold a Soviet style in music. Speaking of this simplistic manner of judging the artistic value of a symphony, Shostakovich remarked in 1935, "If you write down a poem—it seems you have content; if you don't write one down—then it's formalism." It was now said that the poem was not everything, that the music was also important. "Today the main thing, so to say, in Soviet music is to explore the region of the most different genres," said Dmitri Kabalevsky. Victor Bely stressed that "a Soviet symphonic style does not as yet exist. . . . We do not yet have compositions broadly reflecting stylistic and ideological-emotional cross-sections of our life in a beautiful form." The symphonic scores already created by that time, he claimed, "were the result mainly of tendencies to form a new musical language, a new musical thinking."

But less than a year after that discussion in February 1935 Tikhon Khrennikov's First Symphony was played and six months later, Nikolai Myaskovsky's Sixteenth. And a year previous, Dmitri Kabalevsky's Second Symphony had had its debut. These events give reason to be more tolerant than the discussants were in appraising the initial period of the development of the Soviet symphony. The explanation is simple: they did not have, nor could they have had, the hindsight we possess today.

Nevertheless, it is within the context of the severe judgments expressed in the discussions that we gain a better understanding of the true importance of Khachaturyan's First Symphony, for his own work and for the future of Armenian music and Soviet music generally. Many of the musical ideas contained in the score were developed and given new dimensions by the composer in his more mature works. The wonderful secondary singing theme played by the cello in the first movement heralds many examples of Khachaturyan's musical idiom in his piano, violin, and cello concertos. The lyricism of the second movement is echoed in the revelations of *Gayane* and *Spartacus*. In the Second Symphony the dynamic surge of the dance finale, the unrestrained nature of the dance, threatens to become more and more impressively forceful. In the First Symphony the beautiful colors of the Armenian landscape serve to confirm the birth of a truly great composer-painter, one of this century's most significant masters of the orchestra. In commenting on the First Symphony, Lev Oborin remarked that

Khachaturyan was lucky to have avoided a tedious search for his own artistic identity. Although he started to study music rather late, he immediately spoke out in his own voice, becoming the Khachaturyan that we all know today. I believe the secret of the artistic success that has accompanied him for so many years now is to be sought in this great flood of talent.

# Rise to Fame

*I was totally immersed in the atmosphere of the*
*upsurge of socialist culture. I was at the very center*
*of a mighty movement for realism in art, for a*
*people's, Soviet art.*

ARAM KHACHATURYAN

Aram Khachaturyan's rise from a gifted musician to one of the
top composers of our time was swift indeed. His great talent,
his phenomenal capacity for work, his persevering efforts for
professional perfection, and his excellent teachers all contributed to his rise to fame. His success was also due in great part
to the general situation in Soviet music in the 1930s. It would
be difficult to understand Khachaturyan's work outside this
context. As a matter of fact, it would hardly have been possible
outside this context. Soviet music critics speak of the 1930s as
one of the richest and most fruitful periods in the development
of Soviet musical culture.

It was in that decade that the compositions that came to
form the "golden treasury" of Soviet music began to be created:
Dmitri Shostakovich's Fifth Symphony and the opera *Katerina
Izmailova,* Sergei Prokofiev's oratorio *Alexander Nevsky* and his
ballet *Romeo and Juliet,* and the songs of Isaac Dunaevsky, Vladimir Zakharov, and Matvei Blanter, to name but a few. Here
also should be included Khachaturyan's piano and violin concertos, for his work was the direct outcome of this country's
flourishing musical art, and also convincing proof of the really
great achievements of the national schools of music. From its
very beginning, music in the USSR developed as a multinational
art. Traditions were assimilated and the age-old experience of
such different cultures as the Ukrainian, Georgian, Kazakh,

and Azerbaijan were developed; the successes of professional musical cultures and the wealth of folk music traditions were summed up and synthesized. This was a great leap forward in the musical development of a huge territory peopled by various nationalities, a process unprecedented in its complexity.

This process was not without its conflicts. Whereas in the 1920s the struggle between various tendencies, especially between RAPM and AMM, was confined to disputes between groupings, it now emerged in the contradictory works of certain composers. There were also exaggerations in evaluating certain works—it is enough to recall some of the critical articles that appeared in newspapers and magazines in 1936 on the problems of music. Today it is quite evident that "notwithstanding some correct critical remarks and ideas of a general nature, the sharply categorical tone in appraising certain artistic trends was unfounded and unjust." This is stated in no uncertain terms in the *History of Soviet Music*. "Their unequivocal and categorical tone," it continues,

> obviated any possibility of a free creative discussion of the essence of the problems. As a result many talented, though possibly controversial compositions, were excommunicated from Soviet cultural art and unconditionally ascribed to the hostile formalistic trend.

Such criticism in the 1930s did not touch Aram Khachaturyan. When analyzing his work, however, one must take into account all the complexities of the creative process of those years, as well as the fact that the atmosphere of general creative upsurge was the determining factor (this includes all of Soviet art of the 1930s). For the first time the people definitely felt themselves the creators of a new life, the creators and absolute masters of all spiritual values. Music greatly influenced the new audience by the unprecedented force of its immediacy. And Khachaturyan had the incomparable gift of such immediacy. As an exceptionally sensitive artist, he was able to perceive what the most democratic audiences thirsted for; this, very possibly, was one of the chief reasons for his rapid rise to the heights of nationwide recognition.

Photographs of Aram Khachaturyan taken in those years—he was just over thirty—show him to have a prepossessing appearance, black eyes peering out from under thick eyebrows, and a mass of curly hair. At times he is smiling; more often he seems to be listening to himself. He is an optimist, an epicurean, an exceptionally active person who finds time for everything. He makes friends easily and has many friends, particularly among musicians, poets, and people of the theater and film world. He attends almost every interesting concert and musical, or theatrical premiere.

The period from 1935 to 1941 was among his most fruitful. He completed his postgraduate studies at the Moscow Conservatory. He wrote and successfully performed his piano concerto and composed incidental music for two films, *Pepo* and *Zangezur*. His *Poem to Stalin* had its first performance. The composer kept in close touch with Armenia and was elected deputy to the Armenian parliament. He was appointed to executive positions in the organizing committee of the Composers Union. He was awarded the Order of Lenin for his music for the ballet *Happiness,* performed during a ten-day festival of Armenian music in Moscow. He wrote incidental music to the Moscow productions of *The Widow of Valencia* and *The Masquerade*. And, finally, he married composer Nina Makarova, who had studied with him in Myaskovsky's composition class. She was a musician with a very sensitive feeling for his artistic personality, and the mother of his beloved son.* All this in just over seven years. *Happiness* could have been the name not only of his first ballet but also of this period of his life and work. As a musician, Khachaturyan benefited greatly from his close association with prominent Soviet composers. His friendship with each of them is a subject in itself; his association with Prokofiev, Myaskovsky, Shostakovich, and Gliere will be dealt with in later chapters.

Of all his meetings with Soviet and foreign cultural emi-

*This was his second marriage. By his first wife, the pianist Ramella Khachaturyan, he had had a daughter, Nune, for whom he always showed a touching concern. She too became a pianist and music teacher at the Moscow Conservatory Music School.

nences during those years, Khachaturyan particularly singles out those with Maxim Gorky and Romain Rolland. During his visit to the Soviet Union in the summer of 1935, Romain Rolland stayed at Maxim Gorky's country home near Moscow. Khachaturyan recalled one day in particular because it was so hot. Gorky had invited a large group of writers, painters, musicians, and artists to meet Rolland. Among them were Heinrich Neuhaus, Alexander Goldenweiser, Yuri Shaporin, Dmitri Kabalevsky, and Samuel Feinberg. The German antifascist composer, Hans Eisler, who lived in Moscow at the time, was also there. Aram Khachaturyan was most likely the youngest of the guests, and it was certainly not pure chance that Gorky had invited him. At the turn of the century Romain Rolland was very interested in the music of the East. At get-togethers he organized in 1906 in Paris, within the framework of the courses of the school of social sciences, Russian, Persian, Georgian, and Armenian music was played. "The national distinctions were clearly expressed in the music," wrote Rolland.

> Even in dreams the Armenian is deep, tragic, and courageous; the Georgian is clear and sunny, almost Italian; the Russian is dynamic, variable, and gentle. What wonderful music! These people are somehow differently gifted in music than we are and I am certain that sooner or later European art will feel the influence of this art. . . .

The details of his meetings with Gorky and Rolland remained fresh in Khachaturyan's memory to his very last days.

> We met Gorky in the garden; he was crushing bricks to spread over the paths. A courteous host, Gorky entertained his guests and asked about their work. While talking he held in his hand the ever-present wooden holder for the cigarettes he rolled himself.
>
> Romain Rolland did not feel too well, and came to the table a bit late. Tall, stooped, and thin, he wore a suit buttoned to the top with a plaid shawl thrown over his shoulders. He listened carefully to each of us, all the while observing us. For some

reason I had the impression that he was looking for Dmitri Shostakovich among the musicians.

When I was introduced—a young postgraduate student who, I believed, had been invited as a fill-in—he asked me:

"Are you Armenian?"

"Yes, I am."

"I have been interested in Armenian music for some time. Have you any samples with you?"

"Not with me, I'm sorry."

"Could you send me a collection of Armenian folk songs?" Rolland asked, stressing the word "folk."

I sent him a collection arranged by Komitas and received a letter from him, thanking me for the wonderful songs and expressing a great interest in Armenian musical culture.

Gorky, who was standing near us during this conversation, suddenly said: "Composers should study folklore. Folklore must be studied seriously. Folklore is the beginning of everything."

I can still hear Gorky's slightly hollow voice saying—"Folklore must be studied seriously."

Judging by Rolland's description of Armenian music, he must have enjoyed the Armenian folk songs as arranged by Komitas. We can only regret that the writer, who had such feeling for music, never heard the works of Aram Khachaturyan. For it is in them that we so clearly see the influence of Eastern music on European music, about which Rolland wrote so prophetically.

Khachaturyan devoted more and more of his time to social and professional activities. In 1937 he was appointed to the important and honorable post of Vice Chairman of the Moscow Composers Union. Two years later he became Vice Chairman of the nationwide association of composers—the Organizing Committee of the Union of Soviet Composers. Any music institution could have been proud of such widely representative events as the ten-day festivals of Soviet Music that won such wide acclaim before the war; or the interesting discussions about the future of certain musical forms; or the analysis of symphonic works and operas by Soviet composers. The Union dealt with a wide range of problems. It established a Music Fund in 1939 whose function it was to publish the works of Soviet composers. Another important aspect of its work was to provide out-of-town retreats where composers could work in quiet and pleasant surroundings, an atmosphere rarely available in large cities. These were situated in Staraya Ruza, not far from Moscow, later at a farm near Ivanovo, also at Repino close to Leningrad, Vorzele near Kiev, Dilizhan in Armenia, Sukhumi in Georgia, and Sortavale in Karelia. A great deal of wonderful music was written in these retreats.

Aram Khachaturyan was one of those who initiated such facilities. Together with Nikolai Chemberji and the Director of the Music Fund, Levon Atovmyan, they located "a place in Staraya Ruza, which at that time was an impenetrable forest," recalls the composer Zara Levin.

> The first residents were Yuri Shaporin with his wife and children, Khachaturyan and Nina Makarova, Nikolai Chemberji with his wife and daughter. A wisp of smoke rising from a samovar helped us locate Yuri Shaporin, who was writing his opera *The Decembrists.* The wonderful sounds of the violin meant David Oistrakh was rehearsing Khachaturyan's Violin Concerto.

Aram Khachaturyan, energetic, sociable, and emotional, had since his youth always had numerous social obligations, both inside and outside the Composers Union, obligations to which he dedicated himself. He wrote later in an article that he was often asked during tours abroad whether the social activities of Soviet composers hindered their work. "I would explain patiently that for artists who had matured together with their country, social activities were not an obligation but a necessity."

But then, it was Khachaturyan's nature and his unbridled temperament that often kept him from maintaining a balance of his time between social activities and composing. Khachaturyan came to realize this much later but it changed little in the general tenor of his life.

While working in the Composers Union, he associated closely with the union chairman. The Moscow branch and the national union were then headed by Reinhold Gliere.

The Union was first housed in a large room divided by plywood walls. We all worked tirelessly. The organizing committee was given one year in which to prepare for the Constituent Congress of the USSR Composers Union. Through no fault of ours, the Congress was not convened in 1940 nor in the first half of 1941, for the war started and although the organizing committee was very active even in those grim war years, plans for a congress were postponed. It was not held until 1948.

Aram Khachaturyan and Reinhold Gliere: student and teacher, musicians with an age difference of more than a quarter of a century.

Gliere was a very kind and thoughtful person. He invariably tried to satisfy the numerous personal and professional requests of musicians and always remained very fair. Though strict and demanding, he was also kind. He believed that a high level of professionalism was an absolute must for a composer; he made no allowances in this.

Reinhold Gliere was exceptionally intelligent, well versed in all the processes of artistic work. He had a sharp tongue and, if need be, could put a braggart in his place or clear up an argument or conflict with just a few words. He enjoyed immense authority in the Union; his integrity was beyond question.

Khachaturyan was attracted to Gliere by his outstanding skill as a composer—"It was a simple matter for him to improvise a five-part fugue." But, as Khachaturyan pointed out, "Craftsmanship never overshadowed the main idea in his compositions; he invariably tried to achieve the clearest means of musical expression, most accessible to the masses."

This is one of the reasons why his ballet, *The Red Poppy*, was so popular and why another of his ballets, *The Bronze Horseman*, is still playing to this day.

His capacity for work was another feature that always astounded Khachaturyan. "During the war," wrote Khachaturyan,

I evacuated my family to Sverdlovsk while I remained in Moscow.

Reinhold Gliere would often invite me over for dinner. Knowing that I had an ulcer, he was touchingly concerned for me. When it came to working he was something of a fanatic. I was able to observe this while still a student, but it was most evident during the war. When I joined my family in Sverdlovsk for a short time Gliere and his family were also there. For the first few weeks his family didn't even have beds. They slept on the floor. But a piano stood in the center of the room; Gliere would place a candle on the piano (electricity was scarce in those days), and work, oblivious of all else.

In 1940 Moscow musicians marked Gliere's fortieth anniversary as a composer; Khachaturyan headed the anniversary committee. Many of Gliere's former students were still living, among them such celebrities as Nikolai Myaskovsky, Sergei Prokofiev, Boris Lyatoshinsky, and Lev Revutzky. It was on this occasion that Khachaturyan wrote the very affectionate article about Gliere that appeared in *Pravda*. A touching concern for his teacher is evident also in a letter written soon after the war to Anastas Mikoyan, then Deputy Chairman of the USSR Council of People's Commissars (Deputy Prime Minister), with whom Khachaturyan was well acquainted since before the war.

"Dear Anastas Ivanovich, he wrote,

I consider it my moral obligation to remind you of our conversation last year on the day the Stalin Prizes were awarded. We discussed our senior citizens and the concern shown them. We also spoke of our senior composer, author of the famous ballet, *The Red Poppy*—Reinhold Gliere, who was not among the senior laureates.

He has now been nominated for the Stalin Prize for his Concerto for Voice and Orchestra. Nevertheless, I feel it necessary to write you because you asked me to remind you of this in good time.

Reinhold Gliere is seventy years old. He has written numerous symphonies and chamber works well known here and abroad; he is a master craftsman and pedagogue who has taught an entire generation of Soviet composers. I would especially wish to stress his merits in helping to develop the national arts in our non-Russian republics. Gliere's work was particularly productive in developing the national music of Azerbaijan and Uzbekistan. . . .

The public activities of People's Artist of the USSR R. M. Gliere are particularly important. As you know, he is Chairman of the Organizing Committee of the USSR Union of Composers.

I believe that R. M. Gliere has earned the right to a Stalin Prize for his services to Soviert art.

Gliere received the Stalin Prize that year.

Nina Makarova's name was often mentioned in my talks with Aram Khachaturyan, whether he was speaking of various years of his life, his work, or just recalling some of the places he had toured. He always spoke warmly of his wife. She had passed away in 1976, but he continued to speak of her as a part of himself, his work, his life, of his very existence. His first meeting with her Khachaturyan described in this way:

The door of the classroom where Myaskovsky was teaching opened suddenly and . . . happiness walked in.

Nikolai Sergeyevitch Zhilyev introduced me to Nina. This girl with bangs and beautiful, expressive eyes seemed to me reticent and secretive. She was from the Volga area and resembled the typical Russian woman; there was nothing Eastern about her. We were in the same year of studies. I don't know how it happened, but I was ahead of her. I was attracted by her seriousness and her talent. The three-part symphony with which she completed her postgraduate course with Myaskovsky in 1938 was a great success.

In later years Nina wrote many kinds of music—for the theater and films, and violin pieces played by Leonid Kogan and Victor Pikaisen. Her own performance of Six Virtuoso Etudes for Piano was highly praised by Emil Gilels. Her operas were also interesting, particularly *Zoya*, about Zoya Kosmodemyanskaya, the World War II heroine.

Nina was an exceptionally warmhearted person. Her love of music was absolutely unselfish, she adored Ulanova and Rikhter and worshiped Shostakovich; she attended Conservatory concerts more often than I, not wishing to miss anything worthwhile. Books were her passion; she was interested in art—how many museums and art galleries we visited together all over the world!

I could never shake off a sense of vexation and pain that I and my work involuntarily overshadowed Nina's work and personality. In vain I tried to stop it; it just seemed to happen that way, possibly because Nina was a singularly kindhearted person, and everyone just found it more convenient and simpler to consider Nina Makarova the wife of the composer, Aram Khachaturyan.

In the 1930s Khachaturyan was quite active in the sphere of popular music. After his two Marches, discussed in connection with the days of the Procoll meetings, Aram Ilych composed the "Zangezur March," one of the most interesting and easily remembered pieces of music from the film *Zangezur*.

The decision to have my "Zangezur March" played on Moscow's Red Square for the military parade was a great honor. Regrettably, almost no one could hear it. What happened was that Semyon Chernetsky, the composer and military band conductor, in those years responsible for military music in the country, did not like my march. He even said the music was not suited for marching. He said the second part of one of the themes was quite out of place. Apparently others thought differently, for my march was played, but Chernetsky had it played when the tanks were rumbling over Red Square.

Such songs as "March of the Red Fleet," "On Gogol Boulevard," "Daughters of Iran," "Pepo's Song" from the film *Pepo*, and "Zulfiya's Song" from the film *The Garden*, brought him wide popularity. Many of the most popular songs of the 1930s came from films, and the best composers of the time wrote for the screen. Such films as *Alexander Nevsky* and *Ivan the Terrible*—the result of collaboration between Sergei Eisenstein and Sergei Prokofiev—made film history. Dmitri Shostakovich collaborated with such eminent film directors as Leonid Trauberg, Grigory Kozintsev, Alexander Dovzhenko, and Sergei Yutkevich; he wrote the music for the famous Maxim trilogy—*Youth of Maxim, Return of Maxim,* and *The Vyborg Region*—and for the film *Counter Plan*.

Khachaturyan, too, wrote for the screen at all stages of his career. First, however, we must review his music for the stage, as he wrote for the theater first and only later for the screen.

# Music for Stage and Screen

*My passion for the theater is such that if music had
not, in its time, monopolized my mind, I most likely
would have become an actor.*

ARAM KHACHATURYAN

*I came to films with absolutely no idea of the broad
field of activity it affords the composer. Though
many years have gone by since then, I must admit
that composing for the screen still opens up to me
new aspects of this exceptionally interesting work.*

ARAM KHACHATURYAN

In discussing the various genres Khachaturyan has worked in,
critics have often noted that the theatrical was an organic part
of his music. It was only natural, therefore, that he should start
writing for the stage, a field rich in traditions both in West
European music—Beethoven's *Egmont,* Schubert's *Rosamunde,*
Bizet's *L'Arlesienne,* Grieg's *Peer Gynt*—and in Russian music
—from Glinka's *Prince Kholmsky* to Ilya Satz's music for the
Moscow Art Theater production of *The Bluebird.*

The passion for the theater, which Khachaturyan got from
his brother Suren, was to remain with him to the end of his
days. He wrote the music for over twenty plays, all very different—lyrical comedy, psychological drama, classical tragedy,
Gabriel Sundukyan and William Shakespeare, Lope de Vega
and Mikhail Lermontov, Nikolai Pogodin and Boris Lavrenyov.
Nevertheless, in all his theatrical scores we never fail to hear
his inimitable voice.

Khachaturyan prepared scrupulously for every new stage
production, studying the period and atmosphere described by
the author. His two scores for *Macbeth* are a case in point. He

73

wrote his first *Macbeth*—consisting of twenty-four musical numbers—in 1933 for the production by the Sundukyan Theater in Erevan. Twenty years later, when the Moscow Maly Theater asked him to write the score for its production, he composed twelve numbers based on a completely new approach to Shakespeare's drama. For his work he went to England in 1955, saw the play at the Old Vic in London, and visited the Shakespeare Museum in Stratford-on-Avon. He wrote that

> optimistic confidence in the present and in a good future for English art were largely promoted by London's theaters, particularly the Old Vic, where I attended a performance of Shakespeare's *Macbeth*. This theater won my heart. I was delighted by the actors, who were able to convey their feelings and passions without visible effort.

Khachaturyan believed it was the job of the composer who writes music for the stage to convey the feelings and passions of the characters without stylizing the music to the given age. In those years Khachaturyan already disagreed with the view that music is simply a background for the plot. For him the music was a major component of an integrated whole.

Most of his stage music was written in the 1940s and 1950s, but it was in the 1930s that many of his associations with directors and theaters began. It was then that his basic principles took shape, and he followed them in the ensuing decades when working in what are called "applied musical genres." In the 1930s the Moscow Art Theater, Studio Two, staged a play entitled *A Question of Honor,* which marked the beginning of Khachaturyan's long association with that institution and its outstanding actors. He was subsequently to work with them on five additional productions. An association with Ruben Simonov began with productions by the Armenian drama studio in the Armenian House of Culture. Simonov was soon to become the principal director of Moscow's Vakhtangov Theater and producer of Lermontov's drama *The Masquerade.* The production of *Macbeth* by the Sundukyan Theater cemented his collaboration with his boyhood friend Armen Gulakyan, who in the

1930s headed Armenia's best dramatic theater. In 1922 Gulak-yan, then a modest young actor with Tbilisi's Armenian Theater who had drawn Suren Khachaturov's attention, had made the nearly month-long journey with Khachaturyan to Moscow, where he subsequently studied in Suren's studio. The title role in Khachaturov's first production of *Macbeth* was played by Grachya Narsesyan—a wonderful actor of the Armenian stage and screen.

"You haven't forgotten what I told you about the mutes?" Khachaturyan asked Gulakyan in a letter during preparations for the Erevan premiere of *Macbeth*. "If it is too loud or too soft the mutes can be put on or removed. But don't muffle the music, let it be heard."

His collaboration with such outstanding directors proved an excellent school, one in which he learned to fathom the "secrets" of the stage and its dramatic springs. Khachaturyan always prized the director's opinion of his music. "Please write me your impressions of my music," he asked Gulakyan. "Write me about each number separately, first your general impression of how it sounds, and then whether it is expressive of that particular scene."*

But while learning from directors and actors, he was also teaching them his music. Many stage personalities who worked with him recall this, Yuri Zavadsky among them:

> About 1925 or 1926 a young man, an Armenian, came to my studio on Sretenka Street in Moscow, and timidly offered his services as a piano player. Elena Fedorova, a former actress with the Moscow Art Theater's Studio One, was then conducting

---

*Yuri Zavadsky, the principal director of the Mossoviet Theater, recalls that when the theater started rehearsals of *King Lear* in 1958, the producer, Irina Anisimova-Wolf, asked Aram Ilych to write the music. "Khachaturyan agreed, but, to our surprise, suggested that in the course of her work Anisimova-Wolf should choose fragments from her favorite works of any composers which she thought best suited to express the main idea of the play. He then attended a run-through of *King Lear*, listened to it all put together, left Moscow for two weeks, and wrote wonderful, absolutely Shakespearean music which, I believe, has not yet been fully appreciated."

classes in etudes with elements of pantomime. Our new soloist played at her lessons. I recall that Fedorova was very satisfied with him, praising his lively piano improvisations.

The pianist was of course Khachaturyan. "Many years later," continued Zavadsky, "Khachaturyan told me that he had gained a lot from those improvisations, they released his composer's imagination and awakened his love for the theater."

"Fedorova was teaching the Stanislavsky Method," Khachaturyan explained.

Stanislavsky's books had not yet been published but many actors of the Moscow Art Theater were already spreading this "new faith." When someone was given a sketch to do like this one—"You come home in an excellent mood but on the living room table there is a telegram informing you of the death of someone you love," I would learn its contents at the same time as the student and together we would start to improvise—he by means of his art, I by means of mine. I am certain that these improvisations—there were several a day—sharpened my musical perception and taught me a good deal. I agree absolutely with Dmitri Shostakovich, who said that his work as a pianist in silent films was not only a means of earning a living in his younger days, but an excellent school as well.

For the production of *The Widow of Valencia,* staged in 1940 for the Lenin Komsomol Theater by Ivan Bersenev and Sophia Giatsintova, Khachaturyan wrote six numbers, later to become a separate symphonic suite. This music clearly reveals Khachaturyan's kinship with the work of Lope de Vega, his ability to portray in surprisingly simple and understandable music the democratic spirit, temperament, and bubbling gaiety of the great Spaniard's comedies.

The widow Leonarda, who took a vow of celibacy she was later to break, was played by Giatsintova. Rostislav Plyatt and Arkadi Vovsi competed as her two suitors, Othon and Valerio. They not only compete for Leonarda's hand but also for priority in the brilliant comedy situations, mix-ups, and punch lines with which Lope de Vega was so generous. In the first and main round they both lose, for Leonarda prefers Camillo as an admirer. In the second round—most interesting for the audience—they both emerge triumphant. Giatsintova writes,

> I recall how much Aram Ilych enjoyed it when Plyatt and Vovsi sang his comic songs at rehearsals. Neither had a strong voice but both were very musical. And Khachaturyan's music, sarcastic and showing the heroes for what they are, was so good that the actors seemed to feel themselves opera singers. Everyone laughed, the composer loudest of all. Khachaturyan's music helped the actors greatly; even the well-molded characters created by Plyatt and Vovsi owed something to the music. At times the music conveyed, or more precisely, disclosed the character of the personage in general, and at certain moments of the play, better than even the talented and experienced actor could.

Khachaturyan took his work for the stage very seriously. He always attended rehearsals from the very beginning, along with the director and actors. *King Lear,* however, was an exception. The Moscow Art Theater conductor, Boris Izraelevsky, recalled that

> during rehearsals of Alexander Kron's *Deep Reconnaissance,* whose music was based on three Azerbaijan songs written by Khachaturyan, the composer not only helped the actors learn to play the *tara, kemancha,* and tambourine and sing in the Azerbaijan language, but, sitting together with the director, Mikhail Kedrov, he carefully examined all aspects of the director's ideas on the music and singing. He himself conducted the orchestra in rehearsals of the March in the Finale, working to make it sound just right.

In discussions of Khachaturyan's songs it was stressed that many became popular after being heard on the screen. Songs like "The Baltic Sea" from the Moscow Art Theater's 1942 production of *The Kremlin Chimes* and "Nina's Song" from the incidental music to Lermontov's drama, *The Masquerade,* are still popular. But the suites from *The Widow of Valencia* and *The Masquerade* rank among his best-known compositions.

Khachaturyan's music for the theater reached its peak in the latter. Composed originally for the Vakhtangov Theater production, it was subsequently used by many other theaters.

I shall never stop marveling at the miracles of *The Masquerade*, which Lermontov wrote when he was only twenty-one. I was very serious about my work on this production for several reasons. First of all, I like the Vakhtangov Theater, which had commissioned me to write the music, and I often attended its performances. Second, I knew that *The Masquerade* had been staged in Petrograd many years ago by Vsevolod Meyerhold with incidental music by Alexander Glazunov. When I saw the revival of this production in 1938 I noted with surprise that there was no waltz in his music, though it seemed definitely indicated by Lermontov. Glazunov had instructed Meyerhold to use Glinka's famous Waltz-Fantasy. I must admit that it was the waltz that gave me the most trouble. I was deeply touched by what Nina says after returning from that fateful ball as she remembers the evening. "How beautiful the new waltz is! I whirled ever faster, as if intoxicated. A wonderful desire seemed to carry me and my thoughts to the very horizon; something between sorrow and joy gripped my heart." I kept repeating these words over and over again but could not find a theme that I considered beautiful and new, in other words, appropriate enough. Nikolai Myaskovsky, with whom I shared my doubts, gave me a collection of romances and waltzes of the pre-Glinka era. I looked through them but they didn't inspire me. I was almost frantic; waltzes were all I could think of.

At that time I was posing for Evgeni Pasternak, who was painting my portrait. One day while posing I suddenly heard a theme in my head which became the second theme of my future waltz. I doubt if I can explain where it came from. But I am certain that, had it not been for the strenuous search of the past weeks, there would have been no such discovery. The theme was like a magic link, allowing me to pull out the whole chain. The rest of the waltz came to me easily, with no trouble at all.

This waltz was the "magic" link in Khachaturyan's incidental music for *The Masquerade*. It was a rare success. Yuri Yuzovsky, the prominent Soviet theater critic, wrote,

For centuries, artists, composers, actors, and directors have been attempting to fathom the artistic individuality of the author of *Romeo and Juliet*. I believe the composer Sergei Prokofiev deserves the palm, for in his music to the ballet he lays bare the quintessence of Shakespeare's tragedy. By fathoming the genius of Shakespeare he found his own genius. The same can be said of Aram Khachaturyan and his incidental music for Lermontov's *The Masquerade*. In this music Lermontov's perturbed muse is shown in an unusual, almost physical presence.

There is much more, of course, to the incidental music for *The Masquerade* than the "Waltz." There is "Nina's Song" and "Nocturne," both fine lyrical pieces, and also "Mazurka" and "Gallop"—all providing a general background, as it were, for the ball and masquerade. One of the main reasons for the popularity of this incidental music is undoubtedly its symphonic style. The composer stresses, as though in italics, the theme of the lost bracelet, wherein lies the core of all the main themes we are yet to hear. It was the "Waltz," however, that made Khachaturyan's incidental music famous. Ruben Simonov, who had a fine ear for music, suggested repeating it several times throughout the performance, starting with the ball scene and ending with the sad Finale, where reminiscences are intoned by a chorus backstage. After the dress rehearsal, the writer Alexei Tolstoy approached Khachaturyan, who recalled that "he praised the actors, then said, turning to me, that from the very first time it is heard, one feels in the intonations of the 'Waltz' that Nina's fate is predetermined; a tragic note seems to run all through it."

The feeling of an impending storm in the music for *The Masquerade* captured exactly the atmosphere on stage, but it also corresponded, almost uncannily well, to the atmosphere outside the theater at that time. The dress rehearsal was held on June 16, 1941, the premiere on June 21. The report of the premiere in the papers the next day appeared next to reports of fascist Germany's treacherous attack on the Soviet Union.

Due to the war, the Vakhtangov production had a short run, but the music was often played in those days, and later as well, as a symphonic suite written by Khachaturyan in 1944. Depending on the atmosphere, it sounded either highly dramatic, tinged by the tragic experiences of the war, or exultantly festive, seeming to express a confidence in ultimate victory.

In 1952 Yuri Zavadsky used Khachaturyan's music for his production of *The Masquerade* in the Mossoviet Theater. More than two decades later, Zavadsky wrote, "The music became so much a part of our production that it is not impossible to imagine our *Masquerade* without it."

In this production Arbenin was played by Nikolai Mordvinov—a wonderful actor with a fine ear for music. He also played the title role in *King Lear*. "Mordvinov had a tender love for my music," Khachaturyan said. "He told me many times that it helped him create the role. I invariably found his portrayal of Arbenin wonderful. He was impassioned and sincere at one and the same time. I recall my meetings with Nikolai Dmitrievich with gratitude and delight."

The State Symphony Orchestra conducted by Yevgeni Svetlanov played the "Waltz" from *The Masquerade* at the funeral services for Aram Khachaturyan in the Grand Hall of Moscow Conservatory. None of us had ever been able to understand that tragic elemental force before then. The "Waltz" made everyone in the hall feel with terrifying reality what a great musician we had lost.

Aram Khachaturyan's work for the theater is on a level with the finest Soviet achievements in this field—the scores of Sergei Prokofiev, Dmitri Shostakovich, and Tikhon Khrennikov.

For thirty years Khachaturyan was equally interested in stage and screen; only circumstances can explain his preference for one or the other at various times. In quantity there is a close balance—twenty-one stage productions, seventeen films. But, most important, the same principles went into all of them.

Khachaturyan considered film the most democratic form of art because it reached the largest number of people. He felt that the music should help make the film a work of art—synthetic by its very nature—which would shape the esthetic tastes of millions.

What actor who has dared to play the Moor of Venice has not pondered the essence of his tragedy? Blind jealousy? Betrayed trust? The well-known Soviet screen actor, Sergei Bondarchuk, struggled with these questions during the filming of Sergei Yutkevich's *Othello*. And his conclusion is based on Othello's words: "and when I love thee not, chaos is come again." "Chaos is the antithesis of harmony," commented Bondarchuk.

> But Shakespeare's hero, a true man of the Renaissance, eagerly searches for harmony everywhere—within himself and in all that surrounds him; he seeks an opportunity to unite his own harmonious perfection with the perfection of the world but does not find it. I believe that in his music for the film, Khachaturyan precisely caught and vividly expressed what may be called the dominant trait in the character, that is, the desire for all-embracing harmony and the rejection of chaos.

That was the "bull's-eye" to which the composer Alexander Arutunyan alluded later: "Khachaturyan is jokingly called a sharpshooter in music. It's true, the composer always has and still writes *aptly*." And Khachaturyan himself said: "A composer must be a sharpshooter." This was precision, gained through experience, particularly the experience of writing for films. "I learned to play different roles with the actors in order to understand the hidden emotions in one scene or other."

Thinking of the younger generation, Khachaturyan would often remark that the film industry was a school for composers.

> It is a colossal school, I would even say a second conservatory for the young composer. In the first place, you experiment with a wide variety of the most fantastic combinations of instruments. And the recording sessions are the test—is the tone coloring what it should be? It was in films that I discovered many of my sound effects. You bring your music to the conductor, he looks at it and asks, with a hint of trepidation, "Is this possible?" Second, films discipline a composer (deadlines, timing, etc.) but most important, it brings out the playwright in him. After all,

he is writing for the screen and must reflect the situation appearing on the screen. This visibility, this concrete musical thinking, is very important. Whenever my students show me their music for the stage or screen I always ask, "And what is happening at this time?" The composer must be responsible for every nuance in the music.

His work with many directors and actors helped Khachaturyan achieve precision in his music for the screen. As in the theater, here too the influence was mutual.

Once I asked Khachaturyan who were the most musical film directors he had worked with. He promptly replied: Amo Bek-Nazarov, Mikhail Romm, and Sergei Yutkevich.

Khachaturyan's first incidental music for the screen, Bek-Nazarov's film *Pepo,* was a triumph. The press was keenly interested in this first Armenian sound film long before it appeared in 1935; this first attempt at filming Sundukyan's classic drama brought together a host of prominent craftsmen in the film world, Bek-Nazarov, and a whole constellation of excellent actors headed by Grachya Narsesyan.

In Amo Bek-Nazarov, Khachaturyan found a person who had gone through the school of hard knocks; he had tried many trades, from shoemaker to journalist, before becoming the king of Russian silents; he worked with Vera Kholodnaya, then a film star, and finally became a film director. Bek-Nazarov's thorough familiarity with the professional secrets of the film world greatly helped the novice composer. Then also, the two were lucky to have similar views, particularly on the role of music in films and on how to interpret the national in art.

The plot, based on a conflict between the families of poor Pepo and the rich merchant Zimzimov, was written by Sundukyan in the 1870s. Sixty years later Bek-Nazarov made it more of a class conflict. Pepo, who belonged to the *kinto* social class found in Tiflis, so familiar to Khachaturyan from his childhood, was portrayed by the director, who had also written the script, not as a lazy prankster but as a bearer of the ideas of class protest, although possibly not aware that he is doing so. "While not departing too far from Sundukyan as a whole, we should make the film something of a concentrate of his work" was how Bek-Nazarov articulated his task. The director allotted an important role to the music, for he chose to shoot the film and record the sound simultaneously, a daring experiment at that time, when sound films were in their infancy. "Aram Khachaturyan—a young fellow at that time—and I had a lengthy discussion about the role of music in our film. We wished, above all, to acquaint our audiences with at least a small part of the musical culture that had been accumulated in Armenia over the centuries, particularly the wonderful songs of Sayat-Nova."

Bek-Nazarov later recalled how almost the entire film group would gather in his hotel room. "Aram Ilych would promptly sit down at the piano and improvise. The melodies followed one another while his eyes glowed with inspiration. He was like a young oak in which one could just discern the beginnings of a mighty tree. We would listen quietly to his wonderful playing." The director also shows us the source of Khachaturyan's inspiration—the local taverns they visited in Tbilisi, where they heard the music of the *sazanders*. "We asked them to play the old songs for us, and Khachaturyan would immediately jot down the tunes we liked."

Everything then had to be put together. "Carefully, we would select the melody that best conveyed the emotional coloring of the episode and blended with the rhythm of the movement on the screen and the rhythm of the editing. We attached great importance to unity of the rhythmical movement of the image with the music and sound."

The critics agreed that the integrity of its artistic impression was what made *Pepo* so important. That the director and composer saw eye to eye was equally important. Characteristically, Khachaturyan completely agreed with Bek-Nazarov's urge to give the film a national form. "As a director working with national material, I often found myself wondering what I could do to ensure that the national form should not remain a simple fabric, a shell of the artistic image, but an organic part of it, an essential part of the content," Bek-Nazarov wrote during the filming. This also worried Khachaturyan. Many years later he heard people in Armenia singing "Pepo's Song" as a folk song. This was the highest praise a composer could possibly desire.

There is not much music in *Pepo*, only seven short fragments. But its portrayal of the Armenian bourgeoisie has great dramatic impact. It seems to be a blend of the European idea of Oriental music and the Oriental idea of European music. There is also dramatic impact in the image he creates of the policeman and the Russian autocracy through "March of the Shirvan Regiment," so popular in those years. The scene in the public bathhouse is a masterpiece. In keeping with the unwritten laws of the petit-bourgeoisie of those days, the prospective bride stands naked for inspection, while the camera pans from her face to the caricatures of the women's faces, so suggestive of Goya's old women. Meanwhile, despite this repulsive scene, the music is surprisingly tender, like the songs of the *ashug;* it is a hymn to beauty.

Pepo's song becomes the film's psychological center. Sundukyan's Pepo sings and, according to Bek-Nazarov, his song should express the very essence of his character. This presented Khachaturyan with a problem. The director intended to create on the screen the very essence of all the playwright's works, and so did Khachaturyan. In his incidental music, particularly "Pepo's Song," he seems to infuse the score with the spirit of the great Sayat-Nova without attempting to echo individual melodies from his works. That is why "Pepo's Song" did not come easily to Khachaturyan.

Bek-Nazarov points out in his recollections that Khachaturyan, extremely demanding of himself, "persevered in his search for maximum unity of music and image. For instance, only the seventh version of 'Pepo's Song' satisfied him." But Bek-Nazarov had said earlier: "What kind of a song must it be in order to merge completely with the portrait of Pepo? I could hear the song, but not being a composer I could not create it. I heard it in my head but could not reproduce a single note." Bek-Nazarov recalls that he actually tormented Khachaturyan, rejecting all the proposed variations of "Pepo's Song" one after another, accepting only the seventh version.

So we see that Khachaturyan's "sharp-shooting" was perfected in a persistent—and in Bek-Nazarov's words, an inspired—search for the "only correct artistic solution." In this blend of East and West we see the emergence of Khachaturyan's inimitable style.

The idea of composing the opera, *Sayat-Nova,* probably first occurred to Khachaturyan while he was writing the music for *Pepo*—Bek-Nazarov spoke of it as music that "in style merged completely with folk melodies." The recurring idea kept stirring his imagination.

To audiences in Tbilisi and Erevan *Pepo* seemed a piece of their own lives. This was only natural, since Sundukyan's drama was very popular. That was what made it so difficult to write music for the film. And that is why the success of Khachaturyan and of the entire film group gave cause for such rejoicing. "Were some passerby to look into the movie theater in those days, he would have been surprised at the audience's behavior," said Bek-Nazarov, remembering the first showings.

> The minute the screen came alive the audience became a part of the life and actions of the characters. Pepo sings while heaving his fishing net . . . and the audience sings along with him. The whole hall sings! In the distance we see a raft with people on it making merry and the audience begins to shout greetings. And as the group, floating past Pepo, drinks a toast to his health, we see bottles of wine emerging from the pockets of wide pants.
>
> The audience pours wine into drinking horns and joins in the toast coming from the screen. The *zurna* players [the *zurna* is a kind of flute] had come with their instruments and now start playing together with the musicians on the screen, for it is they who were filmed for this episode, and now, in the hall, they accompany themselves.*

*Khachaturyan recalled that during the filming of *Pepo* he introduced his father to Bek-Nazarov, who liked his face and asked permission to put him into the picture. "Father didn't object, and I also agreed, but later, with all the problems of filming, I completely forgot about this. During a screening of the court scene, I unexpectedly saw my father sitting in the courtroom. "Stop!" I cried, causing surprise and laughter. But I insisted that they rewind the film and show me that scene with my father once again."

The music for this film had a very special meaning for Khachaturyan. "He came to his country with the 'Song of the Fisherman' " wrote the well-known Armenian author, Raphael Aramyan, ". . . and although he was far from home for many years after that, his name was constantly on the people's lips. It was a short song, but how dear it was to the people's heart."

Khachaturyan collaborated with Bek-Nazarov again in 1938, when he wrote the music for the film *Zangezur*, about the revolutionary struggle in Armenia. The "Zangezur March" from the film became very popular. More important, though, as Armenian researchers of Khachaturyan's film music justly observed, was the fact that in *Zangezur* the composer developed the principle, latent in *Pepo*, of music heard throughout the film. The *ashug*'s funeral song, heard in *Zangezur* when the commandant's mother is buried, was later used by Khachaturyan in the slow movement of the Violin Concerto. The dramatic principles applied in *Zangezur* were continued in the "Funeral Dirge" in his music for the film *Vladimir Ilych Lenin,* in the requiem from the film *Ships Storming Bastions*, and in the famous requiem in the ballet *Spartacus*. For his incidental music to *Pepo* and *Zangezur* Aram Khachaturyan was awarded the title Meritorious Artist of Armenia in 1938.

"My most interesting meetings in the film world were with Mikhail Romm," Khachaturyan recalled.

> He was always able to meet the music half way and understand the composer he was working with. His thinking was surprisingly precise, he knew exactly what he wanted and was able to explain it to the composer. He could sit down at the piano and illustrate his ideas. . . . Before starting to work on a film—Romm and I made six films together—we would look at the problem from all sides and only after doing that would I bring him the music.

In 1948, after Khachaturyan had already made two films with Romm—*Man Number 217* and *The Russian Question*—Romm asked Khachaturyan to write the music for *Vladimir Ilych Lenin.*

I remembered my enormous grief in those freezing days of 1924, as I slowly walked through the streets of Moscow, with their many bonfires. Endless streams of people stricken by the same terrible grief were moving, like me, toward the Hall of Columns. Many times, on recalling those people, immersed in deep misery, it occurred to me that I should try to express their feelings. But I must admit that I lacked the courage. The film now placed me in a position where I had to do it. All the material about the life of the great leader that had been collected for the film moved me so strongly that I finally decided to do it.

Prior to the film's premiere in 1949, the music was performed by a symphony orchestra under the title *Ode to the Memory of Lenin.* In 1934, while taking part in a discussion of the Conservatory's Leninist Collection, which included works written by students for the tenth anniversary of Lenin's death, Khachaturyan noted as a general shortcoming that all the music seemed to hover on a single emotional level.

"The theme has been narrowed down," he said. "For Lenin is remembered only in grief, and that is wrong."

In his *Ode,* written fifteen years later, the composer was able to convey how that grief was interwoven in the people's hearts with a determination to go on living and building a new society created and inspired by Lenin's ideals. In the finale, the theme expressing nationwide sorrow is transmuted into a hymn to the great leader of the Revolution.

A two-part film about the Russian Admiral Ushakov, made in 1953, was the last joint effort by Romm and Khachaturyan. It is a film about the nineteenth-century Russian naval victories. The composer had the difficult task of writing music for the excellently filmed battle scenes. In the second part of the film—*Ships Storming Bastions*—one such scene showed the capture of the Corfu Fortress and the burial of Russian seamen.

I felt a special responsibility when I started working on the requiem. That part of the film, made by the director with such deep feeling, depicts the many expressions of grief, and the different perceptions of death. This made me think. Of course, the feelings of the Greek peasants as they accompanied their

Russian liberators to their last resting place differed greatly from those of the dead men's comrades-in-arms, and even of the Admiral himself, who set an example for them in battle and here by the graveside. All this taken together . . . I wanted to convey in such a way as to keep fear of the finality of death from creeping into human sorrow, for it is not typical of the Russian people. That is why it was possible to use fragments from the rousing seamen's songs here, but in a special interpretation.

A director capable of building up his film with a fine feeling for music and a composer equally attuned to the rhythm of the screen image created the impact of the scene showing the storming of the fortress. Romm built up a continuous emotional crescendo, and the sound track—which besides the music reproduced the sounds of the sea, the booming of cannon, and the cries of "hurrah"—merged with and supported it. Besides, the atmosphere and rhythm created by Khachaturyan's music changed Romm's initial scenario; he wrote about this later. It is interesting that the editing of the funeral scene was fitted to the music; there was not enough footage to cover Khachaturyan's music and the director agreed to lengthen the footage by repeating some of the frames. "The exceptional impact of the music in this episode, the beautiful landscape and the expressive faces saved the situation," wrote Mikhail Romm.

Khachaturyan's moving requiem played an important role in the episode. He played an outline, almost an improvisation of the requiem, for us in Yalta, and this provided the necessary emotional spur to film the material. Then a rough draft of the material was sufficient for Khachaturyan to write the final version. When the requiem was played by the orchestra and recorded on film, we finally put the whole episode together. This was an ideal example of collaboration with the composer.

The many episodes the script called for, ranging from palace scenes to close-ups of the people, from the launching ceremony of the first ships to the burial of Russian sailors killed in battle, from battle scenes to lyrical scenes, all suggested to Khachaturyan that the music should be monothematic. That is why, in the overture to *Admiral Ushakov,* we hear the theme of the seamen's marching song, "Make Way, Hostile Forces." It reflects the heroism of Russian seamen, the invincible spirit of the Russian Army, and is repeatedly heard in both parts of the film whenever valor and heroism are shown.

The film *Othello* (1956), mentioned above, was Khachaturyan's only joint venture with Sergei Yutkevich.

> I found my artistic contacts with Sergei Yutkevich, a highly cultured person with a rare intellect, very satisfying. He invariably stirred my imagination. I was very pleased to learn that the invitation to work on such a serious film as *Othello* was Yutkevich's initiative. He later told me that he liked my music, particularly my Piano Concerto.

Khachaturyan's music highlights Othello and Desdemona; his musical images are built on contrasts—courage and sympathy. This was suggested by Shakespeare's text: "She lov'd me for the dangers I had pass'd;/And I lov'd her that she did pity them." True to his principles, Khachaturyan introduced Armenian folk tones in Desdemona's "Vocalese," so well known today. But the "Vocalese" attracts by its very unpretentiousness and the enviable simplicity of its musical expression.

Many singers, like the famous Armenian soprano Goar Gasparyan often include it in their concert programs. However, as in Mikhail Romm's films, the significance of Khachaturyan's music for *Othello* lies not in the success of some of its fragments, but in its active dramatic role. "Yutkevich and I dreamed of collaborating on an opera. He selected Bertolt Brecht's *Caucasian Chalk Circle* as possible material for an opera. The idea, however, was not to be realized."

Khachaturyan had a special affinity for Shakespeare. The incidental music he wrote at different periods of his life for plays and films derived from Shakespeare's works was not accidental. He composed two scores for *Macbeth,* as well as music for *King Lear* and *Othello.* He was also planning to write the music for the 1954 Mayakovsky Theater production in Moscow of *Hamlet*, staged by Nikolai Okhlopkov. Khachaturyan told one interviewer that heroic images and great social conflicts had always attracted him. "In this respect," he said, "my music for the film *Othello*, for the stage production of *Macbeth*, and especially for the ballet *Spartacus* have a great deal in common."

The genius of Shakespeare as a dramatist and thinker whose characters, as Friedrich Engels wrote, "find motives for their actions not in petty individual whims but in the historical stream in which they are carried"—"motives [which] are more vividly, actively, and spontaneously brought to the forefront by the action itself"—the very direction of the dramatist's artistic thinking, have always been consonant with the ideals of Soviet art. Following in the wake of the Russian and foreign classical composers who preceded them, prominent Soviet composers have created many works inspired by Shakespeare's immortal creations; what is most important, they were able, each in his own way, to interpret in these works the all-encompassing world of William Shakespeare.

In his famous ballet *Romeo and Juliet*, Sergei Prokofiev was able to convey a comprehensive vision of life, so typically Shakespearean, and of the clash of opposing passions—love and death, light and darkness, good and evil. But were not the works of the young Prokofiev, who had little respect for any sort of "norms" in art, branded as barbaric?

Dmitri Shostakovich brilliantly expressed in the language of music the bewilderment of man, who, like Shakespeare's Hamlet, witnesses the world's duplicity and crying dissonance. It is in his works that the twentieth century cries out in full voice, with all the force of truly Shakespearean pathos, its devotion to humanist ideals, despite the divisions in the world.

In his music Aram Khachaturyan asserted the high humane ideals so dear to Shakespeare, giving full reign to the bright coloring and theatricality of the action on the stage, and leading us, as in his Second Symphony and the ballet *Spartacus*, through the shock of tragedy to catharsis. A bard of the beautiful, the composer embodies it in the lyrical, personifying it in such characters as Desdemona in his music in the film *Othello*, Nina in the stage production of *The Masquerade,* and Phrygia in *Spartacus.* Whether the literary foundation is Shakespeare's, Lermontov's, or the historical events of the Spartacus revolt in ancient Rome is of little importance.

Having acquired sufficient experience in writing for films, Khachaturyan could speak with authority about its specific characteristics for a composer:

> In no other field of music is the composer so required to be at home in the most different forms, from the monumentally symphonic to songs, marches, dance music, and the like. Films allow the composer to address himself to huge audiences, to constantly undertake new and interesting artistic problems, dictated by the script and the director's ideas, and to resolve them. Films, I repeat, discipline the musician by the subject matter and strict time limits. One must write not just good music, but music which expresses the dramatic focus of every episode.

At the same time, Aram Ilych liked to say, if the music in a film plays the role of first violin it must sound equally good outside the theater. For example, basing himself on his music for the film *The Battle of Stalingrad,* directed by Vladimir Petrov (1949), Khachaturyan arranged a suite for symphony orchestra in which the leitmotiv, just as in the music for the film, was taken from the Russian folk song, "A Cliff on the Volga," symbolizing the invincible spirit of the Russian people.

> I look upon this composition not as seasonal work, but as one more opus. I must admit that every time a new work is performed for the first time, I find myself thinking that it could have been better. But here —one more specific trait of films—no corrections can be made, there can be no second or third editing.

Khachaturyan also stressed how important it is for a composer to select places in the script where the music must complete the story or summarize the action on the screen:

> There is a scene in Romm's *Secret Mission* where the heroine,

fleeing the Gestapo, heads in despair straight into the path of an oncoming automobile. The tense situation is expressed in the music; its emotion climaxes at the moment of catastrophe, when the speeding car crashes into a wall. Though the heroine is killed, the music does not stop. Director and composer find the only possible solution, not called for in the script—the camera pans to the sky and tragic music follows.

When writing music for films Khachaturyan would often say that the composer should not strive to have the music heard constantly—he should ask the director to give the music a dominant place in one or another episode. This is the case in *They Have a Country*, directed by Alexander Feintzimer, where the music seems to continue the story, or, more precisely, conveys the feelings of the audience as they see a Soviet boy, deprived of his country and kept in an orphanage in postwar Germany, slapped in the face for trying to take a photograph of his mother from a desk drawer. This was also the case in Mikhail Romm's *The Russian Question*, where the journalist, Smith, has to decide whether to write the truth about the Soviet Union and risk losing his job and everything he has. He goes behind a glass partition and starts dictating to his secretary. We do not hear his voice. "Turn the sound and text off," Khachaturyan told Romm. "Let me use music to show the audience what Smith has decided."

Of course, Khachaturyan was not always able to make full use of music in films. This often depended on the director's view of music. Sometimes Khachaturyan was not satisfied; he even wrote articles complaining about film makers, saying that directors should know music and that the composer was not always accepted as an equal member of the film group. Khachaturyan had every right to complain, above all because of his serious approach to film work. He insisted that the score not be cut or sound effects recorded over the music without the composer's concurrence. He complained when some part of his music was not included in a film or when the dramatic effect of the music was lost because of someone's carelessness.

Many factors determined the success of Khachaturyan's incidental music for stage and screen—its entertainment value, his love for these genres, and his rapport with directors. Not least was his specific manner of work. When composing, Khachaturyan always needed an outside emotional stimulus, notwithstanding his own emotional character. This could be a talk with the choreographer or director, on a subject close to the subject of the future film or stage production, or just a proposed libretto or scenario. If they struck a responsive chord this sparked off strong impulses. As Khachaturyan confessed,

I love the theater and films. I like to write with a clear dramatic plan before me flowing from the content of the play and the ideas of the director. I attach great importance to this work because the stage, the scene, the episode, the live image created by the actor—all help to mold my idea of the music, giving my work concrete shape and enriching the form.

# The Piano Concerto

*It is here that Khachaturyan's healthy philosophy of life, generosity of feeling, and depth of thought are expressed most strongly and fully.*

DMITRI SHOSTAKOVICH

Aram Khachaturyan's instrumental compositions are among his best known and most often performed works; they fully and vividly embody the most characteristic traits of his style.

When he started work on his Piano Concerto in 1936, he seemed not to have in mind a cycle of three instrumental compositions, and yet, though his Violin Concerto appeared four years after the Piano Concerto and the Cello Concerto six years later, they are all regarded as something of a grand cycle. Khachaturyan's researcher, Georgi Hubov, writes of them as the three parts of a unified "concerto of concertos," where the Piano Concerto is associated with the tone of morning freshness dominating the score, the Violin Concerto with the heat of the midday sun, and the Cello Concerto with the hues of a silvery sunset. Hubov himself agreed that comparisons of this nature may be somewhat subjective. But on hearing these concertos you find that they have a great deal in common, and not only in the details. "One has the impression," writes the Armenian critic Marina Berko, "that the scope of Khachaturyan's creative work is not exhausted by the form of the concerto alone. The reserve strength is used to create a group of concert pieces." That was the case in the 1930s and 1940s with his three instrumental concertos, in the 1960s with the trilogy of concerto-rhapsodies, and with the three solo sonatas in the 1970s.

Khachaturyan's preference for instrumental concertos is most likely deeply rooted in the characteristics of his talent.

Boris Asafiev wrote of his "constant leaning toward a representative, brilliantly virtuoso style both in its colorful oratorial uplift, splendid polish, and luxuriantly rich exposition of ideas." It was only natural that these qualities of Khachaturyan's style should be so vividly apparent in his concertos, which, by their very nature, presume brilliant execution, the captivating element of competition between soloist and orchestra, and sumptuous "attire."

That, at any rate, is how Khachaturyan interpreted the genre. "Apparently my attraction for the 'concert style,' for colorful virtuosity, is characteristic of my creative individuality. I like the very idea of writing a composition with a predominating, joyously vibrant beginning of free competition between virtuoso soloist and symphony orchestra."

His preference for concertos enabled Khachaturyan to portray inimitably the rhythm of the atmosphere and life around him in his concerto trilogy, and to put into sound all that was wonderful in the lives of his contemporaries.

Khachaturyan was probably attracted to concertos because his formative period came at a time when the Soviet performing school was scoring one victory after another with its galaxy of world-class artists. First place at the First International Chopin Contest in Warsaw in 1928 was won by Lev Oborin; the First All-Union Competition of Musicians in Moscow in 1933 brought Emil Gilels and Svyataslav Knushevitsky to the forefront, while at the Second All-Union Competition in Leningrad in 1935 David Oistrakh and Yakov Fliere won top awards. Fliere and Gilels then went on to win the World Competition of Pianists in Vienna in 1936; Oistrakh became Laureate of the Henryk Wieniawski International Competition in Warsaw (1935) and the Eugene Ysaye Contest in Brussels (1937). Daniil Shafran scored a success at the Third All-Union Contest in 1937; a year later, at the Ysaye Piano Contest in Brussels, the winners were again Gilels and Fliere. The All-Union Contest of Orchestra Conductors in Leningrad in 1938 brought fame to Evgeni Mravinsky.

The list could be continued. These are but a few Soviet

performers, but they are the ones who later became closely associated with Khachaturyan as interpreters of his music. He dedicated his piano, violin, and cello concertos to Oborin, Oistrakh, and Knushevitsky, the first performers of these works. After Oborin and Knushevitsky, Gilels, Fliere, and Shafran became the best interpreters of the piano and cello concertos. Gilels was the first to play his Piano Sonata; Mravinsky conducted the Leningrad premiere of the Piano Concerto and was also the first to perform the Third Symphony.

Aram Ilych never forgot the impressions of his first meetings with several of these performers.

*Emil Gilels.* On that day performers were being selected in the Small Hall of the Conservatory for the national piano competitions. Everywhere, in the cloak rooms and corridors, everyone seemed to be talking excitedly about the boy wonder Emil Gilels. I tried to get into the hall, but it was too crowded; I could only make it up to the balcony. I think Gilels was playing Liszt's arrangement of Mozart's *Marriage of Figaro*. His technical brilliance and artistic maturity were astounding.

*David Oistrakh.* I met David Oistrakh in Leningrad in 1935. Armenia had chosen me, a young composer and conservatory postgraduate student, to sit on the jury. I was included in the jury for violinists, possibly because I had played the cello in the past. It was there that I first heard and saw Oistrakh; until then I had only seen his name on posters. The judges, who included some of the Soviet Union's best violin professors, people like Miron Polyakin and Pyotr Stolyarski, jotted down their impressions of the performers in notebooks. I noticed, however, that when Oistrakh began to play, many closed their books and just listened. I, too, closed mine. It was such an inspired, mature, and artistic performance, especially of the Mendelssohn Concerto, that I had no desire to estimate, to apportion the honors; I just wanted to sit back and enjoy this wonderful rendition.

No wonder that the very appearance of Khachaturyan's concertos and their frequent performance were largely due to these outstanding Soviet musicians.

Khachaturyan really came to know the piano only after he moved to Moscow.

> Just a few days after settling down in my brother's home I attended a concert by Nikolai Orlov, a wonderful pianist and a former student of Igumnov's. He played Chopin and Liszt. I was astounded both by the music, which I had never heard before, and by the unusual sound of the piano.
>
> I had never imagined until then that our fingers were capable of such magical strength, such nimbleness and precision, capable of extracting such an array of tonal colors, rhythms, and brilliant passages from the instrument.
>
> Soon after that I attended a performance by Igumnov himself . . . , with Alexander Hessin conducting. We heard Beethoven's Ninth Symphony and Rachmaninov's Second Concerto. I think it was then that I began to try for a differentiated perception of music, by applying to it my experience in analytical reading.

Khachaturyan's piano playing was further stimulated by his lessons with Mikhail Gnessin, who encouraged him in every way. Gnessin believed that every composer should master the piano. "His piano playing improved rapidly," Gnessin recalled, "but his technical abilities lagged far behind his performing requirements; his playing was lively, his fingering was absolutely fantastic." Since then he always used the piano when composing.

Khachaturyan liked to tell of the time when even Konstantin Igumnov was deceived by his playing. He was performing his recently composed Toccata for the professor, a piece requiring excellent technique. He played so skillfully that Igumnov took him for a piano student and inquired what year he was in. He was probably misled by Khachaturyan's bubbling temperament, impressive artistry, and that special performer's gift which made the composer say that he constantly felt a "dormant pianism" in his hands.

Khachaturyan spent a good deal of time analyzing the piano style of Russian, Armenian, and foreign composers and studying the works of Prokofiev. He was particularly attracted to

Rachmaninov, Scriabin, and Medtner. He also made a careful study of the techniques of such outstanding pianists of the time as Alexander Goldenweiser, Heinrich Neuhaus, and Samuel Feinberg, as well as of Igumnov. He even watched his own fellow students at the piano. "I like the universality of the piano, its rich multiform means which make it possible to convey the entire range of human emotions. I should like to stress here that the piano is one of the most widely used and most democratic instruments."

Khachaturyan started working on his piano concerto encouraged by the success of his First Symphony. He already had several piano pieces to his credit—the Waltz-Caprice (1926), Poem (1926), and Toccata (1932), all popular among pianists to this day, but heard more often in those days. They were definitely influenced by the piano music of the French Impressionists and by Armenian folk music. Nevertheless, in these excellent pieces we can already discern the piano style of the composer of the famous piano concerto. Here we find the embodiment of spontaneous folk music, improvisation, treatment of the instrument in a beautifully decorative manner close to the style of a fresco; we also hear the timbres of Eastern instruments which, until quite recently, had seemed impossible to reproduce on the piano, but now ever so subtly and tastefully reproduced on the "Khachaturyan piano."

Of all his earlier instrumental works, the Toccata has proved the most durable. The rhythmic resilience of this ancient genre compounded by skillful imitation of such Eastern folk instruments as the *doira* and *kanon,* the chromatic harmonies, typically Eastern but so individually Khachaturyanesque, the vivid contrast between the compelling fascination of the beginning and concluding sections and the appealing lyricism of the middle part, between the *perpetuum mobile* type of movement and the spontaneity of improvisation—all contribute to the Toccata's success. Its popularity is comparable only to Béla Bartók's Allegro Barbaro. The Soviet composer Rodion Shchedrin, himself an accomplished pianist who played the Toccata many times in Yakov Fliere's Conservatory class, wrote, "Many years have passed since this dynamic and brilliant composition appeared, but it is still enthusiastically received at every performance. Every professional knows it by heart and is fond of it."

It took Aram Ilych just over half a year to complete his Piano Concerto. As a postgraduate student he took the advice of Myaskovsky and of many of his fellow students, among them Alexei Klumov, the talented pupil of Heinrich Neuhaus. In November 1936 Khachaturyan wrote: "I have finished the concerto and sent it off to be copied. Oborin wants to play it; I will send him the notes in a few days. I will also take the concerto to the Union, where it will be played by Klumov." Alexei Klumov and Berta Kozel played the new concerto on two pianos in Myaskovsky's class. As Nina Musinyan recalled,

> Soon after completing his concerto Aram Ilych invited me—faithful performer of his piano pieces—to his apartment, where he played the whole thing for me from beginning to end. Everything in the music was not only talented but incredibly pianistic. It was one of the marks of his talent that, though not too good a pianist, as a composer he had an amazing feeling for the instrument.

On November 28, 1936, Alexei Klumov and Maria Greenberg played Khachaturyan's Piano Concerto at a gathering in the Composers Union. Many prominent Moscow composers, among them Neuhaus and Igumnov, were lavish in their praise. The critic Boris Yarustovsky, who had heard the Concerto in Myaskovsky's class, wrote many years later: "I recall the burst of feeling in the audience. It seemed as though the juices were springing forth from the living earth."

In a long article on this new work, Heinrich Neuhaus wrote: "The Concerto for Piano and Orchestra recently completed by Khachaturyan is a real joy. It shows that the composer is growing, gaining greater mastery of this form, and that his musical language is becoming clearer and more expressive." Such high praise from Professor Neuhaus, who was then Conservatory director, certainly helped to put the Concerto on the student program. Professor Neuhaus was teaching Emil Gilels at the time; the Concerto was also performed by students of Vladimir Sofronitsky, among them the future composer, Andrei Eshpai.

Regarding its first full-scale performance, Khachaturyan wrote,

> When I was working on my Concerto I dreamed of hearing it played by Lev Oborin. My dream came true in the summer of 1937. The wonderful performance by this outstanding pianist ensured its success. For me it meant entering a new area of creation, one very near and dear to me, the area of instrumental concertos.

After voicing his delight with Khachaturyan's First Symphony, Oborin gladly accepted the composer's proposal that he be the first to play the Piano Concerto. Together they went over the score. Aram Ilych said later that his work with Oborin at the piano proved wonderful instruction in piano technique.

The Concerto was first performed July 12, 1937, on the open-air concert stage in Moscow's Sokolniki Park.* The concert was a disappointment to Khachaturyan for several reasons. First of all, the musicians had come from different orchestras; the conductor, Lev Steinberg, could manage only one rehearsal; the instrument on stage was an old upright; the acoustics of the shell were far from ideal; and, to top it off, the audience consisted predominantly of whoever happened to be in the vicinity. The premiere seemed a success but, as Oborin wrote, "when it ended we had a hard time finding the author; he was deep inside the park, crying bitterly with his arms around a birch tree."

Khachaturyan was especially sensitive because he had been well aware of the innovative nature of his idea when he started working on the Concerto. "I am now completely immersed in

*Prior to being played with an orchestra the Concerto was performed several times on two pianos. "Many nice things have been said about my Concerto," Khachaturyan wrote the composer Sergei Balasanyan, "but it has not yet been performed with an orchestra. It has been played on two pianos no less than ten times at public concerts and other performances. . . ."

the Concerto, which should come out brilliantly," he had written in November 1935.

> Every composition should be an event for the real artist. It should pose a problem. My Concerto, being the first national piano concerto, might stir the minds of young people, at least it might induce our master composers of the future to consider this genre from the viewpoint of national material and to proceed from the existing modest attempts in that direction.

The disappointing summer concert was amply compensated by brilliant performances of the Concerto that autumn in Moscow and Leningrad, with Alexander Gauk and Evgeni Mravinsky conducting. For Khachaturyan the performance on November 14, 1937, during the ten-day National Musical Festival, was a especially memorable occasion, as this was also the twentieth anniversary of the 1917 Revolution. The orchestra was conducted by Alexander Gauk. What more could the composer desire? "As a young composer with just a few symphonic works to my credit, I had dreamt of having something of mine conducted by Gauk. I had not yet met him personally but he was very well known by then." The conductor was very serious about rehearsals and went through the entire score with the composer. "Gauk asked for my views on the tempo, dynamics, and ensemble performance; I listened to his opinion on orchestration. I must say we had some heated discussions but, after all, truth is born of argument."

Khachaturyan had enormous faith in Gauk's professionalism and experience; he was impressed by his lively character and tireless quest for new ideas. Their friendship grew, especially after they became neighbors in Snegeri, where they both had country homes.

> It was Gauk who talked me into buying a house there. I remember we were rehearsing for the first performance of *Spartacus Suite* and I was jotting down some ideas. I went to the dressing room during the break to tell the conductor some of my ideas. Alexander Vasilievich did not give me a chance to say a word.

"Just think, your kitchen will be here," he said, starting to sketch on the back of my score, "and here you'll build a porch." And then there was no time left for me to say anything.

Gauk, who subsequently conducted almost all of Khachaturyan's symphonic works, well remembers the preparations for his first performance of the Piano Concerto. He invariably speaks of it as a bright period in his conducting career. Lev Oborin has equally vivid recollections. "What is there in that music that has attracted me for so many years?" he wrote later.

Probably what is so characteristic of all of Khachaturyan's work—a mighty temperament, originality and the brilliant virtuosity of the solo piano and orchestra. I think I may say that Khachaturyan's Piano Concerto is one of the few modern works of its kind that is a true concerto, and not just a composition for piano and orchestra. It has range, sharp contrasts, and a contention between soloist and orchestra.

Khachaturyan's Concerto showed him to be a mature composer at the height of his powers. Its three movements rest on the best traditions of the classical instrumental concerto, but with a new conception and purely "Khachaturyanesque" content. The sonata form, which he always spoke of as a Procrustean bed shackling the imagination, became a pliant means of artistic expression. The durability and grace of the form of the Piano Concerto is ensured by the monothematic principle, so much more convincing here than in the First Symphony, and by the common fabric shared by all the basic themes. There is an enviable continuity in the development of the musical thought, achieved through maximum use of the inner reserves of carefully selected themes and their skillful development, thanks to the ingenious application of dynamics in even those themes which seem absolutely static in the exposition, the second subject of the first movement, for example. Even the transitions of the musical form acquire a rare flexibility here—the coda in the first movement and the reprise of the main theme in the Andante are introduced on the crest of the piano cadenzas. And how impressive are the "pure changes," where the second subject of the first movement immediately follows the principal subject and we unexpectedly hear the principal subject of the first movement in the culmination of the Finale.

Pianists are invariably attracted by the challenge to their virtuosity. Virtuosity is in fact essential to the very spirit of the entire work, a thrilling competition between soloist and orchestra. This is expressed mainly in the constructive function, one might even say the outright dramatic function, of the piano cadenzas. Khachaturyan repeats this in his Violin Concerto, where the cadenza makes up for the none too extensive development of the first movement.

Dmitri Shostakovich applied a similar principle many years later in his First Violin Concerto.

Khachaturyan interprets the "piano image" in a romantic key, as in the works of Rachmaninov and Liszt (the main part of the first movement and the lyrical episode in the Finale are characteristic); neither does he reject the influence of Prokofiev's piano: Recall the theme of the Finale, so vivaciously "Prokofievesque" and naturally associated with Juliet in the ballet *Romeo and Juliet* (a comparison Khachaturyan would not find offensive, as Prokofiev's ballet had not then been written).

Step by step the composer enriches the piano texture "with the aural impression of the specific sound of folk instruments and their characteristic pitch and scale of overtones." Here Khachaturyan has in mind the instruments and musical principles found not only in Armenia, but in all the Transcaucasus and even among many Eastern nations. Orchestrally and in beauty of sound the piano is at an advantage.

The Piano Concerto contains innumerable examples of the composer's boldly innovative interpretation of folk traditions. Though he displays a certain lack of restraint and a penchant for improvisation unusual in European classical music, with the piano cadenzas at the focus of this improvisation, gradually rising to the music-making of the *ashugs*, he nevertheless blends them into the structure of the classical sonata-symphonic forms. Using a simple folk melody familiar to everyone in the Transcaucasus as the main theme of the Andante, his interpretation is radically different.

> By taking this melody as the basis for the central theme of the Piano Concerto I obviously ran the risk of the critics tearing me to pieces when they learned the source of the music. But I departed so far from the original, changing its content and character so radically, that even Georgian and Armenian musicians could not detect its folk origin.

The risk was justified, for critics in the 1930s compared the Andante with such gems of Russian music as the famous Nocturne from Borodin's Second Quartet and the Andante from his own First Symphony.

The Piano Concerto did have some shortcomings. The Finale would have been stronger without the recapitulation of the main subject of the first movement. The music of the Finale was justly criticized as being too wordy. It is interesting to compare the opinions of Dmitri Shostakovich and Heinrich Neuhaus, so similar and yet so different. "The Concerto is a significant step forward compared with the First Symphony," wrote Shostakovich. "It is a brilliant masterpiece with greater depth of thought and even greater symphonic sweep than the First Symphony. In this Concerto Khachaturyan was able to combine great virtuosity with profound content." "Khachaturyan's music is lively, temperamental, and emotional. But, it is not enough," wrote Neuhaus.

> What we say of poetry can also be applied to music: the more thought it contains, the deeper and more significant it becomes. Great art (Michelangelo, Shakespeare, Beethoven, Pushkin) always contains elements of a knowledge of the world. And what is that knowledge if not the "radium" extracted from thousands of tons of the artist's ideas, emotions, experiences, and impressions? It is this radium that Khachaturyan must learn to extract from the rich ore of his great talent.

However, such mild criticism was not meant to decry the

importance of Khachaturyan's Piano Concerto, the first instrumental concerto in Armenian music and a brilliant example of this genre in Soviet music.

The Soviet music critic Valentina Konen drew attention to the interesting coincidence that Khachaturyan's Concerto was composed in 1937, the year when the declaration of the International Conference of Composers in Florence and the series of lectures delivered at Vienna University by Ernest Kshenek (and later included in his book, *About New Music*), asserted that only by ignoring traditions and the demands of the broad democratic public was it possible to create something new in music. The importance of Khachaturyan's music is that it vividly and unequivocally proved the opposite, that in principle innovation is possible where there is respect for the best traditions of musical art, both professional and folk, and for genuine democracy. Equally important, it also proved the possibility of symphonizing Eastern music, a subject dealt with in greater detail below.

Dmitri Kabalevsky wrote after the premiere of the Piano Concerto,

> I believe that of all the major compositions performed during this ten-day festival of Soviet music, the most interesting are Myaskovsky's Eighteenth Symphony, Shostakovich's Fifth Symphony, and Khachaturyan's Piano Concerto. These three compositions, absolutely different in all respects, demonstrate the great progress made by Soviet musical art.

So it was that Aram Khachaturyan found himself on a level with his teachers Myaskovsky and Shostakovich.

Kabalevsky's words were prophetic: For close to half a century now the Concerto has been played all over the world, never losing its attraction for new generations of performers and audiences alike.

Yakov Fliere, who played the Concerto much later than Oborin, always said that Oborin's interpretation had established something of a standard for pianists. Fliere's interpretation, however, proved a surprising departure from this standard. Not all the characteristic traits of Khachaturyan's style accorded with Oborin's musical individuality. Reticent by nature, a subtle interpreter of Chopin, never seeking effects or dynamic exaggeration, in Khachaturyan's music he was faced with the need to display a volcanic temperament, even a certain "barbarism" mentioned by Khachaturyan himself in subsequent discussions of his Concerto.

Opinions differed concerning Oborin's interpretation. Some said he was at his best in the middle part, in conveying the cantilena, at which he was unexcelled. Others, like Nina Musinyan, insisted that "Oborin, with his emotional composure, imparted to the Concerto exactly what it may have lacked at times—incredibly well-balanced proportions and an irreproachable sense of measure." Whatever the case, Khachaturyan himself always cherished Oborin's interpretation of his Concerto. Many years later, in a letter to a young pianist preparing to play the Concerto for her graduation project, Khachaturyan wrote: "When you have learned my Concerto, go to the radio and ask them to play you Oborin's recording. It would please me and help you. Try to keep to Oborin's tempo and interpretation."

Fliere's interpretation of the Concerto was broader and more expressive, the difference from Oborin's apparently lying in their contrasting personalities. Fliere's repertory always leaned toward the works of Liszt and Rachmaninov. Besides, Fliere was able to perceive Khachaturyan's music from the heights of his achievements in the 1940s and 1950s.

As for interest in Khachaturyan's music abroad, the following facts are illuminating. The Concerto was especially popular during the Second World War, when soloists and conductors played Soviet music as an expression of solidarity with the USSR's battle against Nazism. During the 1943–44 season the Piano Concerto was played no less than forty times in the United States alone. In a letter to Khachaturyan on his sixtieth birthday, Samuel Barber wrote,

I am very pleased to recall the stunning success of the Piano Concerto's American premiere. Wherever its first performer,

William Capell, appeared the public would make him play the Concerto. . . . I happened to be in Boston on October 9, 1943, where the symphony orchestra under Koussevitzky was playing my new composition. During the rehearsals Koussevitzky told me with his mysterious and intriguing smile, which he usually reserved for some big event, "You're going to hear something, my friend." He was right. And today, twenty years later, I vividly recall my first impressions of those Khachaturyanesque colors and rhythms. My impressions have not lost their freshness with the years because Khachaturyan speaks with the voice of his country, the voice of his people. It is a rare composer who does this so ingeniously and so naturally.

Among the performers of Khachaturyan's Piano Concerto are such outstanding names as Arthur Rubinstein, Julius Katchin, and Mura Limpany, the last of whom played it in London in 1941 and subsequently many times in the United States.

In 1954 Khachaturyan participated in a month of Anglo-Soviet Friendship, together with a group of Soviet artists which included David Oistrakh and artists of the Bolshoi Theater. "I was not scheduled to perform," he recalled,

but when our English colleagues learned I was in London they asked me to conduct the Royal Philharmonic and I agreed. On the day of the concert the hall was filled to capacity. Interest in the art of the Soviet Union exceeded all my expectations. To tell the truth, I was worried. My skill as a conductor was not very great, while the orchestra was one of the best in the world. I decided to include the Violin Concerto, which David Oistrakh kindly agreed to play, and the Piano Concerto with Mura Limpany as soloist. "How should I address you?" I asked her at our first rehearsal. "Just call me Murka," came the unexpected reply. We had a long rehearsal. The soloist was probably more worried than I; it showed during the concert. On developing the first Allegro, I was horrified by her accelerando. But we were saved by the brilliant and experienced orchestra. On the whole, though, Limpany played well and my Concerto was a success.

I regret to say I was not in Moscow two years later, when

Limpany was appearing in Moscow as soloist with that same Royal Philharmonic, conducted by Sir Adrian Boult. We did not meet again until February 1977, in London. She asked for my new piano compositions, the Sonata and the Concerto-Rhapsody, adding that she was prepared to come to the USSR for me to check her interpretation of these works. We agreed to meet in Paris, where I was soon to visit, but we did not meet, as I was laid up in hospital there and underwent surgery. Not long ago I received a letter from this surprisingly conscientious pianist, who is so attentive to me. She suggested that we meet and perform together in Tanglewood, the American music center. Circumstances permitting, I shall accept her invitation with pleasure.

This was said just a few months before his death.

New generations of pianists will go on discovering something of their own in Khachaturyan's Piano Concerto; this is a guarantee of the music's undying vitality, as with all great works of art.

# The Violin Concerto

*I wrote the music as though on a wave of happiness, my whole being in a state of joy . . . and this winged feeling, this love of life was transmitted to the music.*

ARAM KHACHATURYAN

Khachaturyan's Violin Concerto was preceded by his *Poem to Stalin*. The idea for the poem goes back to 1936 when he, like other Soviet composers, was preparing for the twentieth anniversary of the October Revolution. At the end of 1936 Khachaturyan wrote,

> I am planning some new compositions. Possibly, first, a chorus, with soloists and orchestra, on the text of a letter to Stalin by Turkmen collective farmers. It is a wonderful letter in verse. This letter contains wonderfully descriptive comparisons. This should be a big symphonic ode. Second—I have already contracted with the Azerbaijans for a symphonic composition on themes of their choice. Third—A ballet for the Armenians, based on a subject by Ovanes Tumanyan. Of course, it will be difficult to write all three in one year, but I think I could manage two.

What Khachaturyan says is interesting because it demonstrates that he did not restrict himself to Armenian art alone. At this time he was already arranging Tadjik folk songs and had written three Tadjik songs to words by Lakhuti, rightly believed to be among his best. He was even toying with the idea of going to work in Tadjikistan as his fellow Conservatory student Sergei Balasanyan had done.

His plans also show how creatively active he was in those

109

years, even though he did not do all he had planned. They also show how long the idea of his *Poem to Stalin* took to mature. It is usually associated with his "Song of Stalin," written in 1937 to words by the Azerbaijanian poet Mirza Bairamov. Khachaturyan wrote in 1937, "I am considering writing a symphonic poem, with chorus at the end, for the twentieth anniversary, a *Poem to Stalin.* I am excited as I gather the material, but I don't know how it will turn out."

And here is what he said after completing the score:

> I had been thinking about this *Poem* for some time, but I was not sure what form to use. Then I saw the words of Mirza the *ashug*'s wonderful song and my idea immediately crystallized: The *Poem* must be a symphonic work ending with a song-apotheosis on these wonderful words. I wanted the symphonic part of the *Poem* to be more of an emotional than a thematic introduction to the concluding chorus. The chorus should be the culmination of the *Poem.* The thematic links, however, are clear: All the symphonic themes emerge from the melody of the song.

It took Khachaturyan just forty days to compose the *Poem,* and it was first performed on November 29, 1938, during the ten-day festival of Soviet Music, by the State Symphony Orchestra conducted by Alexander Gauk and the State Chorus under Nikolai Danilin.

Khachaturyan's *Poem* must justly be classed among the best of the many art works glorifying Stalin in the 1930s. Critics stressed that its ideological impact lay in the glorification of the Motherland and the new, happy life of the working people. Georgi Hubov called it a "symphonic ode to the joys of labor." Yuri Shaporin noted the simple and clear musical style, the spare means of expression, the warmth and emotional fullness of Khachaturyan's familiar Azerbaijanian-Iranian melodic style, while Reinhold Gliere considered the *Poem* almost a symphony. "Apart from the indisputable qualities of the musical material so replete with the intonations of folk music," he wrote, "Khachaturyan's symphony is delightful in its accomplished arrangement, symphonic unity, and monumental stature."

Khachaturyan's *Poem* was undoubtedly a success as a natural blend of folk idioms and his own voice. His experience with the *Poem* helped Khachaturyan when he began to write an anthem for the Armenian Soviet Socialist Republic. When it was finished in May 1944, he invited several intellectuals to his Moscow apartment and played it for them. It had not yet been officially sanctioned, because the contest for an anthem was still open and many Armenian entries were still to be heard. Khachaturyan played it several times, then the guests hummed it. Soon after came the announcement that it had won. It is still heard daily on the radio.

The composer started work on his Violin Concerto after the *Poem to Stalin* and the ballet *Happiness.* David Oistrakh, who was the first to play the Concerto, wrote,

> I am proud, as are all other violinists, that Khachaturyan's first composition, his Dance in B-flat Major, was written for the violin, an instrument for which this talented composer has the feelings of a true virtuoso and inspired artist. His first work, dated 1926, reveals many of the young author's attractive traits, which were later developed in other compositions, for example, in his Violin Concerto, one of his finest instrumental works.

Three years after the Dance, Khachaturyan produced his inspired song-poem for violin and piano, "In Honor of the Ashugs." Though these were not yet fully complete pieces (the Dance for all its national characteristics was faintly reminiscent of Wieniawski), their spontaneity and warm sincerity were captivating. You will not find in them the passion and ardor of the Piano Toccata, but they complemented each other and were often played. Written for Avet Gabrielyan, their first performer, they were later performed by David Oistrakh. Khachaturyan recalls that it was Oistrakh who made them popular. The violinist continued playing them even after the Violin Concerto was completed.

> Often after I had conducted the Violin Concerto, and one would have thought there had been enough violin playing, the audience

would not let the soloist go, calling for an encore. The piano would then be rolled out and David Oistrakh would play these pieces. His performance was exceptionally convincing, inspired and of an improvisational nature.

Oistrakh himself said he cherished Khachaturyan's early works. "I played them often and still do. I like them immensely for their poetry and expressiveness, for that peculiar bright light that seems to radiate from everything Khachaturyan creates," the violinist wrote on the eve of the composer's seventieth birthday.

During the many years Khachaturyan and Oistrakh worked together, their great mutual respect and admiration seemed to shed a special light on their recollections about the birth of the Violin Concerto. What better material could a researcher desire?

After the ten-day festival of Armenian music in the summer of 1940, when his ballet *Happiness* was such a success in Moscow, Khachaturyan was in a state in which music seemed to be generated in his mind faster than he could put it down on paper.

I was living in my country home in Staraya Ruza not far from Moscow, in the summer of 1940. My windows faced the woods. I wrote music as though on a wave of happiness; my whole being was in a state of joy, for I was awaiting the birth of my son. And this feeling, this love of life, was transmitted to the music. I wanted a son very much. I worked quickly and easily; my imagination seemed to fly. David Oistrakh came often from Moscow to visit and played those parts that were completed. I was writing the Concerto with him in mind and it was a great responsibility. When it was finished I dedicated it to Oistrakh. I recall one musician congratulating me and saying, "You are lucky, your son was born immediately after you had finished the Concerto."

The Violin Concerto was composed in record time, in just two months.

Oistrakh said he would like to hear the Concerto and invited me to his country home. I played it for him, trying for some degree of synthesis—I would play the harmony with my left hand and the violin part with my right, singing some of the cantilena parts and the violin melody with the entire accompaniment. Oistrakh carefully followed the score. He liked the Concerto and asked me to leave it with him. We agreed to meet again in a few days.

"I cherish the days of my work with Aram Ilych," wrote Oistrakh.

I will never forget them. I came to know him quite well while the Violin Concerto was being written. I remember that summer day in 1940 when he first played the Violin Concerto, which he had just finished. He was so totally immersed in it that he went immediately to the piano. The stirring rhythms, characteristic turns of national folklore, and sweeping melodic themes captivated me at once. He played with tremendous enthusiasm. One could still feel in his playing that artistic fire with which he had created the music. Sincere and original, replete with melodic beauty and folk colors, it seemed to sparkle.

All these traits which the public still enjoys in the Concerto made an unforgettable impression at the time. It was clear that a vivid composition had been born, destined to live long on the concert stage. And my violin was to launch it on its career.

I still remember the enthusiasm with which I worked on that composition," Khachaturyan recalled.

In about two or three days, Oistrakh came to Staraya Ruza to play the Concerto. My little cottage was full of people. It was summer and the door to the porch was open. Many friends were there—composers and musicians. All those present, myself included, were astonished by Oistrakh's enchanting performance. He played the Concerto as though he had been practicing it for months, just as he was to play it subsequently on the concert stage.

Present at that first intimate performance of the Concerto were composers Yuri Shaporin, Dmitri Kabalevsky, Nikolai

Rakov, Nikolai Chemberdji, Vano Muradeli, Nina Makarova, and Zara Levina. "Khachaturyan invited us to his cottage to hear a new and absolutely fresh composition," recalls Dmitri Kabalevski.

> Oistrakh even apologized because he hadn't had enough time to really prepare the Concerto. He need not have, for he played brilliantly, with inspiration. Khachaturyan's new creation captivated us by its originality, freshness, impetuous onward movement, and bold contrasts of unrestrained joy, gentle lyricism, and tense drama. Everyone was greatly impressed by the Concerto. We all stayed on for some time, asking for one or other episode to be repeated. I don't know about the others, but I found it difficult to work for several days after, I just couldn't forget the vivid images in Khachaturyan's music.

Like the Piano Concerto, the Violin Concerto was performed during a ten-day festival of Soviet music regularly held before the war. "We rehearsed a lot and at length," Oistrakh was to write later. "Alexander Gauk, the conductor, took great pains. If I am not mistaken, we had ten orchestra rehearsals. Aram Ilych would make certain changes in the solo score and the orchestration. He was both exacting and quite specific in his requests, he knew exactly what he wanted, knew how best to express a musical thought."

David Oistrakh was being modest. Let's see what Khachaturyan had to say about those rehearsals.

> We made many corrections in details and nuances during the rehearsals . . . in one place we even added a mute; everything was decided on the spot on Oistrakh's suggestion. Oistrakh often came to my home before the Concerto was published and we would carefully go through the violin score, noting many details; many pages of the score still contain his interesting suggestions.

"Working with him was easy and a real pleasure," wrote Oistrakh. "It was simple to find the key to performing the Concerto. The author had a perfectly clear idea of the performing plan. However, he did not restrict the performer, allowing him ample creative imagination and willingly adopted suggestions from the musicians during work on the Concerto."

The Violin Concerto was first performed on November 16, 1940, at the opening of the festival and repeated the next day. The USSR State Symphony Orchestra conducted by Alexander Gauk also played Myaskovsky's Twenty-first Symphony and parts of Shaporin's opera *The Decembrists* for the first time. So, as with the first performance of his Piano Concerto, Khachaturyan's new work was heard together with other works destined to become classics of Soviet music written in the 1930s and 1940s. Of all the "firsts" performed three years earlier the critics had been most enthusiastic about Myaskovsky's Eighteenth Symphony, Shostakovich's Fifth, and Khachaturyan's Piano Concerto. Now again, it was Myaskovsky's Twenty-first Symphony, Shostakovich's Piano Quintet, and Khachaturyan's Violin Concerto. "These three compositions, so different in style, personality of the composer, and degree of maturity," wrote the magazine *Soviet Music*, "may rightly be classed with the best of recent Soviet music."

Any composer would envy the great number of famous persons present at the first performance of the Violin Concerto: Nikolai Myaskovsky, Sergei Prokofiev, Dmitri Shostakovich, Yuri Shaporin, Dmitri Kabalevsky. The list of violinists was no less impressive. "I came face to face with Khachaturyan's music for the first time," wrote Leonid Kogan many years later. "For us young violinists it was a revelation, a new page in violin music. I remember that the Concerto seemed to us to be extremely difficult, almost impossible to perform."

"I was overjoyed at the success of the Concerto," Khachaturyan wrote about that night. On December 24, 1940, Oistrakh and Gauk performed the Concerto in Leningrad, then in Erevan, Tbilisi, Kiev, and Odessa, receiving rave reviews everywhere. "I received many letters from people in the Soviet Union and from abroad," Oistrakh recalled, "all of them expressing admiration for this talented Soviet composer." Alexander Gauk, whose repertoire included almost all the latest Soviet compositions said, "I have not conducted any of the numerous modern concertos as often as I have this one."

Khachaturyan's Violin Concerto, his waltz from *The Masquerade,* and excerpts from *Gayane* were often played at concerts and on the radio during the Second World War. David Oistrakh's recording of the Violin Concerto was very popular abroad; both the composer and performers received numerous letters praising the Concerto and expressing faith in the Soviet Union's ultimate defeat of fascism.

The prominent English musician Walter Legge recalls in his memoirs that after he and his wife, the famous soprano Elizabeth Schwartzkopf, first heard a recording of Khachaturyan's Concerto, he could always tell her mood, for if she was in a good mood she would try to sing the melody, although it was not easy because of the Concerto's high range.

David Oistrakh always insisted, with characteristic modesty, that he owed his fame to Khachaturyan's Violin Concerto. But Khachaturyan thought differently: "On the contrary, Oistrakh's brilliant recording made the Concerto well known here and abroad."

Oistrakh often played the Concerto with Khachaturyan conducting. "We made a recording of the Concerto in London," Oistrakh recalled in 1975. "I especially like that recording, although it was not the last recording of that work. We recorded it again a few years ago, with Khachaturyan conducting the Radio Moscow Symphony Orchestra."

David Oistrakh's rendition of the Violin Concerto affords an excellent object lesson in the interpretation of Khachaturyan's music. To date, almost every soloist follows Oistrakh's interpretation. Possibly the only exception is Georges Enesco. This outstanding violinist first played the Concerto in 1946 in Bucharest and then included it in his program when touring the Soviet Union. He was then sixty-five. In a letter to the violinist, Khachaturyan wrote,

It is truly a titanic effort to learn a new concerto at your venerable age. Your interpretation is original and convincing and I believe many young violinists will follow your example. There is so much poetry and romantic expression in your interpretation. I was greatly moved by your playing yesterday and I now want very much to write a new composition for violin and orchestra.

In Armenia the Concerto was first performed in 1944 by Khachaturyan's old friend Avet Gabrielyan, who subsequently played it again and again.

Khachaturyan's mastery of his art is evident throughout the score. The Concerto's main themes are inspiring and expressive. It has original harmony and artistic modulation, which at times is instantaneous but always seemingly unintentional. His orchestration is brilliant and colorful, achieving an ideal balance between solo violin and orchestra. The entire score is fastidiously measured with a composer's fine ear. And yet the music, particularly the violin part, so virtuoso yet so cantilena, creates the impression that the soloist is improvising. The Concerto, possibly more than any of his other works, gives one the feeling of soaring above the earth. As you hear the music you find yourself visualizing a flowering, jubilant Armenia bathed in sunlight.

In the Concerto the composer remains true to his principles in the interpretation of forms and in the method of dramatic development. The impetuous Allegro of the first movement is replaced by the nocturnelike second movement, followed by the enthralling playful dance in the Finale, a veritable miracle of ornamentation and variation.

As in the Piano Concerto, the main themes are compared rather than contrasted—in the first and third movements it is the singing quality and the dance mood, in the slow movement, the singing quality and recitative. The ceremonial fanfares of the Introduction are followed by the major themes—energetic, rushing onward. The secondary theme, though continuing to follow the main theme, is relegated to the sphere of captivating and languorous lyricism, a world of subjective feelings. It is not surprising that they do not clash as they develop but draw closer together.

Looking ahead, I would say that the second subject of the

first movement acquires more objective overtones when it is introduced in the Finale.

Khachaturyan compensates for the absence of broad elaboration in two ways. First of all, the elaboration itself as a means of development is found in the exposition and the reprise, thereby providing the continuous development of the melodic material which so impresses in the Violin Concerto. Second, as in the Piano Concerto, elaboration is achieved by a grand and masterful cadenza.

During his first acquaintance with the Violin Concerto at Khachaturyan's country place, Oistrakh played the first movement without the cadenza.

> The cadenza seemed a bit too long to him, and he asked me to write another variation. I kept postponing it. Oistrakh then wrote his own cadenza, using the theme of the Concerto. I liked it. I was pleased that the score contained Oistrakh's cadenza as well as my own. It was written wonderfully, with imagination, and very violinistically. It was shorter than mine, which was fine, as I later had to shorten my own.

Oistrakh's cadenza was a natural synthesis of the music's masterfully thematic foundation, an alloy of the microelements of the first movement's basic themes. It was an extension, as it were, of the composer's main line of thought, and Khachaturyan naturally appreciated that.

During the First International Tchaikovsky Violin Competition in Moscow in 1958, Khachaturyan and Oistrakh both sat on the jury. After hearing one of the entrants play his Violin Concerto with Oistrakh's cadenza, Aram Ilych sent a note to Oistrakh saying, in part,

> Sometimes people live near one another in the same town, often in the same house, but seldom meet or don't have the time to tell each other what they think.
>
> I am certain that you would never have written such a wonderful cadenza if you did not like my concerto. I think your cadenza is better than mine. It is a fantasy on my themes, and

convincing in form. You prepare the audience very well for the reprise by providing the elements and rhythms of the first theme.

"I shall continue to claim your cadenza as my own," he added jokingly. "When I die they will announce that the cadenza is Oistrakh's. Small consolation."

In his Violin Concerto Khachaturyan employs another dramatic means already heard in his "Piano Concerto"—he includes in the Finale thematic material from the first movement, thus completing the cycle. The second subject of the first movement introduced in the Finale not only continues its development, in more objective elucidation, but produces a new "offspring"—an exceptionally fresh, pure, and youthful melody.

The composer's line of thinking is interesting. At the moment when the ideal, embodied in the second subject, seems to be attained, a new and more beautiful ideal emerges, giving the impetus for further development of the music. And although the new theme appears at first to be a melodic antithesis of the turbulent dance in the Finale, it is soon drawn into the mad whirl of the dance and later, at its crest, introduces the main theme of the Finale, the refrain. It is this theme of the "high sky" which unexpectedly disappears on one of its cycles, as though entrusted to the memory of the audience; only the ornamental texture remains. This could be done only to a theme with a magnetic effect and hence is rapidly absorbed by it, as though it were a long-familiar theme. Rodion Shchedrin uses this method in his paraphrasing of Bizet's *Carmen*. In one of the toreador songs the famous theme is also left to the imagination of the audience.

The Violin Concerto's melodic wealth contributed to its success no less than its integrated form and striking dramatic principles. Instrumental singing has long been one of the basic traditions of Russian and Soviet violin playing. All the virtuoso violin sections of the Concerto as well as the orchestral accompaniment are very melodious. But the themes themselves are the most captivating. Its overall sound is based on Armenian folk songs and dance tunes. Although there are no direct quotes in the score, some of the themes suggest their folk origin, as in the principal and second subjects of the first movement; the former is faintly reminiscent of the intonations of the folk song "March, March" and the dance "Kochari," whereas the second subject can be traced to the folk song "The Stream"; that also applies to the themes of the slow movement and the Finale, in which one detects a kinship with the Armenian folk song "Little Shoe."

Khachaturyan's Violin Concerto cannot be considered purely genre music or devoid of dramatic conflict, although such views have been voiced. What Dmitri Kabalevsky called "the gentlest lyricism and tense drama" of the Concerto was later rephrased in the *History of the Music of the Peoples of the USSR.* "Notwithstanding the generally festive mood of the music," we read, "we come upon images of grief and drama in the Concerto."

Performers and critics who interpret the slow movement of the Concerto as wholly immersed in a world of personal, subjective emotions underestimate its content. The wonderful theme opening the slow movement is sensual; only at first does it seem to be more restrained than, say, the second subject of the first movement. And although at every turn of its capricious flow its inconstancy never fails to surprise us, the imagery remains within the framework of personal feelings, at times even hinting at intonations of ordinary popular songs.

As the central episode of the Andante emerges, everything changes. The theme of the violas to the accompaniment of the cellos and basses, their pizzicato seeming to measure time, can hardly be likened to "amorous melancholy," to quote Georgi Hubov. The associations it conjures up are quite different. The Armenian scholar Georgi Geodakyan finds here a similarity with the most tragic Armenian songs of the exiled, songs of nostalgia, "Antuni" (The Homeless) and "Krunk" (The Crane).

> Where do you fly, oh Crane?
> Your cry is stronger than words.
> Bring you no word from home, oh Crane,

Wait, there is time to reach your dear ones.
Bring you no word from home, oh Crane,
I left my garden and my home,
My heart burns like fire.
Wait, oh Crane, your cry,
Is music to my ears.
Bring you no word from home, oh Crane?
How slowly the years pass by.
Hear me, God, open the gates.
The life of a *harib*,*
So sad, so full of tears.
Bring you no word from home, oh Crane?
No joys for me, day after day,
Skewered, I burn in fire.
Not the flame that brings me pain,
But memories of what has been.
Bring you no word from home, oh Crane?
You are silent and fly on. . . .
Go away, oh Crane, and leave me be.

There are other associations with the Andante, bringing to mind those horrible scenes at the beginning of the war when our retreating soldiers witnessed the grief and tears of people watching silently along the roadside; they seemed to be the grief and tears of the entire nation. Though the Concerto was composed before the war, something in the music belies that fact. Was it a premonition, born of the sharpened intuition of a great artist? Or was the composer looking back at his people's past, at their suffering and thralldom over the ages?

But here again he brings out the orchestral tonal colors (the violas accompanied by the pizzicato of the cellos and basses) which he will use again in his Second Symphony, written three years after the Violin Concerto at the height of the Second World War; the related theme will form the basis of the mourning procession in the third movement.

Whereas the first movement of the Violin Concerto bursts

*Harib*, an immigrant.

forth in a dominating mood of joy, the opening notes of the second movement are foreboding—the bassoon is heard against the background of the uneasy cellos playing ponticello and the muted French horns. True, this feeling of evil is soon dispersed and the singing of the solo violin is enchanting in its serenity, making one forget the feeling of foreboding for the time being, a feeling that has by now materialized not only in the repeat of the viola theme, but in the lament of the muted violin as well, a violin seemingly pierced by the organlike sounds of the harp and French horn and the insistent sound of "G," particularly in the culmination of the entire movement. It emerges in the recapitulation of the Andante immediately after the reappearance of the main theme. It seems to sum up what has been heard in the orchestra's mighty tutti, as though saying, "Do not forget the tragedies of wars and invasions, appreciate the beauty of the world and of peace on earth." An excellent example of the blending of the objective and the subjective in Khachaturyan's music.

The concept of the slow movement of the Violin Concerto cannot be grasped without dissecting the construction of the dramatic middle episode. However, the music remains dominated by joy and vitality, for that is how Khachaturyan looked upon Soviet reality in the ten years preceding the war.

# Gayane

*I consider the ballet, in its best creations, a great
art. For in the ballet it is possible to express all the
diversity of man's life and wealth of emotions.*

ARAM KHACHATURYAN

At dawn, on June 22, 1941, Nazi Germany's crack troops attacked the Soviet Union. The enemy was strong and dangerous. Spoiled by its easy victories in Europe, it counted on a lightning victory here. This was the beginning of the Soviet people's Great Patriotic War, which lasted almost four years. The destiny of humanity and of a culture built up over the centuries were largely determined by this war. In it, the Soviet Union lost twenty million people.

Soviet literature and art contributed greatly to the all-out war effort. "No other national culture ever experienced such a tremendous creative upsurge in time of war," wrote Dmitri Shostakovich.

This in itself is unprecedented. Art during the Great Patriotic War was an esthetic and social phenomenon. This had never happened before. Past wars affected culture . . . mostly in a tragic vein. During the years of the battle against fascism the mood of Soviet artists was quite different. Art was in the thick of the people's fight. It never avoided the terrible truth of the war; even during the most tragic days it resounded with heroism, challenge, and faith in ultimate victory. Our art was filled with a boundless love for the Motherland; this was the main factor determining its tone.

Many Soviet artists, Khachaturyan among them, matured

as individuals and as artists during the war. The composer now viewed life with a deeper insight and in bolder relief; the boundaries of his music broadened. Together with such feelings as happiness and jubilation, he was now able to handle acutely dramatic emotions, heroism and tragedy. "Tragedy is not born of pessimism," wrote the Soviet critic Ivan Sollertinsky in a discussion of Shostakovich's Eighth Symphony. "Tragedy is the fruit of maturity, strength, courage, moral freedom and the clash of wills. The tragic is not necessarily pessimistic." In some respects this is the key to Khachaturyan's manner of expressing the war years in his music.

In 1943 Khachaturyan joined the Communist Party, whose ideals he had long been expounding as an artist, musician, and public figure.

Writing about the first years of the war, he declared, "We were all eager to show that, although there was a war going on, and the enemy was advancing . . . our cultural life was continuing, cultural values were being created, and the spirit of the people was strong."

"It is now important to write even more music, ranging from songs to symphonies and operas," he wrote in 1941. "We must create monuments to our epoch, to our struggle. All our experiences, all the thoughts and feelings of the Soviet people must find expression in works of art."

"From songs to symphonies. . . ." Soviet songs for mass consumption had reached the heights of popularity in the 1930s. The best of these songs were usually about this country's experiences in building a new socialist life; they were something of a musical emblem of the new world. Songs like "The Marching Song" by Shostakovich, "Jolly Fellows" and "Song of the Homeland" by Dunayevsky, "Meadowlands" by Knipper, and "Katyusha" by Blanter still convey to us the joy of creation and the spirit of the first years of the Soviet five-year plans, years of outstanding achievements. Many of the songs acquired a second life in other countries. For example, Italian guerrillas took Blanter's song "Katyusha" for their own during the Second World War.

In later years it was Solovyov-Sedoi's "Moscow Evenings" that won worldwide popularity. During the war, however, songs played a different, more serious role. The Composers Union set up a song headquarters with Gliere and Khachaturyan in charge.

> During the first days of the war I spent my days and nights at the Composers Union. From all the rooms and halls came the sound of new songs and marches being tried out by composers and poets. Moscow composers and poets alone produced more than forty songs in the first two days of the war; by the fourth day there were over a hundred, among them Alexander Alexandrov's "Sacred War," which became the musical expression of the very essence of the Great Patriotic War.

New songs were played over the radio almost as soon as they were written; they were sent to the front lines, printed in army newspapers, and performed by the numerous army bands. They imbued the soldiers with a spirit of heroism and courage and faith in ultimate victory.

> Soviet songs are a fighting weapon and it is our duty to forge this weapon with all the passion, responsibility, knowledge, and talent at our disposal.
> We shall give the front songs throbbing with wrath and fury, songs of revenge, songs of victory, and songs of glory worthy of our heroic Soviet soldiers.

Throughout his career Khachaturyan wrote songs; he was against the idea of composers specializing in one genre only: "Songwriters should always turn to neighboring fields and, refreshed, return to writing songs."

Among the many reasons for Khachaturyan's interest in songs were his childhood recollections of the *ashugs* and their tradition that whatever the *ashugs* sing today will be sung by the people tomorrow. The *ashugs* put heart and soul into their songs and their singing. In Arabic the word *ashug* means "one in love," "one possessed by passion." It was Khachaturyan's deep conviction that a good song, accepted and sung by the people, becomes a powerful artistic and ideological force. That is why, in his comments on his own songs, we find a recurrent wish that they be sung by the people.

Referring to "The Armenian Drinking Song," Khachaturyan wrote to his friend Tatal Altunyan, leader of the Armenian State Song and Dance Ensemble, "My goal is for this song to be heard in the streets."

Khachaturyan was partly successful in this, for "Pepo," "Song of Erevan," and "The Armenian Drinking Song" were popular in Armenia. His "On Gogol Boulevard" was heard often in prewar Moscow, and "Into Battle, Camarados" was sung in Spain during the Civil War, while his "Baltic Sea" was popular in this country. His "Anthem of the Armenian Republic" was also an achievement.

Khachaturyan remained in Moscow until October 1941, when the organizing committee of the Composers Union was evacuated to Sverdlovsk in the Urals. He joined his wife Nina Makarova and his little son Renik, who had been awaiting him there.

> I left Moscow together with Dmitri Shostakovich, his family, and many other prominent musicians who had recently arrived from besieged Leningrad. I remember we had trouble boarding the train. Shostakovich changed his mind; he traveled only part of the way with us and then headed for Kuibyshev, where the Bolshoi Theater had settled. In a few months his famous Seventh Symphony was performed there for the first time. The trip to Sverdlovsk was agonizing. My ulcer acted up soon after I arrived in Sverdlovsk. This was especially inopportune, because I had big plans at the time and the ulcer required a strict diet, while food shortages were steadily growing worse.

Khachaturyan occasionally complained of his health in letters from the Urals.

> I shall be going into hospital in a few days. My ulcer is really troublesome. I don't eat anything, am hungry, and in pain. The doctor says one of my ulcers requires surgery.

> I am really suffering here. I have several attacks a day.
>
> I've really got it bad. . . . Severe pains in the stomach. I stayed in bed with hot water bottles for five days. It's a little better now and I am working again. I eat porridge without salt.
>
> Oh, my stomach aches . . . I'm in a terrible mood. I'm afraid it will start up again . . . in which case the ballet and the symphony will be lost.

Not all his thoughts, however, were centered on himself. His letters of those years express deep concern for the fate of his country and joy at the news of every victory at the front. He helped improve living conditions for his colleagues and busied himself with affairs of the Composers Union. He was concerned for his wife and little son and also for his daughter, who had remained in Moscow. The minute he felt better he started working again, trying to make up for lost time. He was about ready to start work on *Gayane*. However, as luck would have it, the trunk with all his manuscripts and the only copy of the score of his ballet *Happiness* was lost somewhere between Moscow and Sverdlovsk. It was finally found.

> I have great plans for work, but I must have some treatments first, then I shall start writing.
>
> All of us are very happy at the news from the front. It gives us colossal energy and faith.

But he also had his creative joys in those grim years. His music was played on July 2, 1942, in the Sverdlovsk Opera Theater at a concert featuring the works of Soviet composers. "Oistrakh played my Violin Concerto in Sverdlovsk on August 2. The hall was filled to capacity despite the heat and the driving rain. I am pleased with the performance and the success of the Concerto."

Khachaturyan soon left for the city of Perm to work with the Leningrad Opera and Ballet Theater on *Gayane*. The story of this ballet goes back to his other ballet *Happiness*, written in 1939. Writing in the early 1970s, when his ballets *Gayane* and *Spartacus* had become world famous, he said,

I consider the ballet, like the opera, the supreme synthesis of art. Music, dance, choreography, pantomime, drama, theater, stage sets, painting, architecture, songs and poetry—what a wealth of means, what truly boundless opportunities to depict reality, to embody broad ideological and artistic concepts and reveal strong characters, passions, and moods! What a variety of possibilities for esthetically influencing the audience!

When I started working on my first ballet score, I knew absolutely nothing about the specific features of the ballet as a musical form. But I quickly began to grasp and understand its characteristic features in the course of my work.

Khachaturyan's admission takes us back to the days before *Gayane*, before *Spartacus*, when he first began to master what for him was a new form of art.

Ten-day festivals of national art were very popular before the war. They brought the best soloists, performing groups, both professional and amateur, composers, poets, artists, and theatrical companies to the capital. Ukrainian, Kazakh, Georgian, Uzbek, Azerbaijan, and Kirghiz festivals had already been held in Moscow. It was Armenia's turn now in the latter half of 1938 to demonstrate its achievements.

"All of us still remember the wonderful productions by the Georgians, Kazakhs, and Uzbeks," wrote Khachaturyan, full of admiration for the Azerbaijan festival. "These performances gave us a new and acute understanding of the depth, force, and significance of the great Leninist nationalities policy that opened the doors wide to the development of the Soviet people's socialist culture."

In a conversation with Khachaturyan, Anastas Mikoyan, the government leader of Armenian origin, expressed the wish that a ballet be written for the Armenian festival—it would be one of the first in Armenian theatrical history and the first such production to be shown at a festival. Since the suggestion was very much in tune with the composer's own plans and time was short, he immediately started work on it. As he already had an idea for the ballet, Mikoyan advised him to get in touch with the prominent Armenian director Gevork Ovanesyan, who had done the book for *Happiness*.

I spent the spring and summer of 1939 in Armenia gathering material for the ballet *Happiness*. I took Maxim Gorky's advice and started on a deep study of Armenian melodies, folk art, and music.

Thinking back to those days, I refer to my stay in Erevan as a period of exile, in jest, of course, but I really slaved, at least that's how it seemed to me then, for I was a young man who had completed postgraduate work just two years previously and was interested in all aspects of life. The people at the Spendiarov Theater did their best to make me comfortable. I was given a good apartment, which I rarely left during my work on the ballet. Alexander Dolukhanyan, a wonderful, erudite musician who later wrote many popular songs, lived on the floor below. Shortly before my arrival in Erevan he had returned from a very interesting folklore expedition throughout the republic. He brought back many Armenian folk songs and dances which he readily put at my disposal. Later, when I had already started writing, he would take the fragments of the score and arrange them for four-hand piano, thus making it possible for me to start rehearsals while composing.

The world of folk music proved a wonderful source of inspiration to Khachaturyan. Completely absorbed in Dolukhanyan's notes, he also listened to many folk musicians and went to concerts at the Armenian Philharmonic. Many years later Khachaturyan told how much he had been impressed by the folk song "The *Pshatov* Tree."

*Happiness* was to be about a village girl, Karine, her love for the border guard Armen, and about the life and work of collective farmers and border guards, and their patriotism. "Although ballet music is strictly for dancing I aimed to symphonize it. I wanted the songs and dance melodies created by the people to become a natural part of the ballet, inseparable from the ballet music." This shows that at that early stage in his ballet Khachaturyan had already found the key to creating a truly musical, truly artistic theatrical production.

The score took just half a year to write. The conductor, Konstantin Saradjev—a well-known musician, an enthusiast of Armenian culture, and Rector of the Erevan Conservatory

—rehearsed the ballet. Aram Ilych had met him when he taught conducting at the Moscow Conservatory. It was Saradjev who chaired the jury at a contest for the best arrangement of Armenian folk songs in 1922, at which Khachaturyan—just beginning to study music—won first prize. It was Saradjev also who conducted the orchestra at Sergei Prokofiev's concert in Moscow that made such a great impression on Khachaturyan, especially Prokofiev's *Love for Three Oranges* and his Third Piano Concerto, which the composer himself played.

Saradjev was quite a personality: thin, very lively, with burning eyes, a short beard, and long mustache, invariably dressed elegantly and in good taste. Musicians respected him; he was excellent company, very attentive to his colleagues and students. Khachaturyan had often met him at Armenia House and knew that he always took an interest in new works by Armenian composers. They had rarely met after Saradjev moved to Erevan in 1935, although they would get together to talk about their work whenever Khachaturyan was in Armenia. And now Saradjev was to conduct his ballet.

> Every effort was made in Armenia to ensure the success of the Spendiarov Theater's Moscow tour. Saradjev organized a wonderful orchestra which received special mention from critics during the Armenian Festival in Moscow. Armenian instrumentalists from Moscow, Leningrad, and other cities responded to the appeal to make the Armenian Festival a success. Among them were performers I knew from the Komitas Quartet. Saradjev threw himself into the work, transmitting his enthusiasm to the entire orchestra.
>
> When he liked something he expressed his joy with a childlike naturalness that inspired me. He displayed boundless initiative, artistic talent, and skill, as well as an excellent feel for the orchestra. However, he would never force his own taste on others, respected the composer's ideas, and always asked if what he was doing was what I wanted.

Saradjev was delighted with the score of *Happiness*, particularly its folk character. Khachaturyan himself said once that

*Happiness* could be considered a folk ballet not only because of the seven genuine Armenian melodies in it but also because the music "is full of the sounds of ancient Armenian songs."

Saradjev heard the score in the very same way. "In arranging folk melodies (Armenian, Ukrainian, or Russian), the composer created his own themes concomitant with the folk themes," wrote Saradjev. "These themes are so related in style (Dance of the Cranes, the Hopak, the Russian Dance), that they amaze and delight." Saradjev also noted the symphonic qualities of *Happiness*. The second and fourth scenes, he said, were pure symphony. The fact that composer and conductor agreed on almost every question certainly contributed to the production's success.

The ballet master, Ilya Arbatov, was an ally of both Khachaturyan and Saradjev. It is remarkable that as a result this was perhaps the first ballet on record to be staged exactly as written. However, many years later Khachaturyan wrote that Arbatov was more successful in individual dances than in ballets as a whole.

*Happiness* had its first fun in Erevan in September 1939 and proved a major event in Armenian musical culture. That same year, on October 24, the ballet charmed a huge audience in Moscow's Bolshoi Theater. It was an exciting day for Aram Khachaturyan.

The many reviews of the Erevan and Moscow performances included articles by such prominent persons as the poet Avetik Isaakyan; the author Marietta Shaginyan; the conductors Alexander Melik-Pashayev and Konstantin Saradjev; the director of the Armenian Festival, Ruben Simonov; the director of the Armenian Opera Theater, Armen Gulakyan; the composer Vano Muradeli; the ballet master Igor Moiseyev; and Khachaturyan's biographer and critic, Georgi Hubov. "We are used to poetry and colors on the stage of the Bolshoi Theater," wrote Marietta Shaginyan.

We have experienced the panorama of *Sleeping Beauty;* we have seen the fluttering of swan's down in the most tender and divine of ballets—*Swan Lake;* the conductor's baton has brought us the fabulous melody of the Lilac Fairy and the rippling waltz from *Coppelia*—and now a new Soviet ballet, *Happiness,* has burst triumphantly into this world of beauty. Aram Khachaturyan seems to have poured music onto the audience from a horn of plenty.

An undoubted achievement, though not fully realized, was his symphonization of the dance. The subject line unfolded in full choreographic scenes as in Tchaikovsky's ballets. But there were also many individual numbers in the score that charmed the audience with their melodic wealth and highly professional arrangements of Armenian folklore. Though herself not a professional musician, Marietta Shaginyan was the first to note the individual manner in which the art of the East and the West were interwoven. As she wrote,

> Even Spendiarov, to say nothing of other composers who used the music of the East, brought the national elements into the broad sphere of European musical means. Khachaturyan, in his ballet *Happiness,* brilliantly did the exact opposite. Basing himself on Eastern sounds and colors, but standing firmly on Armenian ground in his own musical feelings, on the rhythms and melodies of Armenian music, Khachaturyan attempted to sum up, or more exactly, to graft onto it, by the strength of this Eastern culture, European—i.e., Russian and Ukrainian—folk melodies. One does find in Khachaturyan's ballet the Eastern fulfillment of European melodies (in all their originality). This is seen not only in art, but in life itself, a phenomenon reflecting the new beginning in culture and a means of equal intercourse between Westerners and Orientals.

And so it was that back in 1939 Khachaturyan's music brought to the forefront the same problem that in the 1960s and 1970s became a priority for the development of world culture, the heated debate between those who stood for isolating the musical cultures of the Eastern nationalities and those who advocated their development within the framework of the international traditions of the modern cultural process.

The success of *Happiness* did not hide from the music world or from Khachaturyan himself the shortcomings of the score, and later they induced him to radically rewrite it. The book was rather sketchy and loosely hung dramatically, and some situations were unfounded. Not all the musical images were well developed; the fragmentary nature of some parts contrasted sharply with the composer's intention of symphonizing the dance; also, the vivid coloring at times verged on overillustration.

"I think the criticism of *Happiness* was just and well founded," said Khachaturyan in later years. He probably thought the same back in those years when the flow of praise and the success might have gone to his head. Otherwise he probably would not have agreed immediately after the festival to participate in a production of *Happiness* with a new book, as the Leningrad Kirov Opera and Ballet Theater proposed. Painstaking work began which due to circumstances continued for many years. The score of *Happiness* was practically forgotten but the final result was the creation of *Gayane*.

The Kirov Theater took the production very seriously. Everyone realized the artistic value of Khachaturyan's music. They realized also that the theater that had successfully staged such ballets as Alexander Krein's *Laurencia* and Prokofiev's *Romeo and Juliet* had now to consolidate its success. Many outstanding soloists were in the cast of *Gayane*—Natalia Dudinskaya, Konstantin Sergeyev, and Tatyana Vecheslova. The theater tried to obtain the services of Martiros Saryan and Ruben Simonov as well. Saryan's sets, together with Khachaturyan's music, would have been an additional guarantee of success. Simonov at the time was working successfully on the production of Lermontov's *Masquerade* at the Vakhtangov Theater and so had to decline the invitation.

Konstantin Derzhavin, the well-known critic, philologist, and connoisseur of the ballet, wrote the new book. His subject—the struggle against lawbreakers and traitors—was very appropriate for the prewar period. However, the fact that the music had already been written weakened the book's dramatic force.

Working with Derzhavin was a very interesting experience. I often traveled to Leningrad, where I met with Derzhavin and his wife, Nina Anisimova, who was to stage the ballet. I had already seen her many times on the stage of the Kirov Theater. She was a brilliant performer of character dances, especially Spanish, and often danced with Sergei Korenya, also a wonderful dancer. I did not know what she was like as a choreographer, for my ballet was her first attempt in this field.

Anisimova had never seen a production of *Happiness* and was not too familiar with the music. She was overjoyed at the opportunity of studying the score and meeting the composer, who played the music for her on the piano. "The lilting, graceful music and unusually sharp rhythms, the many lines of counterpoint, the vivid melodies and dancing mood of all that I heard absolutely amazed me and won my heart immediately," she wrote. "*Happiness* contained a wealth of material. I thanked my lucky stars for having sent me such a wonderful composer for my debut as a ballet master."

The production of *Happiness* was no simple matter; a language of the dance had to be found that would correspond to the language of Khachaturyan's music, so unusual and new for the classical ballet. The individual choreographic character of the main roles had to be shaped and a balance found between the length of the music and the phrasing of the dance, which did not always coincide. As Anisimova explained,

Khachaturyan's musical phrasing was unusually long and wordy and had to be cut for the choreography. The theater's pianist, Mikhail Karpov, helped me in this. Endless repetitions of one and the same melody were not suitable for the ballet.

We would prepare long in advance before editing the music. The composer, who at first was lenient and allowed us to cut the music, by the end of rehearsals often became our bitter enemy. He did not like to cut his music, and grew angry and morose. "The great Anna Pavlova would never agree to dance such a long variation," Karpov would say in my support. Aram Ilych would pace from corner to corner, then mumbling something under his nose would sit down at the piano and say in conciliatory tones: "Well, let's see what we can do!" I would sit quietly, waiting. The composer would look in my direction, eyes blazing and say: "This is your responsibility, Nina Alexandrovna. I am committing sacrilege for your ballet."

For the choreography Khachaturyan had to cut the music, but for the ballet he had to provide additional segments. Carefully, Anisimova "extracted" the line of the second dancing pair, Noune and Karen, from the composer.

Once after rehearsals we went with Aram Ilych to the Nord cafe, where we continued our discussions. The composer was deep in thought, for he had to compose variations for Noune. This was required by the performers and made necessary by the form of the second act. I tried to explain to him what I wanted and accidentally tapped the coffee cup with my spoon. Aram Ilych tapped his cup too, and we got a fine melodic phrase. Khachaturyan found the sounds interesting. A day or so later he brought Noune's variations for the second act. The music was playful and coquettish.

Anisimova finished working on the first act in April 1941. It was reviewed and approved by the theater's art council, which praised her work. During the discussions Konstantin Derzhavin remarked that "the people of the Transcaucasus have preserved the traits of a noble and ancient simplicity," while the theater manager, Evgeny Radin, stressed that "Khachaturyan's score is neither the East nor exotic, it is music that allows the production to be staged in any Soviet republic on a local theme."

The ballet was to be ready by June 1941.

"I went to Leningrad on June 16, 1941, immediately after the dress rehearsal of *Masquerade*, recalls Khachaturyan. "I had time before leaving to sit and chat with Ruben Simonov and members of the cast while enjoying a *shashlik* in the canteen. From there I went straight to the railroad station to board the train for Leningrad. Who could have imagined then that war would break out just six days later?"

The Leningrad Opera and Ballet Theater was evacuated to

the city of Perm with a repertory of twenty-one operas and ballets. In the course of one year—1941–1942—it gave more than a thousand concerts for the troops on the Northwestern Front.

It was during those terrible days that Khachaturyan again met with the cast of the Kirov Theater, far from Leningrad and Moscow, deep in the Urals. He decided it was time to resume work on *Happiness.*

> I resumed work on the ballet in the autumn of 1941, when Hitler's hordes were pushing toward Moscow. It may seem strange today that it was possible to think of a ballet production in those days of severe trials. The war and ballet? Two concepts so incompatible. However, events soon showed that there was nothing strange in my plans to express in music and choreography the theme of great national upsurge, of a people united in the face of a foreign invasion. The original idea for the ballet was the expression of patriotism, loyalty, and love of country.

Tatyana Vecheslova, the well-known ballerina who danced on opening night, aptly described the atmosphere in which Khachaturyan's ballet was born with these words: "We were looking for spring in the autumn." Letters and documents help reconstruct the story of its birth.

> *August 8, 1942.* My Kirovites are in Sverdlovsk. . . . On the thirteenth I will leave with them for Molotov [as Perm was then called].

> *August 1942.* On arriving in Molotov I worked on the ballet score with a hot water bottle at my side and a plate of porridge before me. Luckily, I ate at the theater's canteen which, for those days, was very well supplied. In the hotel my only furniture was a piano and a stool.

> *August 23, 1942.* I work a lot here. I am engrossed in the music I am writing. The attitude to me here is ideal . . . all my requests are carried out. I live in the hotel, which is noisy and not very comfortable, but I have a good room and a piano. I

stay home for days on end and leave the room only to eat lunch in the canteen. . . .

*August 26, 1942.* Am working on the ballet. I must write two new scenes and doctor up a few places. I have to compose fifty minutes of music. I am writing in ink right on the score. No time to think and make drafts. The hotel is very noisy and there are radios everywhere, making work difficult.

*September 4, 1942.* I have been given some extra work; the music for the ballet will be almost entirely new.

*September 1942.* This is not the old ballet *Happiness,* but a new one which will be called *Gayane,* the name of the heroine. It is a new ballet, with 60–70 percent of the music quite new. I have completed a new scene here, about thirty minutes of music, two hundred fifty pages of the score. The theater and the ballet company are very pleased with the music and praise it too much. This worries me; I am waiting impatiently to hear how the orchestra sounds. I am even experimenting in places. Unexpectedly, I am compelled to write a whole new closing scene which includes only five of the old dances. All told, there are close to twenty-five numbers. The last scene is being made over into an entire act. I am very disappointed and angry. They do whatever they like with me, but there is no other way out. I'll be composing here for at least another month.

*Autumn 1942.* [The ballerina Tatyana Vecheslova recalls:] We would often drop in on Khachaturyan for some fun. Once he even treated us to a bottle of red wine, a rarity in those days. Aram Ilych was a cordial host, full of fun. He loved to watch the talented Nina Anisimova dance. He appreciated the fine skill of Natalia Dudinskaya and laughed heartily at Nikolai Subkovsky's comic gifts. His music could stir even the most indifferent of actors.

*September 1942.* I am highly offended that my ballet is considered an old piece of work. . . . What I am doing now is big, difficult, appropriate, and interesting. Please explain to certain persons that my ballet is almost completely new and that this is my latest opus. I'm so terribly pressed for time, I write music twelve to fourteen hours a day. I am so tired I often cannot think straight. But it is a pleasant sensation for it is creative.

*September 20, 1942.* Absolutely no free time. Am writing night and day. Not enough time.

*October 10, 1942.* I am writing from morning to night. There is enough work for another three weeks. Am finishing the last act. Should be completed by the end of October. Then I will attend the orchestra rehearsals and compose a symphony. Working fourteen hours a day. . . ."

*October 24, 1942.* "Will finally finish the ballet tomorrow. All told, in my two months here I wrote two acts of absolutely new music. One hour and ten minutes. Close to five hundred pages of score. They say it is the strongest music of the entire ballet. Now everything is in the hands of the orchestra and the stage. The cast is working with great enthusiasm. The theater will soon complete rehearsals of Marian Koval's opera, *Emelyan Pugachiov,* after which the entire company will be occupied only with my ballet. There are parts in the new music where I experimented and I am very worried and impatient for the orchestra to begin rehearsals.

*End of October, 1942.* Busy from morning to night. Three rehearsals a day and endless discussions with the conductor, ballet-master, artists, etc. I am quite satisfied with what I have written, but less satisfied than those around me. One must be here to see what is happening in the theater and among the cast when the orchestra plays. It was a very exciting day when the cast, thoroughly familiar with the music played on the piano, was to hear it played by the orchestra for the first time. I wish all my friends such a day. Pazovsky* told the management that his next work would be an opera with Khachaturyan. . . .

*November 1942.* Everyone in the theater is pleased with the

---

*Ari Pazovsky, prominent Soviet conductor, at that time head conductor of the Kirov Theater, a skilled musician and master at staging operas.

music, but I think much still remains to be done. I am suffering terribly. . . .

*November 1942.* [The ballerina Tatyana Vecheslova recalls:] I was the first to dance the role of Noune." Aram Ilych composed the variation for me and dedicated it to me. He composed it just before the performance, quite effortlessly, in just thirty minutes."

*November 1942.* At the theater's request, after completing the score, I wrote the Dance of the Kurds . . . what later came to be known as the Saber Dance. I started at three in the afternoon and worked until two AM. The next morning it was arranged for orchestra and we had a rehearsal. In the evening there was a full dress rehearsal. The Saber Dance immediately impressed the orchestra, the dancers, and the audience. I recall that I couldn't help scribbling in the score of the Dance, where the three-part rhythm is sharply syncopated: "Just to please the ballet, damn it." At first I wanted to end it in a long and gradual diminuendo, but Nina Anisimova and the dancers persuaded me to end it with a gradual crescendo.

*November 1942.* [Nina Anisimova recalls:] I had a little argument with Aram Ilych just before opening night. It is easier for the dancers to count in three in the Shelokho dance in the fourth act. But the orchestra was obviously playing in two, and the dancers were having trouble. I started to count three loudly, and the orchestra stopped. Khachaturyan called out from his seat, "Stop counting in three, or I'll sink you." "That's all that count is good for," I retorted. We argued for some time. We made up only after the war, in Moscow. But both two and three are possible in the Shelokho dance.

*Beginning of December, 1942. Gayane* was produced by the theater in one of the country's largest munitions centers. While working on the ballet we were inspired by the example of the intensive work for the front we saw at the plants and factories in the city of Molotov and the surrounding region; they were working night and day forging the weapons of victory over the enemies of our country. Working on the ballet we kept in mind the heroic defenders of the North Caucasus, the epic battle of Stalingrad, and the valor of the great city of Leningrad.

*December 9, 1942.* [Nina Anisimova recalls:] Despite all the horrors and consequences of this terrible war which I witnessed, I can say that never before had I created dances as easily as in *Gayane;* never before had I loved and admired music as much as in that ballet. And if my dances were a success it is due only to Aram Khachaturyan. His talent inspired and helped the producer. . . . Opening night was wonderful. There were many curtain calls. On stage Aram Ilych kept kissing me furiously on the cheek, almost biting me. "I'll never forgive you," he kept whispering with a smile.

*December 1942.* [Nina Makarova:] I have just returned from Molotov, it was wonderful. Never before have I seen such an attitude, such attention from the theater, the management, and the entire cast. Aram's ballet is wonderful. I would even say that it sounds more mature somehow than anything he has written so far. . . . The performers are quite enchanting and the production is beautiful. . . .

*December 1942. Gayane* was produced at the very same time as the great battle of Stalingrad was taking place. The soldiers attending the performances went off to the front practically the next day. I received many letters from them. I particularly cherished one from Vera Stafeyeva, who was with reconnaissance, for she wrote about the meaning of my music.

*January 1943.* Upon leaving Molotov I would like once again to thank all of you and express my satisfaction with the production of *Gayane.* The Kirov Theater is a time-honored theater that to this day has reverently preserved the glorious traditions of Russian art. And all who cherish these traditions must understand the enormous joy one experiences at having participated, even modestly, in the growth of this wonderful theater.

I should also like to add that in these days of an unprecedented war that is destroying cultural monuments, the creation of cultural values and works of art is particularly important. This is not only a war of machines, of motors and tanks, it is also a war between two cultures—the progressive, all-conquering Soviet culture, and the so-called fascist culture, a decadent, obscurantist culture. In these difficult wartime conditions the wonderfully friendly, close-knit cast of the Kirov Theater was able to prepare in a short time two anniversary productions —*Emelyan Pugachiov* and *Gayane*. This is something quite out of the ordinary and extremely gratifying for Soviet art.

Whether attending a performance or listening to recordings of the music of *Gayane*, one is immediately impressed. The thought occurs that another composer would find sufficient material here for several large works. Khachaturyan added an entirely new third act to his old ballet, *Happiness*, a large part of the second and several new episodes to the first and fourth. His wonderfully lavish melodies, orchestral arrangements, and harmony, the thoughts and feelings expressed in the score, certainly ensure the success of this work. And successful it was, both at its premiere in Molotov and in later years throughout the world.

*Gayane* owes its renown chiefly to three symphonic suites Khachaturyan arranged from the score of the ballet. "I shall never forget the first performance of the First Suite from *Gayane*, recalled the well-known Soviet soprano Natalia Spiller. "The Radio Moscow Orchestra was conducted by Golovanov. Neither before nor after October 3, 1943, have I ever heard such a storm of applause, nor witnessed such unqualified success of a new work as on that evening in the Hall of Columns." Six years later Dmitri Shostakovich, then in New York for the All-American Congress of Scientific and Art Workers for Peace, said much the same thing. Khachaturyan's music was on that occasion conducted by Leopold Stokowski.

The language of Khachaturyan's music was simple and easy to understand, and he worked well with Nina Anisimova. She did not pretend to have a good knowledge of Armenian folk dance music; she was able to visit the republic only after the war. "I seem to feel Armenia intuitively," she said at a meeting of the cast. And Khachaturyan commented: "I like what Nina Anisimova said about not knowing Armenian folklore but feeling it intuitively. Too much knowledge may even be detrimental. . . . For myself and for Nina folklore must be a motivation." He spoke of three basic elements in the score of *Gayane*—the dance, drama, at times tragic, and lyricism. "I am all for dancing in ballets and singing in operas."

Anisimova agreed with him in this, too. The Kirov Theater pointed out that in staging *Gayane* it had sought "to make maximum use of the effective and dramatic possibilities of the language of the dance in every way—the symphonic construction of the music was regarded as the guiding principle for the producer in the production both as a whole and in interpreting particular scenes."

Khachaturyan attained a good balance between classical and character dancing. Maxim Gorky, who greatly admired Armenian folk dancing, wrote about the male dance of the Sasun Armenians: "Never before have I seen or imagined such absolute fusion, such a blend of many moving as one. No less original and just as charming was the dancing of the women—each separately, the gestures individual and yet ideally preserving the rhythms and unity of movement."

Khachaturyan's music, which captured the very essence of the Armenian dance, was an excellent guide for Nina Anisimova. "The rhythm of our ballet," she instructed the dancers, "demands precise and expressive movements. You must feel and understand that an Armenian woman cannot turn suddenly or jerk her hand sharply . . . she invariably retains the silhouette of a running deer. She always seems slightly mysterious. The gestures of the Armenian men are energetic, distinctive, and supple."

Just as Khachaturyan's music helped Anisimova stage the various dances, so also did it suggest the style for the classical dances. For example, in the duet of Gayane and Kazakov from the fourth act and the Gayane and Armen duet from the first, the traditional adagio of the classical ballet is heard, reminiscent of the breadth of Glazunov's *Raymonda* ballet, while in others the character dance dominates.

Anisimova maintained that the French and Italian classical

traditions—the foundations of Russian ballet—were not appropriate for the choreography of Khachaturyan's music in *Gayane*. She considered the older, more plastic dance styles far more suitable. And how prophetic was her opinion! Fifteen years later Leonid Yakobson was to apply the same principle in his production of *Spartacus*.

The idea of dance portraits for the leading personages in the ballet is characteristic of the composer. He had great faith in the possibilities of the dance and continued the ideas of Komitas, who asserted that "the distinctive traits of a nation, particularly its customs and level of cultural development, merge in the dance."

Such are the dances of Noune and Karen—the embodiment of carefree, happy youth; of Gayane—the captivating lyricism of her monologue, the touching sincerity and warmth of the Cradle Song; of Armen—steadfastness, courage, and willpower; of Aisha—languid, as though born of the music of sunrise in the mountains.

Gayane is a blend of spiritual beauty and nobility, a determination to fight for her happiness, of charm, tenderness, and moral purity. The development of her role from a woman deceived and suffering to a woman glowing with happiness, through a difficult struggle in which she risks her own life and the life of her baby daughter, brings to the forefront the philosophical theme of the indivisibility of happiness in personal and social life. In *Gayane* Khachaturyan faced the difficult task of creating on stage a picture of the positive hero of our times while avoiding all bombast or schematism. Although the title of the ballet was no longer *Happiness,* the meaning remained. For the composer *Gayane* became the embodiment of the immutable moral ideal of all ages, which Phrygia continued in *Spartacus.* In his search for the most moving music to express Phrygia's grief in the epilogue, Khachaturyan naturally settled on motifs that harked back to *Gayane*.

He was fully aware of the difficulties facing him even when he was working on *Happiness* in 1939. "Symphonizing the ballet music presented difficulties, but I was determined to do so, for

I believe that anyone writing a ballet or an opera must do just that."

While creating *Gayane* the composer devoted much thought to the specific features of ballet as a form of music; he carefully unfolded the dramatic line in the score and studied the music and structure of Tchaikovsky's ballets. The influence on *Gayane* of Russian classical music is seen in the emotional frenzy of the Dance of the Kurds (the Saber Dance), whose prototype may be found in the Dance of the Polovtsians from Borodin's *Prince Igor;* it is seen in Khachaturyan's score, which joins Borodin's epic traditions with Tchaikovsky's tradition of laying bare man's psychological inner world. It is likewise seen in the symphonic development of folk music and in the very interpretation of ballet as a musical production that follows symphonic rules. In the score of *Gayane* Dmitri Kabalevsky noticed the same principles of "undulating dramatic development" so characteristic of Tchaikovsky's symphonic and scenic works.

Khachaturyan achieved that broad symphonic sweep in his ballet music first by greatly broadening the scenes, which the structure of the score allows. One notes this in the cotton picking scene in the first act; in the second act it is the carpet weavers. The music for the cotton pickers is built around the wonderfully pliant and emotional folk melody "Pshati Tzar" with which the first act opens and closes, creating an ideal setting for Gayane.

Second, the leitmotivs of the main roles contribute to the symphonic sweep. Third, the composer groups individual dances in small cycles with a definite form, for example, in three parts, as in the Dance of the Kurds, which is preceded and followed by Aisha's Dance. Fourth, the contrasts between the acts and scenes enhance the ballet's breadth. The musically optimistic first act is momentarily clouded over by the appearance of Gayane's tipsy husband, Giko; this massive choral scene then segues into the more intimate second act, which, with its comic Old Man's Dance, resembles an Oriental miniature. The first scene of the third act immerses the audience into the untouched beauty and primitive passions of the camp of the Kurds. This prepares the audience for the dramatic exposure of the conspiracy and takes us to the tragic second scene of the fire. And, finally, the fourth act—a completely different world of people and emotions—is made up of scenes of a collective farm reborn, of colorful dances and three weddings.

Further contrast, but on a different level, is achieved in the first act by the dances of Noune and Karen, Gayane, and then Armen. In the score Gayane's dance is bracketed by the other two, and though they seem to be equally carefree they stress Gayane's concealed anxiety, lending her an air of mystery.

The dramatic climax in the ballet is provided by the scene of the fire. When it seems that all symphonic resources have been exhausted we hear the tolling of the bell—a sound symbolic of tragedy. The fire is the culminating scene, unraveling all the intrigues. Giko, who started the fire, is about to savor his victory when he is exposed by Gayane, an act of heroism expressive of her love for her country and her people. Dmitri Kabalevsky, who saw the Kirov Theater's production in Molotov, compared it to an ancient tragedy. "Everything was monumental," he wrote, "everything was elevated to the heights of great, tragic art."

The strong and impressive fire scene gradually subsides and is soon followed by the soothing divertissement of the fourth and last act. It is announced that Gayane, who has recovered from her wounds, is to be married to Kozakov, the commander of the border guards. The dances, each more colorful than the last, including the Saber Dance, were not written solely for effect. "In the epilogue, which expresses true friendship and the strength of love," wrote critic Georgi Hubov, "Khachaturyan proclaimed the indivisibility of happiness and the national good."

Khachaturyan once said during rehearsals of *Gayane* that he considered rhythm the main element in his music. This may be a slight exaggeration, though it is true that rhythm plays an important part in his work. Could that be the explanation for the great popularity of the Saber Dance, which has for many come to symbolize Khachaturyan's music? Popularity polls have shown that the Saber Dance was for several years the most frequently played piece in the world. The composer was not as pleased as might be expected, for he always said there were other melodies in the ballet equally deserving of attention: "I would prefer other works of mine to be as popular as the Saber Dance.... I remember speaking about this with Sibelius in Finland and Arthur Bliss in London; we agreed that pieces often become popular of their own accord, as it were. People remember the Saber Dance when Khachaturyan is mentioned. This is pleasing but also annoying."

Nina Anisimova was not exaggerating when she said, "The premiere was wonderful." The entire group under her coauthored the ballet.

Many critics noted her talent as a ballet master. In the 1930s, when she danced Theresa in Boris Asafiev's ballet *The Flame of Paris,* her dancing was likened to a passionate appeal; it was also said that the entire pattern of the role she created was frenzied tempo itself. Now her talents were able to find further expression in Aram Khachaturyan's music.

The greatest success naturally fell to the performers. Natalia Dudinskaya created a wonderful Gayane, in whom courage and femininity, determination and charm, were well balanced. Gayane was later danced by Alla Shelest, who, in the words of Dmitri Kabalevsky, "keeps the audience on the edge of their seats. Her mimicry and gestures are natural and wonderfully expressive."

Excellent performances in the first production were also given by Tatyana Vecheslova as Noune, Konstantin Sergeyev as Armen, Boris Shavrov as Giko, and Nina Anisimova as Aisha.

The experienced conductor, Pavel Feldt, surpassed himself in this production "by the inspired passion which he sometimes lacked in other productions," in Kabalevsky's opinion.

Nathan Altman's sets contributed greatly to the success of the ballet. Altman had illustrated books and also had made a name for himself in monumental art. Although some say that opera and ballet were not his forte, *Gayane* was nonetheless one of his best stage creations.

There was also criticism of the new ballet. The roles of Giko,

Kazakov, and Karen were too sketchy it was said, the book somewhat prosaic and too loose, and the contrast between Gayane's dances and the more static movements of the rest of the cast too sharp. However, the ballet won high praise from the Composers Union and such outstanding composers as Prokofiev and Shostakovich; both wished to see the ballet staged in Moscow as soon as possible. Prokofiev, however, was not completely satisfied with Khachaturyan's music. He was very exacting of his colleagues and invariably spoke his mind. He had some critical remarks to make about Shostakovich's Eighth Symphony at a plenum of the Composers Union. Although he was quite sincere, some believe he was too categorical. His remarks about *Gayane* were in a similar vein:

> This summer [1943], I was in Molotov and had the opportunity to attend many performances of *Gayane* by the Kirov Theater. It is an interesting and decorative ballet. It should be shown in Moscow. However, I would like to make a remark, not by way of advice to Khachaturyan, but I would like it to concern other composers using national material. This concerns Khachaturyan's methods of developing Armenian material. Once, while walking along the embankment in Baku, I saw an old beggar playing on a pipe. His music strangely resembled "Sheherezade."
>
> I believe that when such a vivid means of elaborating Iranian or related Armenian material exists, the composer, if he really wishes to create a truly worthwhile composition, must first decide how to handle this material; because if he does so in the manner of "Sheherezade," it will still sound like a copy of Rimsky-Korsakov or Borodin no matter how hard he tries.
>
> I think that Armenian material can be handled in many ways; Khachaturyan's chief mistake was that he did not give the question enough careful consideration, did not settle on his own point of view and therefore found himself influenced by Borodin and Rimsky-Korsakov to a certain extent.

This criticism does not reflect Prokofiev's views on Khachaturyan's music in general. Prokofiev and Khachaturyan met for the first time in 1933, when Prokofiev was already famous and Khachaturyan just a student.

Nikolai Myaskovsky often spoke to us students about Prokofiev, referring to his compositions and demonstrating certain of his methods in composing. He never went into raptures, but behind the restraint of this wonderful musician could be sensed a sincere admiration for the genius of a master, a trailblazer in music. So you can imagine our excitement when Myaskovsky told us Prokofiev would be coming to the Conservatory to see what we students were doing.

Khachaturyan had closely followed Prokofiev's career long before 1933. He had attended all of his concerts, even when Prokofiev was just visiting the capital before returning to settle down in Moscow for good.

His vivid works, his splendid, bold innovations, held a special attraction for us young composers. Prokofiev's music was constantly in our hearts, affecting our musical consciousness. Sometimes we became aware of his influence on us only much later, and most unexpectedly. I, personally, was greatly impressed by Prokofiev's *Symphonie Classique* and *Visions Fugitives,* his piano concertos, the *Old Wives' Tales,* his *Scythian Suite,* his First Violin Concerto played in Moscow by Josef Szigeti, and his unparalleled piano playing.

Khachaturyan at that time was already intrigued by the fact that the complex novelty of Prokofiev's music was so easy to understand. He thought the explanation lay in the composer's close bonds with Russian classical music and in the inexhaustible store of good spirits found in all his works. We can easily see the parallel here between the music of Prokofiev and Khachaturyan, who said that although Prokofiev was no teacher, he did to a large extent influence his outlook and work. "The lessons of Prokofiev's work had a great effect on me. His music excited the imagination; it was fascinating in its originality, strength, bold fantasy, and inventiveness.*

*Shostakovich expressed similar thoughts when he said that although Prokofiev does not teach and cannot be said to be a teacher and educator of our younger generation, he nevertheless exercises a great influence on many composers.

In April 1933 Prokofiev was expected in the director's office of the Moscow Conservatory, an event recalled by Khachaturyan:

> On the day Prokofiev was to attend a lesson, Nikolai Myaskovsky was excited and kept looking at his watch impatiently. He was worried both for us and for Prokofiev. Exactly on the dot, Prokofiev's tall figure entered the director's office. He walked quickly, continuing a lively discussion with Myaskovsky and taking little notice of us, who were staring at him with burning curiosity and barely restrained excitement.
>
> He immediately started listening to our work. . . . My trio for clarinet, violin, and piano was played. It is difficult for me to recall today just what he said then, but I do remember that all his remarks were friendly, concrete, and concise. He approved of my Trio and even asked for the parts to send to France. You can imagine what an effect this meeting had on me.

Prokofiev first visited Armenia in the spring of 1933. He gave a concert in the capital, Erevan, visited Echmiadzin and beautiful Lake Sevan. He met with the young Khachaturyan and listened again to his Trio, which so spontaneously and colorfully expresses the very spirit of Armenia. Prokofiev wrote to Myaskovsky from Paris that same summer, saying that a concert of Soviet music might be held in Paris, and would like "to have the score and parts of Khachaturyan's Trio and the *Oriental Suite* by Schwartz, two sets of each, because there may be a demand for them." The Trio was later published in France.

When Prokofiev returned to Moscow in the autumn of that same year he started coaching sessions for student composers. Khachaturyan also attended these master classes at the National Hotel:

> I never did feel that Prokofiev could teach. As a great artist he could, of course, tell us what was good and what was bad, but I could see no pedagogical inclinations in him, no ability to place a young composer on the right path.
>
> All his remarks were the remarks of a professional composer. He never examined a composition in all its parts as a teacher

usually does (form, tonal plan, polyphony, arrangement, etc.). He would take the theme, its measure, the harmony, and polyphonic methods and say, "This is good," or "And what is this supposed to mean?," striking a chord and turning to the student. He was very exact about the time he spent with each student; this precision, this punctuality, could be seen in everything he did.

But his own composing plans engulfed him and the master classes soon ended. Khachaturyan continued to see Prokofiev, but on another basis.

After Prokofiev finally settled in the Soviet Union he often attended musical evenings in the home of his friend Vladimir Derzhanovsky, whose house was open to all, both the famous and those still to attain fame. The more daring played their new works. Once I mentioned to Prokofiev that I had started work on a piano concerto and played a few fragments for him. Prokofiev listened very attentively, even a bit suspiciously, I thought; after all, as an outstanding pianist, piano music was particularly dear to him. My attempts to write a piano concerto might have seemed quite audacious to him. As a matter of fact, it really was, for I was no pianist.

"It is no simple matter to compose a concerto," he told me. "You must always have a new idea. I suggest you jot down new musical thoughts without waiting for the whole idea to mature. Write passages, and interesting pieces in any order you wish, then use these bricks to build the whole."

Whenever we met, Prokofiev would ask about my concerto and listen carefully, making subtle remarks which gave me much food for thought.

He commented rather sarcastically on the first draft of the second movement: "Here," he said, "your pianist will have nothing better to do than catch flies." He was referring to my simple and easy exposition of the solo part.

Much later, in commenting on Khachaturyan's Piano Concerto, Prokofiev said that it lacked symphonic scope, something he found later in the *Symphony with Bells*.

Khachaturyan's association with Prokofiev continued for over twenty years, and although he could never really reconcile himself to Prokofiev's sharp judgments, his love for his music and respect for the man never diminished, Khachaturyan was particularly impressed by Prokofiev's steady progress in his art while maintaining his own inimitable style in the most diverse works. Khachaturyan invariably mentioned Prokofiev when he urged young composers to be skilled in all genres—from songs and marches to operas and symphonies; all of them, he said, should be treated with equal respect and seriousness. He often quoted Prokofiev on the composer's responsibility and the importance of making art accessible to all.

Khachaturyan attended all of Prokofiev's concerts and premieres and even wrote about them for the press. Among the works Prokofiev wrote after settling permanently in the Soviet Union, Khachaturyan took special note of such "mighty patriotic works," as he called them, as the cantata *Alexander Nevsky,* the opera *War and Peace,* the oratorio *On Guard of Peace,* and the Fifth, Sixth, and Seventh symphonies. After the Bolshoi Theater's one hundredth performance of Prokofiev's *Cinderella,* Khachaturyan wrote to him:

> My dear Sergei Sergeyevich. Allow me to congratulate you on this one hundredth performance and say that you are an amazing composer. The music of *Cinderella* is wonderful. So many brilliant, talented pages. I cannot find words to express the pleasure I experienced listening to *Cinderella,* watching the wonderful Ulanova and seeing the sets by Williams. The Adagio from the second act; the search for Cinderella; the clock . . . and so much more—all really splendid. And the waltzes. I would like to say much more but it is difficult to put it all down on paper.

Khachaturyan was just as ecstatic over the ballet *The Stone Flower,* which Prokofiev composed late in life.

Prokofiev kept track of Khachaturyan's progress just as closely. Though he sharply criticized the development of the Armenian theme in *Gayane,* he always considered Khachaturyan one of the Soviet Union's most talented composers. In December 1940 he spoke of the violin concertos by Shebalin and Khachaturyan as "excellent and very different in style." He welcomed Khachaturyan's work in the ballet, which he himself was very fond of. Writing to congratulate Khachaturyan on the award of a State Prize in 1943, Prokofiev said he remembered *Gayane* from the prewar production of *Happiness* and would very much like to see what had been changed or added to the score. Prokofiev finally attended a performance of *Gayane* in the summer of 1943.

In the summers of 1944 and 1945 Khachaturyan, Prokofiev, and several other composers—Gliere, Shostakovich, Kabalevsky, Shaporin, Muradeli, and Myaskovsky—lived in the Union's country house near the town of Ivanovo. Prokofiev followed a strict schedule of work and strolled in the woods in all kinds of weather. Khachaturyan recalled that "we often joined him on these walks, on which we were able to savor his lively wit, his charm, and his love of nature."

This was a favorite spot with the composers, for it was a beautiful part of the country, with its rolling fields and little stream, the woods in the distance, and the comfortable cottages. "It was easy to work there," Kabalevsky noted,

> and we had ample time to walk in the woods, gather mushrooms, play volleyball and charades, and improvise skits. In those days volleyball was not simply fun for us but a real contest between teams with good and bad players. That's why a fifteen-year-old local boy, whom we nicknamed "the mortar" for his excellent playing, was much more highly prized as a sportsman than heavy, slow-moving Yuri Shaporin or near-sighted, awkward Prokofiev. . . .

It was here that Shostakovich wrote his Eighth and Ninth symphonies, Myaskovsky his Twenty-fifth, and his Violin Concerto, and Shaporin his oratorio *On Kulikovo Battlefield*. Gliere wrote his Fourth String Quartet there, Kabalevsky his Second, Prokofiev his Fifth and Sixth symphonies and his Eighth Piano Sonata, and Khachaturyan his Second Symphony and the Cello Concerto.

On the eve of the thirtieth anniversary of the October Revolution Aram Khachaturyan and Sergei Prokofiev were awarded the title People's Artist of the Russian Federation. "I am happy," Aram Ilych wrote on this occasion,

> to be living in a country that loves and appreciates Prokofiev, a country where Sergei Prokofiev lives and works. I find it difficult to express all my thoughts and feelings, but I do want to say that every new composition of yours . . . is a festive occasion for us musicians. I have learned and continue to learn from your works. They excite the imagination, break down all standards and induce the artist to dare, that is, they make him compose, make him think.

Prokofiev's death in 1953 was a terrible blow to Khachaturyan; it was an irreparable loss for Soviet music and the musical culture of the twentieth century. A quarter of a century later, on March 5, 1978, Khachaturyan, himself very ill by then, agreed to attend a memorial meeting for Sergei Prokofiev in the old Composers Club in Moscow. It was to be his last public appearance.

"There are so many memories connected with this club," said Aram Ilych.

> Here Prokofiev and I sat on the executive of the Composers Union, here we discussed the problems of Soviet music. It was here that all his colleagues listened to his new compositions, and it was from here that we accompanied him in March 1953 to his final resting place.
>
> Prokofiev lived abroad for fifteen years and like all artists could not escape the influence of an alien environment on his work, habits, and character. What a great citizen he must have been to break away from the West in 1943, where, mind you, he certainly was not poor, where his music was often played, and, at the height of his genius, to return to his native land, knowing that at that time not everyone approved of the direction he was working in. How strong must have been the blood ties with his country and its culture for him to be able to adapt so rapidly and so brilliantly to the new musical milieu, to the standards of Soviet musical life.

We know of many talented composers whose music is often played during their lifetime but remains within the boundaries of their time and nation. Prokofiev, who during a period of rampant cosmopolitanism emerged as a truly Russian composer, in whose works Russian tonalities dominated, became a truly international artist. And we are happy to say now that Prokofiev's music is played more and more often with every passing year and is steadily winning people's hearts the world over.

Could Khachaturyan have been thinking of his own work, of the future of his own music? Could he have been thinking that his own compositions, based on such vivid Armenian tonalities, could become, as they did become during his lifetime, truly international?

Despite its minor shortcomings, *Gayane* was in great demand among the country's musical theaters; overcoming these shortcomings became something of a challenge for choreographers and dancers. Regrettably, they were at times a bit too zealous in reshuffling the book and the score. According to one scholar, this was part of a thirty-year history "of the search for a script worthy of the music, whose popularity was growing with the years."

A certain measure of success was achieved by the Sverdlovsk (1944), Leningrad (1945), and Erevan (1947) productions of *Gayane,* all produced by Nina Anisimova. Except for minor changes, all these productions kept very close to the Kirov Theater's original staging in Perm.

The Spendiarov Theater's production in Erevan became a national art festival for Armenia. Erevan newspapers and magazines praised Nina Anisimova's fine work and her understanding of Armenian national dances. "I am happy that my stay in Erevan enabled me to learn more about Armenian folk dancing," she wrote. "I gained a better understanding of its style and character; this enabled me to introduce certain modifications in the Leningrad production."

In 1952 the Kirov Theater presented a new production of *Gayane* in Leningrad; in 1957 there was the long-awaited production in the Bolshoi Theater, and in 1972 by the Stanislavsky-

Nemirovich-Danchenko Theater in Moscow. Each of these productions was a headache for Khachaturyan. There were, of course, other productions in this country and abroad which left him more or less satisfied. However, we can understand this now world-renowned composer, the composer of *Gayane* and *Spartacus,* when he complained in a letter in 1975: "My works are being produced in five countries, and everywhere the score and the book are muddled, with distortions and arbitrariness everywhere."

But it should be admitted that the composer was in part responsible for this state of affairs. He remained true to his principles at first. In 1950 he wrote to Konstantin Derzhavin, who was preparing the new book for the Kirov Theater:

> As soon as a variation of a scene or a dramatic situation appears it should be seen immediately to determine whether or not it suits the music, and what it would be like if staged to the existing music. That should be our method. The music should guide and control the imagination of the creators, it should be the point of departure. . . .

Strange as it may seem, the composer had to convince professionals of these seemingly obvious truths. In that same letter to Derzhavin he declared, "I consider it my duty to repeat that I speak at such length and am afraid of the music being reshuffled only because if the numbers are shifted around the ballet will perish as an integral dramatic composition."

Stranger still is the fact that in time Khachaturyan moderated these principles, so natural to a musician. If earlier he had written "just to please the ballet, damn it," on the margin of the score of the Saber Dance—a wonderful orchestral composition but a questionable "compromise" for the composer—he now agreed to far greater compromises "just for the ballet" and also to satisfy his overwhelming desire to see it on the stage. He seemed to be caught between frustration, a desire to protest, to turn away from everything, and the all-conquering urge to see his ballet on the stage once again.

Of course, the 1940 production of *Gayane* by the Kirov Theater was already outdated and the very traditional choreography particularly obvious. The absurdities in the book were also no longer acceptable. However, it does not seem acceptable to change the story line and the dramatic functions of the main roles in new versions of *Gayane*, as was done, in order to turn the heroine, Gayane, into a victim, or to portray the happy-go-lucky Giko as a hero. Neither was there any justification for deleting Gayane's wonderful lullabye or for making the music of the fire scene express the "heroism" of Giko, who captures the saboteur, rather than expressing the drama of Gayane's feelings. In other words, everything was muddled and, strangest of all, with the composer's approval however reluctant.

In the 1957 Bolshoi Theater production almost a third of the music was changed; Boris Pletnyov's new book required even more changes in the score than Derzhavin's had. Oppressed at the same time by the Bolshoi Theater's excessively prolonged rehearsals of *Spartacus*, Khachaturyan wrote to Kara Karayev: "I want *Gayane* to compensate me. If I do not facilitate the production of *Gayane* now, I will never have such an opportunity again. A completely new book has been written for *Gayane*. I resisted at first, but agreed in the end. I don't know what the outcome will be. It's terribly unpleasant and messy work."

Happily, Khachaturyan's new score was well symphonized, though the style of the music, apparently influenced by this production, was changed, but not for the better. Earlier versions of the ballet opened with the calm and imperturbable strains of "Pshati Tzar"; in the new reading the production opened and closed with a flashy musical fresco—a colorful and perhaps overarranged version of his own "Song of Erevan." Although one of his best songs, it certainly did not suit the fine musical fabric of *Gayane*.

The production by the ballet master, Vasili Vainonen, whom Khachaturyan knew from his work on *The Widow of Valencia* and *The Masquerade*, was colorful and festive but somewhat heavy and extravagant. The sets were by the famed scenic designer Vadim Ryndin. The dance and pantomime blended naturally, and the ensemble scenes were well planned. The Bolshoi orchestra under Yuri Feier played brilliantly, and Raisa Struchkova's interpretation of Gayane was excellent. On the whole, however, the production was not able to overcome the absurdities and gaps in the plot. Heated discussions flared up around the new production; the more sober critics urged that the original version should not be abandoned.

But what about Khachaturyan himself? Apparently his compromises were taking their revenge. A production of such dramatic force should never have been subjected to endlessly changing concepts, book writers, and producers. "Now that so many years have passed and *Gayane* is but a memory," wrote Nina Anisimova in the 1970s, "I believe it would have been best to return to the original version of the plot." Apparently she also had in mind the original score. There is a hint of this in the composer's preface to the score of *Gayane* published by the Bolshoi Theater. In a brief history of the ballet and its different versions, Khachaturyan wrote,

> As the composer I am not certain which of the plots is better or more correct. I believe time will decide that. For this reason I decided to publish the ballet with Pletnyov's book, and the piano score in accordance with it. This publication, together with the existing first edition, will give theaters and ballet masters a choice for future productions.

Interest in the ballet has not waned, either here or abroad. It has been produced in Kiev and Ulan-Bator, Voronezh and Tallin, Leipzig and Sofia, Budapest and Berlin. Interpretations and productions differed, depending on the theaters. Some added music from other works of Khachaturyan, whereas the Stanislavsky-Nemirovich-Danchenko Theater in Moscow preferred to make a one-act choreographic suite of the ballet.

Two other productions of *Gayane* deserve mention—one in Erevan by the Armenian choreographer Vilen Galstyan, and the other in Leningrad by the ballet master Boris Eifman.

"What is most important in Galstyan's new production of *Gayane*," wrote a critic, "is the choreographic image of the people as a whole and of every role in the ballet." The success of the 1974 Spendiarov Theater production in Erevan and its 1976 tour of Moscow was in large measure due to the excellent dancing of the main roles, the work the conductor, Yakov Voskanyan, did with Khachaturyan on the score, and the exceptionally colorful sets and costumes by Minas Avetisyan, which correspond to the music, though more restrained and balanced. Khachaturyan wrote,

> Minas Avetisyan's work on *Gayane* astounded me. I met him on that production. I think the theatrical designs of this original artist rank among his finest creative achievements. True, I did have a complaint. Though his costumes for the main roles were colorful and interesting, I think they were a bit cumbersome, making dancing difficult. During rehearsals bit by bit we had to undress the dancers. As for style and color, I believe Minas is a follower of Saryan, although his language is entirely his own.

Boris Eifman's concept of *Gayane* can be divided into three stages. The first was in 1972, at the Maly Opera Theater in Leningrad. Then a young graduate of the ballet class of Leningrad Conservatory, he considered Derzhavin's and Pletnyov's books outdated and wrote his own. In later years he was to say: "The book was not too perfect because it had not sufficiently shaken off the influence of earlier plot developments."

Accustomed to the fact that every choreographer wanted to discover "the true Khachaturyan," the composer was rather skeptical of Eifman's work; he was not quite satisfied with his book either. During the Leningrad rehearsals, however, he realized that his score was the fabric around which everything revolved, and, sitting in the empty theater, was happy to discover the links between the music and the dance, up to and including counterpoint and polyphonic lines. He changed his views on Eifman. "Still, something bothered Khachaturyan," Eifman recalled. "I think it was the same thing that bothered me—the production was not wholly independent."

In his 1975 production of the ballet in Poland, Eifman no longer had the plot tied down to any definite locality, making it more general and symbolic—the problem of power, the fight for power in an ancient Oriental tribe between two forces representing the old and the new, and the idea that an endless struggle was capable of destroying simple human happiness.

Khachaturyan's music withstood the test of even the choreographic interpretations based on the dance language of the 1970s.

"I have always understood Khachaturyan's music," said Boris Eifman.

> I understood its emotional tensions and national spirit. I imagine Armenia not only as a riot of colors, and Khachaturyan not only as a feast of music. I always look upon Armenians as a people with a tragic history, expressed in the manners and behavior of all Armenians. When an Armenian laughs, his eyes retain a tinge of grief. I hear all this in Khachaturyan's music, especially in *Gayane*. That is why I never doubted that from the artistic viewpoint the risk I was taking in turning to this celebrated score was permissible.

Khachaturyan actively helped prepare the production of *Gayane* in Lodz, Poland. It was a great success, and the theater toured many cities in Poland and abroad.

On December 27, 1976, the Polish version of the ballet was presented by the Latvian Opera and Ballet Theater in Riga, and in 1980 this theater gave two performances on the stage of the Bolshoi Theater in Moscow. It was an interesting though not always smooth interpretation. Its chief merit consisted of a very fine musical understanding of the score and a good balance between music and dancing. The Saber Dance, earlier no more than a divertissement, now became a key dramatic episode, a duel between Giko and Armen for the hand of Gayane. The musical counterpoint in the middle corresponds to the dance counterpoint—Gayane attempts to stop the duel. The Riga production was filmed for showing in the United States.

Not all the scenic problems were solved in the Galstyan and Eifman productions, but they did show that *Gayane* had a long life ahead of it. For Khachaturyan they compensated in some measure for his many years of suffering which, late in life, led him to speak of "the tragic history of my ballet."

# The Second Symphony

*My conscience, so persistent, beats at my heart. Like a tocsin, it warns of approaching doom. Arise, ye all, for battle prepare.*

OVANES SHIRAZ

In the summer of 1942 the Soviet people's war against fascism was a year old. Far from the front, deep in the Urals, Khachaturyan was completing *Gayane* and already planning ahead, despite the wartime hardships and his troublesome ulcers. "I am so pregnant with music that I could give birth to twins, triplets, even more," we read in one of his letters.

> I must write so much this year. I will complete my symphony by December, not earlier. Let it be late but let it be good. I am banking on it. It should cause a stir among honest people. But even if it goes unnoticed, it will not disappear and in some way will remain a monument of our times. An artist must have faith; this faith is a guarantee that he is sincere.

In other letters from Pern, he wrote,

> I am in such a creative mood here, and my nerves are so calm that after completing the ballet I would gladly continue working on the symphony, especially here. But I shall have to return to Moscow.

> I will complete the first movement of the symphony in ten days and want to send it off to the radio, but I'm not sure I'll make it or if there will be someone to send it off with.

The first letter was dated August 1942, the second, September, and the third, October. Much of what he planned for the symphony was ready, but the greater part of the work still remained to be done. Soon after the premiere of *Gayane* in January 1943, Khachaturyan returned to Moscow with his family and was immediately immersed in the work of the Composers Union. He was also Vice Chairman of the musical sector of the All-Union Society for Cultural Relations with Foreign Countries. (Myaskovsky was Chairman; the other Vice Chairmen were Prokofiev and Shostakovich).

It was not till the summer of 1943 that he again found time to work on his Second Symphony. He worked quickly and easily in one of the Union's retreats not far from Moscow. "I wanted my symphony to embody everything that the people think and feel today: The Second Symphony is a requiem of wrath, a requiem of protest against war and violence."

He completed the first movement by July 31, 1943. It took him four days to write the Andante, six for the Scherzo, and seven for the Finale. In conversations he mentioned that he had been inspired by the Red Army victory at the Battle of the Kursk Bulge. He completed the symphony on September 7, and by the end of November the score was ready.

Boris Haikin recalls,

I had been evacuated with the Maly Opera Theater when a summons suddenly came for me to come to Moscow in 1943. At that time it was possible to get into the capital only if summoned by the government. I was being called by Mikhail Khrapchenko, the Chairman of the Committee on the Arts. Khachaturyan's Second Symphony had been nominated for the State Prize and I was asked to conduct the symphony at a concert, and also at a special performance for the Committee on State Prizes. I was naturally very interested and spent a good deal of time with Aram Ilych discussing the score.

The symphony had its premiere in Moscow on December 30, 1943, with Boris Haikin conducting the State Symphony Orchestra. Though the premiere was a success, Khachaturyan made some changes in the score, placing the Andante with its funeral march before the Finale, as in Chopin's B-flat Minor Piano Sonata, and gave the brass section more leeway in the Finale. The symphony was performed on March 6, 1944, by the same orchestra, conducted by Alexander Gauk. Commenting on this composition, Khachaturyan once said, "If the First Symphony, written ten years ago, concluded the early stage of my work, the new symphony sums up, as it were, the period which began with the Piano Concerto."

During the traditional music festival "Moscow Stars" in 1979, one of the concerts was dedicated to Aram Khachaturyan, who had passed away the year before. This was the first time his Second Symphony was performed in his absence. The State Symphony Orchestra was conducted by Alexander Lazarev, who was about the same age as the symphony. Tikhon Khrennikov spoke in the Grand Hall of the Conservatory about the undying significance of Khachaturyan's work.

From the opening bars the music bursts forth like molten lava. The sounds of the tocsin draw the audience into the suffering it expresses. But the action has not yet begun. The music is foreboding, as though told by a narrator before the action begins. The short prologue is vivid, containing not only the musical ingredients of the subsequent development but the emotional content as well.

Suddenly the curtain seems to part and the sounds of the bass clarinet introduce the principal subject of the first movement, played by the violas unhurriedly, somberly, concealing a deeply rooted pain. The nonchalant pizzicato of the accompanying cellos and basses seems to be marking time. Then we hear the harp and the theme is repeated, this time by the violins. It seems to be more radiant, but this is not so; the violas and clarinets follow, relentlessly weaving triplets around the theme. There it is, the undercurrent of alarm, the precursor of tragedy, a hint of which is heard in the middle episode of the slow movement of Khachaturyan's Violin Concerto.

The dynamic flow of the music leads into the somewhat untamed dance episode, followed by the second subject, based on the theme of recollections heard in the prologue. It is brief, appearing like a ghost of the past, and is quickly swept away.

Tension increases; the themes are woven together, revealing their harmonic relationship. Then comes the dynamic culmination promised in the prologue, bringing to mind the terrible scenes of the fascist invasion. The dark overtones of the dance are laid bare in the original "danse macabre," leading into the second theme—the emotional culmination. As though to make up for its brevity, it expands in the exposition to the dimensions of the independent Largamente. The music is like a prayer—the victory of evil is bound up with virtue trampled. It flutters like a caged bird unable to escape. From the very beginning the theme seems penetrated by the first theme rising in counterpoint from the basses. The sounds of the bass clarinet are heard, an instrument the composer associates with evil in the Violin Concerto, *Gayane,* the prologue to the Second Symphony, and in his future *Spartacus.* The music alarms and excites. Its tragic tones color the reprise which soon appears.

The first theme, brought out again by the violins and violas, is now more dramatic, but the newly developed episode does not attain the sharpness of previous culminations—the tension is now receding. Just before the coda of the first movement, the curtain seems to fall and we hear sounds similar to the prologue, summing up what has been said, signaling that the struggle is not yet over; the muted peeling of the tocsin is heard. . . .

In the second movement, the Scherzo, we are immersed in the charming and temperamental atmosphere of the dance, so astonishing in its rhythmic pattern and flexibility. The touching terzetto of the English horn, violas, and cellos in the middle episode is again a prayer for happiness. For Khachaturyan this Scherzo is not only a brilliant orchestral piece, it is also a strong bond with the central idea of the symphony. The very indefatigability of the dance seems to have been anticipated by the "danse macabre" of the first movement, and the theme of the Scherzo is close to the theme of recollections—an integral part of the cycle. As for the orchestra, it is truly Khachaturyan's all the way—magnificent, colorful, full-bodied.

Khachaturyan had the following to say about the third movement, the Andante:

In my third movement I turned to the genre of the requiem. This is a requiem of wrath, of protest against war and violence. I made use of an Armenian folk theme my mother used to sing to me, the theme of a lament.

She usually sang quiet, very sad melodies. I recall how she would cry when singing "Vorskan Akhper"—song of the hunter. Not so long ago I learned that this folk song was composed to words by the great Armenian poet, Avetik Isaakyan, something most people had no idea of. So it is that a poet returns to the people the fruit of an art created by the people.

> Oh, hunter, alone in the hills.
> Have you seen my son,
> My boy, my little deer?
> Yes, I saw him early,
> Heading for a wedding feast.
> On his heart a red poppy I saw.
> Tell me, hunter, who is she
> Who took my son away,
> Where does he lie wed with her?
> Your son lies on a stone,
> Struck down.
> To a bullet he is wed,
> Not with a doe he lies.
> The swallows fly high,
> The clouds like a mist.
> Quietly the grass whispers
> Over your boy so dear.

Khachaturyan uses the poem in the third movement to symbolize the people's suffering, the mother figure weeping for her son killed in battle. "I did not want the audience to seek any concrete illustrations of the scenes of inhuman suffering the fascist monsters inflicted on the Soviet people. But I must admit that while composing the Andante I kept seeing the tragic scenes of Nazi brutalities."

Armenians usually mark sad and festive events alike by processions, their approach announced by the sound of a bass drum and the *zurna*. So it is in the Andante. The main theme is heard after three bars played by the woodwinds, which mark the regular rhythm of the mourning procession, creating a sound faintly reminiscent of the inimitable, plaintive nasal twang of the *zurna*. Khachaturyan did not like symphony orchestras to use real folk instruments, though the young Armenian composer, Avet Terteryan, did so later with good effect.

In the third movement, the effect of renunciation and deep mourning of the lament is extremely moving, even frightening, possibly because the intricate, meandering Armenian melody runs parallel to the seemingly indifferent and incessant rhythm of the procession. The music casts a spell, it hypnotizes, and the unexpected happens: The emotions are sharpened, and the second hearing of the theme is now not just music sounding very close, but music that has become subjective, personal feeling. The first impression is of Eastern tonalities, the second brings the music closer to the classical passacaglia.

Finally the entire orchestra is involved in the lament; the procession is all around us, we are drawn into its rhythm and can resist neither the rhythm nor the people's mood. Suddenly the second theme of the Andante appears, and we recognize the famous cadenza from Thomas Celano's "Dies Irae." Like the lament, it is repeated and interspersed with episodes that heighten the dominating mood. There is an urge to interpret these episodes as timid attempts by the people in the procession to shed the anesthesia of grief and regain their identity. The recurrence of the "Dies Irae" theme accompanied by the counterpoint of the first theme, the lament, subtly alters our perception of the idea of the music. For Khachaturyan it represents the theme of inevitable retribution, of determination and opposition.

As the procession recedes we again hear the first theme, the Andante, but no longer is there any grief, for it has been neutralized by the call for vengeance. It has come full cycle from an objective to a personal interpretation of the tragedy which sears the heart, and back to an objective interpretation, but on a higher level.

The Finale is announced by the brass section, followed by a short introduction. Brilliant arpeggios by the strings usher in the hymnlike main subject of the Finale, stately and victorious in the majestic sounds of the French horns and trombones, its proud serenity symbolizing the joy of peace. At one point intonations of the second theme of the first movement are clearly heard, which the author used at the beginning of his symphonic narrative to depict tranquil scenes of prewar life. Now the main subject of the Finale is heard, played by all the brass led by the horns and accented by the clashing cymbals. This is Khachaturyan at his best, a master of sweeping orchestral frescoes. However, the impression is conveyed that the second theme of the Finale is not as vivid as the first, and the emotional tension seems to ebb. The situation is remedied by the reprise of the first theme, sounding like a general culmination of the entire symphony. This is not yet victory, for the war continues to take thousands of lives although its outcome is already determined. And here we feel Khachaturyan's sense of the dramatic, for he introduces the main theme of the first movement in counterpoint to the theme of jubilation. The blazing horizon, hazy but menacing, concludes the symphony; again the tocsin is an austere reminder of events, while at the same time proclaiming the imminent triumph of justice.

As the echoes of Khachaturyan's Second Symphony die away, one involuntarily recalls the composer's statement that "the Symphony will remain a monument of our times." How true. It lives on because it was written with the heart's blood and, as Khachaturyan said, "the tocsin in the Second Symphony is a call for vigilance and for struggle against the forces of evil."

An appeal so relevant today. It lives on also because the tocsin is so much a part of Armenian culture. "Khachaturyan's mighty Second Symphony," wrote Dmitri Shostakovich, "has forever been inscribed in the annals of our music. A heroic and tragic epic, it is full of a lofty, humane, and patriotic pathos. This symphony has become one of the great and never-aging monuments of the glorious and severe epoch that was the Great Patriotic War."

The Second Symphony did not diminish the importance of Khachaturyan's earlier works. The war did, however, change a great deal in his art and in the man himself. "Like the tolling of a bell, the terrible tragedy of the war perturbed the artist's picture of peaceful and serene beauty," wrote the critic Georgi Hubov. The scene of the fire in *Gayane* and the Second Symphony showed us an entirely new side of Khachaturyan. The composer lost none of his vitality and optimism, but his music now gained depth, with a much greater impact on the audience. He now took a more serious philosophical view of events, and the Second Symphony showed this more than any of his other compositions. It also showed that his style had matured.

This was the first of his works in which he demonstrated a monolithic and naturally developing symphonic form, an organic blend of Armenian musical traditions with the classical European symphonic style and a brilliant display of polyphony.

"A symphony," wrote the Soviet critic Boris Asafiev, "is a chain of the tempos of life and alternating stages of poetry—drama, buoyancy, contemplation, and the epic of a people's heroic deeds and triumphs. When a composer prepares to write a symphony, he is aware that he is facing reality, reflecting his view of that reality in his music, and, thereby, exposing himself."

For Asafiev the symphony was the highest stage in the hierarchy of musical genres, adding weight to his evaluation of Khachaturyan's *Symphony with Bells*.

How many symphonies have been and still are being written? Many of them are not only well constructed and clever, with a good distribution of technical resources; their beautiful music also attracts. But few are universally accepted as symphonies —undoubtedly the highest form of musical thought—so few that it is possible to single out in the overabundance of symphonic literature those symphonies whose artistic individuality and designated number become a proper name that requires no further explanation.

Khachaturyan's Second Symphony has every right to be called a symphony in that sense.

Criticism after the premiere was mild. Myaskovsky, who thought highly of the symphony, mentioned only that there were certain passages in the Finale which he found too long and that "the material in the last movement seemed somehow denuded." Reply to critics who found that the material in the symphony did not follow the standard lines of development, he said "from the point of view of the genre this is certainly a special type of symphony. . . . I do not know why a symphony must follow a set pattern. The composition seems to flow in large pieces united by a common idea."

The symphony does contain many contrasts at varying levels and within separate parts, contrasts that deserved more criticism. For example, one episode in the second movement does not blend with the general spirit of the music; it is even alien in style. The sensual, spicy harmonies, magnificent orchestration, and sultry temperament are reminiscent of a ballet scene, though it is restrained by Khachaturyan's ostinato harmonic accompaniment and repeated rhythmic patterns.

Sergei Prokofiev called it a "highly talented but uneven symphony"; nevertheless, he agreed with Asafiev and Myaskovsky that it was truly symphonic.

It is an important stage in his work, because his earlier compositions do not show any particular love for symphonism. I have already said in a comment on one of his concertos [the Piano Concerto], that, notwithstanding its excellent material, the absence of symphonism is disappointing. I believe that Khachaturyan intentionally searched for values in other directions. This change of direction was obviously influenced by Shostakovich. One can see that symphonism, or the opportunity to achieve what Shostakovich did through the symphonic manner of composition, had a particularly favorable influence on Khachaturyan in the sense that he turned to the method of symphonic music.

That Prokofiev, who himself greatly influenced Khachaturyan by his compositions, and by his personality as a citizen, musician, and patriot, should speak of Shostakovich's influence on Khachaturyan is quite noteworthy. Khachaturyan greatly respected Shostakovich's work, especially his symphonies, and naturally wished to learn from them. Khachaturyan sent Shostakovich a warm letter on his fiftieth birthday, saying,

> I am writing this letter with trepidation and joy, not only to congratulate you on your birthday, but to express a few thoughts about you.
>
> I am grateful that I have your friendship and am your contemporary. I am grateful to you for raising Soviet music to such unattainable heights by your extraordinary art. We all strive to match you, although it is impossible. You are our leader whether you like it or not. You have a great historical mission.
>
> The history of Russian, Soviet symphonism, as a deeply philosophical category, will hold a special place of honor for you. In this way you will occupy—and already have occupied—a worthy place in the history of music.
>
> Your wonderful art, your great and inimitable talent, the depth of your musical thoughts and highly original thinking, are extraordinary qualities recognized by the whole world.
>
> When I hear your music, I want to compose. Your music excites my artistic imagination, it makes me think, it encompasses tremendous human passions, wisdom, a sea of inimitably organized sounds, iron-clad logic, conflicts . . . all cemented by the force of your dramatic talent.

Aram Khachaturyan and Dmitri Shostakovich were contemporaries. Both lived in the same house in Moscow for many years: Shostakovich—master of time and space in music, a born symphonist with a deep feeling for the dramatic—and Khachaturyan—an artist whose emotional perception of the world and sense of life as a holiday remained his dominant trait to the very end.

Khachaturyan composed his Second Symphony and Shostakovich his Eighth at the Composers Union retreat in Ivanovo at the same time. Khachaturyan recalled those days:

> We all worked diligently and met to exchange ideas only in our free time. Shostakovich once invited Nina Makarova, Grigory

Schneersohn and myself to his little cabin to play us the Eighth Symphony, which he had just completed. I shall never forget the impression it made on us. I believe it will be among the best compositions ever written about the Great Patriotic War. An all-encompassing masterpiece of symphonic drama, a natural joining of heroism and subjective lyricism and a tremendous ethical, spiritual strength are all vividly portrayed in the score. The composer himself said of his symphony that it was "an attempt to express the feelings of the people, to reflect the terrible tragedy of the war." This deeply patriotic concept was entirely successful. The proud, courageous music is an expression of the great truth of life which emerged victorious over death and destruction through all the torments and tragic experiences.

More than any other of his works, Khachaturyan's Second Symphony came closest to the elements in Shostakovich's work just mentioned. That is why, of all the compliments about his Second, Khachaturyan cherished most of all the comparison to the highest attainments of Soviet symphonism invariably associated with the name of Dmitri Shostakovich.

Shostakovich and Khachaturyan first met in Leningrad in 1936, on the eve of the premiere of Khachaturyan's First Symphony. "I well remember what a strong impact Khachaturyan's First Symphony made on me," Shostakovich wrote subsequently.

I don't remember many occasions when the new work of a young composer made such a strong impression on me at first acquaintance. On that unforgettable evening in the hall of the Leningrad Philharmonic . . . I experienced to the full the joy of meeting face to face a wonderful, original, and forceful artist who was destined to occupy one of the most outstanding places in the ranks of our country's composers.

Shostakovich wrote of the First Symphony,

I was impressed by the unusual melodic wealth of that composition, the splendid and vivid instrumentation, the profound content of the musical material and its overall festive and joyous atmosphere. It may be said that the music of the First Symphony is true ecstasy at the beauty and joys of life.

I was very pleased to know the works of a composer who possesses such a lively and daring mind, who is capable of dealing in his own way with the most complex problems of modern symphonism.

Many musicians present at the premiere of the First Symphony felt as I did—joy at the emergence of a very great and talented composer.

Shostakovich spoke warmly about almost all of Khachaturyan's works, but it was only natural that he should be most interested in the composer's growth as a skillful symphonist. Shostakovich was particularly attracted to the Second Symphony, which revealed Khachaturyan's maturity as a symphonic composer and his changed views on life: "The Second Symphony is most likely Khachaturyan's first composition in which the tragic element reaches such heights. However, notwithstanding its tragic essence, it is full of a deep optimism and faith in our just cause and our victory."

In one of his letters to Shostakovich, Khachaturyan wrote:

I often ask myself why it is that I am so constrained in your presence. I am unable to say what I want or to play, although I play my own compositions rather easily. People in love often become tongue-tied and awkward.

I believe that it is due to your great authority, the charm of your noble and wise personality. It neither upsets nor disappoints me. I experienced something like it with Myaskovsky. I am glad that a person exists with whom I am bashful out of respect and admiration. I do not trouble you much, though I often need to communicate with you.

This is truly a case of one great artist being enamored of the work of another great artist. Although Khachaturyan was three years older than Shostakovich, he always looked upon him as his teacher and greatly respected him as a musician and thinker. "Shostakovich would listen to my compositions and often criticize them severely," wrote Khachaturyan. "But he was always right."

Khachaturyan was eager for any opportunity to meet and talk with Shostakovich and listen to any new work of his. Shostakovich played his Fourth Symphony for Aram Ilych in Moscow in 1936. "Nina Makarova and I were not yet living together at that time. She had a small room in the Conservatory dormitory and Shostakovich came there and played his entire symphony on the piano. We were astounded by its tragic spirit and the sincerity of what it conveyed."

Not long before the premiere of Shostakovich's Fourth Symphony, highly biased and erroneous articles appeared in the press with false accusations against the composer. This caused Shostakovich to cancel the premiere. The symphony was not played until a quarter of a century later. Khachaturyan was among the very few musicians who were familiar with the Fourth Symphony in the intervening years. "It is sometimes rumored that there was some sort of 'conflict' between Shostakovich and the public," wrote Khachaturyan in 1956. "This is wrong, I think. People who look for an expression of great ideas and strong feelings in music, who strive to understand the complex and deep feelings expressed in sounds, are profoundly affected by the music of this outstanding Soviet composer."

Summarizing his impressions of Shostakovich's music in an article that regrettably appeared only after the composer's death Khachaturyan wrote, "Only future generations will be able to comprehend the full historical significance of his monumental work and of his great life, which was so deeply affected by trials and tribulations."

Aram Khachaturyan took pride in the fact that he had attended almost every premiere of Shostakovich's works: "I well remember the Moscow premiere of his wonderful opera, *Lady Macbeth of Mtsensk,* staged by Vladimir Nemirovich-Danchenko. I attended one of the first performances of his Fifth Symphony, conducted by Evgeny Mravinsky in Leningrad. It was an unforgettable evening of modern classics."

Khachaturyan understood and cherished all of Shostakovich's fifteen symphonies: "Each contains something new as compared with the previous one. . . . In each is heard the voice of the times, the voice of our turbulent epoch with all its tragic conflicts and great reaching out toward the light."

The Seventh: "We received a telegram from Khrapchenko to submit the Seventh Symphony for the 1941 Stalin Prize at once. Just imagine . . . the Seventh is up for the Stalin Prize! It was my suggestion and it was accepted."

The Ninth: Many expected this to be a monumental continuation of the symphonic trilogy started in the Seventh and continued in the Eighth. "It is a radiant and joyous composition expressing the composer's festive mood at the victorious conclusion of the war by the progressive forces of the world. It is possible—and we really believe it—that the Ninth Symphony is only a sidestep prior to the gigantic leap."

The Tenth: Khachaturyan's forecasts are correct.

> This symphony differs in its great assertion of the value of life, in the significance of its emotional and philosophical content. Its four movements depict a world of bright, emotionally elated images, irresistible in the force of their impact, radiant and tragic, lyrical in their grief, exultant in their joy. Again and again we see Shostakovich's ability to create dramatically contrasting images, his skill at drama, his ability to construct a large form and fill every part of the symphony with movement and maintain tension in the audience, a quality that I as a composer greatly admire.

The Eleventh, or *1905* Symphony:

> How it differs in principle from what we, regretably, still come across—an outwardly formal view of the drama of this genre, when the program is viewed simply as a literary subject, and in the order of musical subjects, to match the alternation of events it contains. The Eleventh Symphony is a brilliant example of Shostakovich's love for and understanding of the folk song. He does not use it thoughtlessly, he uses it creatively. In folk melodies he selects the most expressive thematic material and boldly develops it to fit the idea of the composition, including it in the tense, symphonic flow of developing thoughts. The intonations

themselves become an endless source, the motive force of symphonic development.

The Thirteenth: Created together with the poet Evgeny Evtushenko and based on his poem, *Babi Yar.*

Even in chamber performance* [this work] creates a prodigious, powerful impression. There is not even a shade of exaggeration here, for this is truly a great composition by a great artist. Yes, great, because Dmitri Shostakovich, first among the best of our composers, is, like no one else, endowed with a special, acute, I would even say conceptual feeling of the times. The artist with all his creative ideas is tightly intertwined in Shostakovich with the citizen and patriot.

The Fifteenth:

When listening to the works of Shostakovich I always wonder at the secrets of his individuality as a composer, the might of his technique and his original solutions of creative problems. It started with his marvelous First Symphony, written when he was nineteen years old, and continued right up to his astonishingly unexpected and exciting Fifteenth Symphony.

Khachaturyan was also attracted to Shostakovich as a person: "If I were asked what chief trait of Shostakovich's character particularly endeared him to people," wrote Khachaturyan, "I would say—his kindness. His kindness and readiness to help, his sincere compassion, his sense of commitment and punctuality in business matters."

When Nikolai Myaskovsky died in 1950 and Sergei Prokofiev in 1953, Shostakovich wrote Khachaturyan that Soviet art had suffered a great loss. "Do you understand the enormity of the responsibility that falls upon us now?" he asked.

In an open letter to Dmitri Shostakovich on the eve of his

---

* Khachaturyan heard the Thirteenth prior to its premiere at the composer's apartment performed on the piano with a vocalist.

sixtieth birthday, Khachaturyan replied, "We all realize that the lion's share of the responsibility falls on you, with your sensitive conscience of a Soviet artist and citizen, with your kind heart, your great and incomparable talent. And you are fulfilling that mission with a high feeling of responsibility to your people and your beloved art."

A year after the Moscow premiere Khachaturyan's Second Symphony was performed in Leningrad, conducted by Alexander Gauk. In Armenia the Second was heard at the end of 1945, conducted by Mikhail Tavrizyan, an excellent interpreter of Khachaturyan's works. He also conducted the first performance in Tbilisi, Georgia.

Leonard Bernstein conducted the Second Symphony in New York on April 13, 1945, just one day before its Leningrad performance. Since then it has been featured regularly in the repertoires of the best orchestras in Europe and America.

"I myself," Khachaturyan recalled,

> have conducted the Second Symphony in many countries. The orchestras like it and willingly play it, as it contains something for every group of instruments. Whenever I compose symphonic music I never forget that it should be interesting for every member of the orchestra to play, that their parts should contain something to attract them, to interest them, not only in the musical sense but technically, as well.

The Rumanian conductor George Georgescu, was one of the best interpreters of the Second Symphony. Anatole Vieru, the Rumanian composer who studied under Aram Khachaturyan, wrote in his memoirs, "Georgescu conducted the Second Symphony in Bucharest in 1949; the audience was very impressed. Georgescu liked this symphony very much . . . and late in life it became one of his great achievements. I witnessed the joyous meeting between George Georgescu and Aram Khachaturyan in Moscow in 1952."

The future Catholicos Vazgen first heard Khachaturyan's music at the Bucharest premiere of the Second Symphony.

> I was very highly impressed with the Second Symphony, as were

all the others present in the hall of the Aetheneum. A few months later I was invited to a reception at the Soviet Embassy in Bucharest on the anniversary of the October Revolution. Georgescu was there too, and we were introduced. I told him how delighted I was to have heard the music of Khachaturyan. "Don't you think he belongs among the most outstanding Soviet composers?" I asked. "To tell you the truth," the maestro answered, "he belongs among the greatest of Soviet composers."

In a message to Khachaturyan on his sixtieth birthday, Georgescu wrote, "I believe that the Second Symphony expresses all the feelings that agitate people's hearts. In its sounds are wrath, indignation, and grief rising to despair, but full of energy and lyricism at once intimate and solemn. And this entire range of feelings is replaced by a festive mood announcing the triumph of the joy of life." The conductor seems to have released the Second Symphony from the confines of the period with which it was always associated because of its content as a war symphony; he approached it from purely human positions, just as the ballet master Boris Eifman did in his production of *Gayane*.

Today, too, when we hear the Second Symphony within the context of other Soviet compositions dealing with the war years, including those created in the past fifteen or twenty years, it remains as fresh as ever. A good deal is said today about the merits of what is called the new war prose. Among these are books by Konstantin Simonov, Yuri Bondarev, Grigory Baklanov, Vasili Bykov, Oles Adamovich, Jonas Avijius, Alim Keshokov, and many others. People stress how deeply the authors probed the psychology of the heroes; they stress that the events described are authentic and cite historical facts and documents of those years—letters, diaries, and recollections of participants; they stress the polyphonic picture of the national tragedy as a tragedy of the masses and of the individual. It would be wrong to compare works created during the war with those about the war appearing in the 1960s and 1970s. "No matter how noble our motives, the war remained a human tragedy for us from the very first to the very last day, in times of defeat and in times of victory," wrote the prominent Soviet author, Konstantin Simonov. "If we forget this, we will not be able to write the truth about the war." These words are confirmed by the experience of all of our art, particularly the art that was created during those years and depicted in Alexander Tvardovsky's poem, "I Was Killed at Rzhev," Pavel Antokolsky's poem, "Son," Dmitri Shostakovich's Seventh Symphony, and Aram Khachaturyan's Second Symphony.

Khachaturyan's symphony is not simply Armenian music, just as Tvardovsky's poem, "Vasili Tyorkin," is not just Russian poetry. The theme of the people's lament used by the composer was a concentrated expression of the Armenian people's age-old grief and the tragedy of the whole country plunged into war. And this theme, long before Adamovich wrote his *Tales of Khatyn* or *The Blockade Book* written together with Daniil Granin, marked the beginnings of documentation through music. The grief and tragedy that Khachaturyan melted down into a grim desire for retribution, as symbolized in the symphony by the ancient Catholic hymn, was a sign of the great social optimism so characteristic of all Soviet art. "We tend to paint the front in idyllic colors," said Semyon Lazovsky, one of the executives of the Soviet Information Bureau at the outbreak of the war.

> But this is war . . . and we must show that we are overcoming the difficulties of this war, and are moving forward despite the blood and the deaths. Our country's strength lies not in the fact that we are doing everything easily, but in the fact that, despite the tremendous difficulties and sacrifices, we are moving forward with resolute moral unity. This would really show just what the Soviet Union is and wherein lies its strength.

That is exactly what Aram Khachaturyan did in his Second Symphony. In today's war stories the figure of a woman partisan holding in her arms a child doomed to die is viewed by critics as a sign of acute tragedy, but Khachaturyan already showed us the symbolic figure of a mother weeping for her son killed in battle in his symphony of 1942 and 1943.

However we may try to draw parallels between Khachaturyan's Second Symphony and Soviet works about the war appearing in the last few decades, for us this symphony remains associated with those grim days of the war. It is of undying importance among Khachaturyan's works, in the history of Soviet music, and in the history of twentieth-century music. Together with such works as Shostakovich's Seventh and Eighth symphonies, Prokofiev's Fifth and Sixth, Arthur Honegger's Second and Third symphonies, Benjamin Britten's *War Requiem,* Igor Stravinsky's Symphony in Three Movements, and Béla Bartók's Concerto for Orchestra, Aram Khachaturyan's Second Symphony forms part of the golden fund of twentieth-century antiwar music.

"As I think of my father I reach the conclusion that he was truly a talented person. . . . There was nothing about my mother to distinguish her from the environment in which I grew up. She was a wonderful woman who gave herself up completely to her home, her children and husband."

At 19, come to study in Moscow . . . .

In the family circle. Aram Khachaturyan is in the second row, second from the right.

He visited Tbilisi many times, walking the old streets and finding the houses where at different times he lived with his parents.

"Borisyak, an experienced teacher who studied under the famous Pablo Casals, was well known and highly respected among musicians." Aram Khachaturyan is second from the right, Professor Andrei Borisyak is in the center.

Suren Khachaturov. "He was 14 years older than Aram."

"Well educated, exceptionally smart and perceptive, Mikhail Gnessin contributed a great deal to my artistic development" (Aram Khachaturyan). Professor Mikhail Gnessin is seated in the center, Aram Khachaturyan stands on the left.

Aram Khachaturyan, Alexander Spendiarov, Gevork Budagyan, 1927. "Spendiarov opened the way to the development of national symphonic music in its deepest sense" (Aram Khachaturyan).

In Myaskovsky's class. From left to right: seated, Vissarion Shebalin, Nikolai Myaskovsky, Nikolai Zhilyaev, Heinrich Litinsky; standing, Yuri Yatsevich, Aram Khachaturyan, Samuil Sendrei, Yuri Biryukov.

... he married the composer Nina Makarova, who studied with him in Myaskovsky's class.

Out-of-town retreats were made available to composers where they could concentrate on their work in quiet and pleasant surroundings, an atmosphere rarely available in large cities. Dmitri Shostakovich, Aram Khachaturyan, and Rheinhold Gliere, Ivanovo, 1943.

Aram Khachaturyan, late 1930s. "He resembled a young oak tree in which one could just discern the beginnings of a mighty tree" (Bek-Nazarov).

Aram Khachaturyan, Nina Makarova, and Dmitri Shostakovich with the score of Khachaturyan's Second Symphony. Summer of 1943, Ivanovo. "Khachaturyan's mighty Second Symphony has forever been inscribed in the annals of our music . . ." (Dmitri Shostakovich).

With Sergei Prokofiev and Dmitri Shostakovich, 1945.

Aram Khachaturyan and David Oistrakh. "Many years of great mutual respect and admiration. . . ."

Aram Khachaturyan and Nina Makarova on the eve of *Gayane*'s first performance. ". . . I am impatiently waiting to hear how the orchestra sounds"
(Aram Khachaturyan).

Aram Khachaturyan (in the center) with performers of his instrumental concertos. Left to right: Svyatoslav Knushevitsky, David Oistrakh, Aram Khachaturyan, Alexander Gauk, Lev Oborin, 1946.

The Rumanian conductor George Georgescu was one of the best interpreters of the Second Symphony." With Anatole Vieru and George Georgescu, 1952.

Aram Khachaturyan,
the 1950s.

Session of the USSR Supreme Soviet; as a delegate from Armenia, 1958.

With Ruben Simonov and Nina Makarova at the Moscow Vakhtangov
Theater.

With Arthur Rubinstein, 1964.

Warm meeting. . . .

"My whole life, everything that I have created belongs to the Armenian people . . ."

Lake Sevan

Hotel Armenia
with Ilya Kevorkov . . .

In
Echmiadzin . . .

"What can be more attractive for a composer than to establish contact with the musicians, to lead them and to hear the music played as you hear it in your heart?"

He met many interesting people . . .

. . . with Igor Stravinsky.

. . . with Samuel Barber.

. . . with Herbert von Karajan.

. . . with Arturo
Beneditti Michelangeli.

. . . with Nadia Boulanger and Nina Makarova, Paris, 1974.

Дорогому Большому
Композитору
Араму Хачатуряну
в память о
пребывании в
Брюсселе
6 декабря
1960 г.
Елизавета

. . . with Queen Elizabeth of Belgium.

. . . with Pope John XXIII.

. . . with Catholicos Vazgen.

. . . with Yuri Gagarin.

. . . with Gina Lollobrigida.

With Ernest Hemingway and Nina Makarova in Finca Vijia, San Francisco de Paula, Cuba, 1960.

"It was interesting meeting him and especially discussing music for I knew that he had written much of the music for his films." With Charlie Chaplin and Nina Makarova near Geneva, 1965.

"Khachaturyan's music has never left me indifferent" (Leonid Kogan). Khachaturyan and Kogan before the first performance of concerto Rhapsody for Violin and Orchestra, 1962.

Aram Khachaturyan and Tikhon Khrennikov.

Aram Khachaturyan
in the 1960s.

"I often strolled down the places where Spartacus walked with his comrades." Rome, 1960.

В несгораемому другу Мердаку
моему дорогому другу и коллеге в
первого ознакомления замечатель
сонат ДД видящему
Верю! Люблю! Благодарю
Арам Хачатурян 19 13/IV 67. Москва

"It's difficult to understand the work of an artist without understanding his inner world."

A highly successful tour of the United States in 1967.
In Washington, D. C.

Khachaturyan's apartment in Moscow is a good reflection of the man
himself.

Before Khachaturyan's concert on Lenin Square in Erevan, 1973. Left to right: Director and Chief Conductor of the Armenian capella, Oganes Chekidjan, Aram Khachaturyan, and Edgar Oganesyan.

Aram Khachaturyan and Edward Mirzoyan, 1963. "[Y]ou are a great talent, . . . you must compose."

Khachaturyan always visited Saryan when in Erevan.

"When I painted you the first time your hair was black, now I see you have turned blueblack. I say this as a painter. But if I am lucky to see your hair gray, then I shall paint your third portrait" (Martiros Saryan).

Spartacus. The Kirov Ballet Corp. Leningrad, 1954.

" . . . Autumn colors seem to tune me in to working . . . "

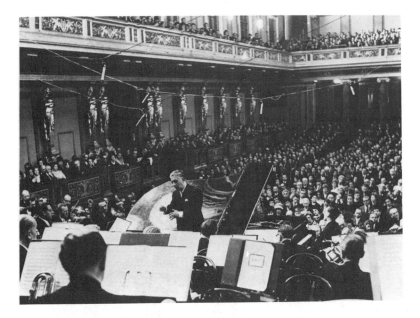

With the Vienna Philharmonic, 1961.

After rehearsal . . . .

Athens Symphony in the Acropolis. Greece, 1965.

# After the War

*I hunger to bring my Armenian heritage out into the mainstream. In that mainstream there are many channels; Russian music is one of the big channels and I want mine to join that big channel called Russian music.*

ARAM KHACHATURYAN

The last work begun by Khachaturyan during the war and completed after the war was his Three Concert Arias for High Voice and Orchestra (1944–1946). After his dramatic Second Symphony, Khachaturyan dreamed of writing an opera. He called the Three Arias

> my first experiment in large vocal forms. . . . In length of music and difficulty of performance I would put the Three Arias on a level with my instrumental concertos. One critic called them a symphony for voice and orchestra, and I quite agree. After all, the orchestra is not insignificant; it does more than merely support the soloist. At any rate, I tried to create a true duet, a concertolike contest between vocalist and orchestra.

Khachaturyan did not quite succeed in creating a "true duet." The vocal score was too obviously part of the orchestration and rarely rose above the orchestra. "The orchestra fired his imagination," wrote Georgi Hubov; "the development of an expressive folk melody, captivating in its simplicity, was suppressed by the elegant and decorative architecture of sounds."

Natalia Spiller, who first performed the Three Arias, noticed this shortcoming, although in her memoirs she speaks not so much of the voice-orchestra balance as of the excessive use

180

of the high tessitura. Nevertheless, she considers the Arias excellent and still not fully appreciated. "During rehearsals for the premiere," she wrote,

> I and my husband Svyatoslav Knushevitsky—who at about the same time was rehearsing for the first performance of Khachaturyan's Cello Concerto —argued at length with Aram Ilych about the vocal score of the arias, the abundance of episodes in the high register so difficult for the performer. We gave as examples several well-known arias from Verdi's *Aida* and *Othello,* to which Khachaturyan would fire back: "And how about the soprano part in Beethoven's Ninth Symphony? Is that any easier?" The changes he made as a result of our arguments were insignificant—five bars of the vocal cadenza before the end of the first aria and a few episodes in the second and third arias, slightly lowering the tessitura. Otherwise the score remained unchanged.

Of the three, the middle aria is the best. However, all three have many beautiful passages, and the few shortcomings certainly do not justify the fact that it is performed so rarely. The famous Polish soprano Eva Bandrowska-Turska was very fond of this work. "I have translated Khachaturyan's Three Concert Arias into Polish. They are difficult for the vocalist but I love to sing them," she wrote in a letter from Warsaw in September 1978. She was the first to record them with the Warsaw Radio Symphony Orchestra conducted by Gregozh Fitelberg. Regrettably, they were never recorded by Zara Dolukhanova, a wonderful Soviet singer who performed them many times in this country and abroad.

Khachaturyan dedicated the Three Concert Arias, telling of a passionate, rapturous, gentle, and tragic love, to his wife, Nina Makarova.

While writing the Arias Khachaturyan was also composing his Cello Concerto, which was to complete his instrumental cycle. He continually put off working on the Concerto, one reason being that he, himself a cellist at one time, was well aware of the specific difficulties of the dynamic relationship between a concert cello and a symphony orchestra. However, work progressed rapidly after he had completed his Three Arias, for he was constantly in close contact with Svyatoslav Knushevitsky. The famous cellist was a professor of the Moscow Conservatory and a member of the piano trio that included David Oistrakh and Lev Oborin, the first performers of Khachaturyan's violin and piano concertos.

"Svyatoslav Knushevitsky will always be my favorite cellist," wrote Khachaturyan, "not only because he gave life to my Cello Concerto and played it many times subsequently. I loved his beautiful, pure and resonant sound, I loved to appear with him when I started conducting. I will always revere the memory of Knushevitsky."

Reinhold Gliere was writing his Cello Concerto at approximately this same time. Khachaturyan wrote him, "I am interested in your concerto . . . because I am writing one myself."

It is an interesting coincidence that Gliere started his Cello Concerto after completing his Concerto for Voice and Orchestra, while Khachaturyan started his after completing the Three Arias. Be this as it may, it is a fact that both concertos brought out most explicitly the cantilena quality of the cello. At any rate, in view of what had been said, Svyatoslav Knushevitsky was without a doubt the best choice as a performer, and Khachaturyan's dedication of the concerto to this splendid master of the instrumental bel canto was more than just a gesture of courtesy to the first performer.

Khachaturyan composed most of the Concerto in Ivanovo, where he always worked very productively; "I did not write a single note in Moscow," he wrote Gliere in 1946. By autumn he had completed the entire score and immediately showed it to Knushevitsky. The latter suggested a few changes, to which Khachaturyan agreed.

The Concerto had its premiere on October 30, 1946, in Moscow, and on November 13 it was played in Leningrad, with Alexander Gauk conducting. Not long after that, all three of Khachaturyan's concertos were performed on the same program in Moscow. The soloists were David Oistrakh, Lev Oborin, and Svyatoslav Knushevitsky, and the orchestra was conducted by Alexander Gauk, who had conducted the premieres of all three works. These celebrated musicians were photographed together on that memorable evening.

The premiere of the Cello Concerto was a success, though not quite as much as the premieres of the piano and violin concertos. Audience perception was probably slightly dampened by having heard too much of the Waltz from *The Masquerade* and the Saber Dance. An even stronger emotional impact was expected of his newest composition, but it turned out to be very different. It was full-bodied and sincere in typical Khachaturyan style, but not quite as striking as the earlier concertos of the trilogy. The score was heavily influenced by the classics, especially Russian classical music. A fine ear and sensitive soul were required to understand it; admiration was not enough.

True, the introduction did not disappoint the audience, for they heard the rhythms and melodic patterns familiar in Khachaturyan's works. However, as the introduction ended the picture changed completely; the melody seemed to expand and the proud diatonic fanfare motive, modest and unassuming, reminded us of Khachaturyan's love of Russian nature.

The greatest difficulty for the composer lay in the elaboration of the Concerto. For although he did say once that new tonal colors needed to be found for the cello and orchestra to blend well, he did not find them.

The soloist faced the dilemma of either bringing the cello score to the forefront, stressing the sounds that are a part of the melodic outline of the Concerto's main movement, or of attempting to hide behind the sounds of the orchestra. That may be the reason why Daniil Shafran, one of the best interpreters of the Concerto, prefers, as he puts it, "the tempo of a squall" for all the toccata episodes of the first movement. "Aram Ilych would usually tell me that it should be played slower in order better to bring out the polyphonic voices," he recalled. "But I honestly could not agree with him and played slower, out of respect for his wishes, only when he was conducting."

The middle movement of the Concerto —Andante sostenuto —is beautifully written, languorous music, full of the passion of restrained emotions that are more impressive than the theme itself, though seemingly not as expressive, built as it is on four or five chromatic intervals. Listening to this music so appropriate for dancing, it is difficult to shake off the illusion of a grand ballet adagio in which the director, following in the composer's wake, strives to prolong the development, attempting in vain to hold back the emotions that threaten to burst forth. "Khachaturyan always is impetuous," wrote the well-known Soviet ballet master, Fedor Lopukhov. "He is always impetuous, whether the music is contemplative or seems to be dreaming. But within that seeming serenity passions are seething, about to burst forth and create havoc." And Daniil Shafran remembers that "Aram Ilych particularly liked my suggestion to bring the static part of the second movement to an explosive, ecstatic pitch."

The Finale is a summary of the concept of the entire composition, for which purpose the main part of the first movement is reintroduced. "The middle episode always affected me," Daniil Shafran recalled. "No matter how many times I played it, I never failed to detect its impact on the audience, and I myself seemed to perceive it as though from the hall." As a whole, however, the Finale does not leave as strong an impression, because it is repetitious.

Khachaturyan's Cello Concerto disclosed yet another side of his talent, which matured in his later instrumental work, particularly his Concerto-Rhapsody for Violin and Orchestra. The Cello Concerto undoubtedly deserves greater popularity than it has attained thus far. This is proved by its success whenever it is performed and the fact that such distinguished cellists as Svyatoslav Knushevitsky, Daniil Shafran, Andre Navarra, Adolph Odnoposov, and many others are so interested in it.

Following on the works of Myaskovsky, Gliere, and Vasilenko, Khachaturyan's Cello Concerto was a sign of renewed interest in this instrument. With the passage of a decade or two, the idea that the cello "will gradually recede into the background of the musical republic, the orchestra, just as its predecessors, the wind instruments, did" will seem hopelessly outdated, even though it was articulated by Tchaikovsky, who, incidentally, later composed his famous Variations on a Rococo Theme for Cello and Orchestra. Prokofiev and Shostakovich, Hindemith and Piston, Foss and Jolivet, Kabalevsky and Khrennikov, as well as many brilliant performers, completely changed the status of the cello in the "republic" of musical instruments.

Myaskovsky's influence on Khachaturyan is most evident in the Cello Concerto. There are many similarities in their works, for example in Myaskovsky's Sonata for Cello and Piano. Though the latter was composed three years later, the teacher and the student are clearly seen in both.

"Congratulations on your splendid, first-class composition," wrote Aram Ilych after attending the preview of Myaskovsky's Sonata in the Composers Union.

> A truly profound and realistic composition, very beautiful and emotional. The great skill with which it is written for this difficult instrument and its youthful temperament, especially in the Finale, are astonishing. . . . The Sonata is fresh and the cello is really heard. . . . I am also astonished at how quickly you wrote it and how ably you handle the tonality and register of the cello.

Gone were the days when their association was that of teacher and student. They never really were that, even in Khachaturyan's student years. Many of Myaskovsky's students, after graduating from the Conservatory and postgraduate courses, continued their association with him, becoming colleagues and friends. Myaskovsky always took a great interest in the work of his contemporaries and in everything that was new in music. He also followed the development of his former students with keen interest, while they in turn retained a warm and sincere respect for their former teacher. Every year the Khachaturyans would send warm and touching birthday greetings to Nikolai Myaskovsky. Such were the relations between Myaskovsky and Khachaturyan.

In 1936, when Myaskovsky was fifty-five, Khachaturyan

thirty-three, and Kabalevsky thirty-two, Myaskovsky wrote in his diary, "On the insistence of Khachaturyan and Kabalevsky I made certain changes in the coda of the third movement of the Sixth Symphony." That same year we read in Khachaturyan's diary, "The number one event in this year's musical season is Myaskovsky's Sixteenth Symphony. His success was outstanding. A wonderful symphony."

In the summer of 1940, Myaskovsky played his Twenty-first Symphony for his colleagues at the composer's retreat in Staraya Ruza. The informal gathering included Aram Khachaturyan and his wife Nina Makarova, Dmitri Kabalevsky, Vissarion Shebalin, Vano Muradeli, and Zara Levina. In November 1940, Khachaturyan wrote, "I remember very well the festive atmosphere at the premiere of Myaskovsky's Twenty-first Symphony, which disclosed so well the composer's personality and yet was so unusually open in its emotional mood, so sociable, not at all like Myaskovsky."

Khachaturyan says nothing of the fact that the premieres of the Twenty-first and his own Violin Concerto took place on the same evening.

In 1943 the musical world was being introduced to Khachaturyan's new ballet, *Gayane*. The composer received a letter from Myaskovsky highly praising his work. "Your letter gave me new energy and a desire to justify your hopes, your faith, and your high opinion of me," Khachaturyan answered. "The thoughts you expressed about my work are very dear to me because you are my highly esteemed teacher and one of the greatest musicians of our age; everything you say about me fills me with joy."

That same year Khachaturyan had another occasion to write Myaskovsky:

My dear friend and highly esteemed teacher, Nikolai Yakovlevich. After completing a business letter to you I learned that you had been awarded the Order of Lenin. My dream has come true. I am happy to have the opportunity today of expressing my very sincere, heartfelt congratulations on this high honor, which you have fully earned. . . . It is also wonderful that this event coincided with the completion of the Twenty-fourth Symphony. It is marvelous. I am elated and proud of you, proud also to be your student. Your wonderful, profound, and original compositions will remain over the ages as an example to many generations to come.

The friendship between Khachaturyan and Myaskovsky was molded of that rare combination of human feelings and professional integrity which is seen in Myaskovsky's acceptance of criticism of his work from Khachaturyan, a former student.

Nikolai Myaskovsky was posthumously awarded the USSR State Prize for his Twenty-seventh Symphony in 1950, but Khachaturyan wanted his music to be more widely known. "The author of many wonderful compositions," wrote Aram Ilych, "he was always just as serious, unassuming, and highly intellectual in his music as he was in life. That may be why his music is not played often enough in our day. I have no doubt whatsoever that Myaskovsky's time is yet to come; it is our duty to do all in our power to bring that about as soon as possible."

Khachaturyan started writing his recollections of Myaskovsky and corresponded with his sister, Valentina Menshikova, visiting her almost every year on the anniversary of Myaskovsky's death. "I want you to know," he wrote her,

> that if on that day we, or I, am unable to come to see you, I am, nevertheless, with you heart and soul and thinking of Nikolai Yakovlevich.
>
> I think of Nikolai Yakovlevich almost every day. I speak of him either with my students, with Nina, or in conversation with friends. Yesterday we met the composer Jolivet. Kabalevsky and I told him proudly that we had studied under Myaskovsky. We *never* forget his behests.

The war ended in May 1945; the Soviet Union started on the Herculean task of restoring its war-torn economy. One thousand seven hundred ten cities and towns and more than 70,000 villages had been destroyed or burned down, 32,000 plants and factories put out of action, 40,000 hospitals and medical establishments and thousands of schools and colleges reduced to rubble, and 44,000 theaters and cultural centers and 43,000 libraries wrecked beyond repair—such was the damage caused by the fascist invasion, to say nothing of the more than twenty million people killed.

However, by 1950 the country had already reached its pre-war level of industrial and agricultural production. Science and culture prospered. The first postwar decade saw the birth of Myaskovsky's Twenty-seventh Symphony, Prokofiev's Sixth and Seventh symphonies, Shostakovich's Ninth and Tenth, Sha-porin's opera *The Decembrists,* Shebalin's *Taming of the Shrew,* Khrennikov's *Frol Skobeyev,* Gliere's ballet *The Bronze Horseman,* and Khachaturyan's ballet *Spartacus.* Soviet music had reached maturity by its thirtieth anniversary.

The postwar years were difficult, with many contradictions in domestic affairs and on the international scene. Leading composers and other artists wished to depict life in all its diversity and complexity. They searched for new ways of expressing their ideas, and found them. This was not a new problem. Musicians had experienced the same thing at other times. The composer Alexander Serov wrote, back in the nineteenth century, "It is wrong to believe that anyone can enjoy music and judge it correctly without the slightest preparation, without a special musical education. This kind of thinking lies at the root of many misconceptions about music." His words have lost none of their impact a century later. Dmitri Shostakovich quoted them in an article.

Realistic musicians were concerned with the future of their art and the need to make it more accessible to the people at large without oversimplifying it or artificially reducing the means of expression to the median level.

"Many questions concerning musical art have accumulated during the war years and need to be examined," Khachaturyan said, opening a plenary meeting of the organizing committee of the Composers Union in 1944.

The variety of styles in Soviet musical culture certainly testifies to its versatility. It is not our task to start some sort of abstract struggle between creative trends, but to join together all truly viable, strong, creative trends with an individuality of their own that have emerged in the course of Soviet musical development. We cannot speak of the musical language of one composer or another in the abstract without taking into consideration the vital content of his work, his ideological intentions, and the social role played by his work.

Addressing a plenary meeting of the organizing committee in 1946, he again dealt with the problems facing Soviet music; he spoke of the need to write music on contemporary themes, of shortcomings in the field of symphonies and operas, and the unsatisfactory state of music criticism. Many of these problems occasioned sharp criticism from the Central Committee of the Party soon after that plenary meeting. However, prior to the appearance of the "Resolution on the opera, *Great Friendship*, by Vano Muradeli*," the concept so deeply felt by Soviet artists, that art is rooted in the people, was oversimplified and misinterpreted. Dogmatic assessments of this kind could only be a hindrance to creative artists.

That is exactly what happened at the end of the 1940s. The above-mentioned Party resolution appeared on February 10, 1948. The first congress of Soviet composers was convened in April and, one after the other, prominent Soviet composers were accused of "following an antipopular, formalistic trend." This was the outcome of artificially narrowing down the concept of realism, of a subjective approach to art. Composers whose works were the pride of socialist culture were subjected to groundless criticism. Several years later the Central Committee of the Party admitted that in those years there had been "unjust and unwarrantedly sharp assessments of the work of several talented Soviet composers."

Does this book about Aram Khachaturyan need to recall the events of 1948, especially since the tendentious nature of many of those events is confirmed in documents? Yes, it does. In the first place, because it is not possible to ignore these events when studying the history of Soviet music. In the second place, because Khachaturyan himself was accused of being a formalistic composer together with such men as Myaskovsky, Prokofiev, and Shostakovich. And, third, because certain books on Soviet music published abroad paint the ten years from 1948 to 1958 in the blackest of colors, and the composers themselves are depicted as mute creatures who did not quite understand what was happening.

True, the atmosphere of those years was extremely complicated. However, both before and after 1948 there was no shortage of excellent Soviet compositions and of sober criticism and constructive deliberations. Addressing a conference of Soviet musicians, Mikhail Gnessin said, "Music easy to understand . . . does not mean offering the masses hackneyed tunes." "I believe," added Shostakovich, "that with all its shortcomings and failures our music is, nevertheless, progressing along a broad front made up of symphonies, oratorios, chamber music, and songs."

And what about Khachaturyan? Well, he experienced many an unpleasant day. His Symphonic Poem was sharply criticized together with the Cello Concerto, and even *Gayane* and his Second Symphony. He also came under attack as one of the executives of the Composers Union. Of all those who were wrongly criticized he was least prepared: as a composer he was used to having his works praised and quickly accepted by the public, and as an individual he was acutely sensitive to his surroundings and viewed the world first emotionally and only later analytically. "Not for a moment did Prokofiev surrender to despair or bewilderment," wrote Israel Nestiev. Khachaturyan, however, reacted quite differently. As he wrote,

Those were tragic days for me. I gave eleven years of my life to the organization and leadership of the Composers Union. How we all waited for our Constituent Congress! And it was here and at this time that I was clouted on the head so unjustly. My repenting speech at the First Congress was insincere. I was crushed, destroyed. I seriously considered changing professions.

Though the criticism of Khachaturyan's work was an obvious injustice, the failure of his Symphonic Poem was due to the composition itself, its outwardly pompous and heavy academic style. This was a postwar tendency that left its mark on Khachaturyan's work. The Symphonic Poem, much later renamed by the author the Third Symphony, composed on the eve of the thirtieth anniversary of the Revolution, was first played in Leningrad on December 13, 1947, with Evgeny Mravinsky conducting. In Moscow it was played on December 25. It was written for a huge symphony orchestra with thrice the usual number of wind instruments, an organ, and fifteen soloing trumpets.

"I sincerely wanted to compose something big, ceremonial, and unusual," Khachaturyan recalled.

> I searched for the means to express my big ideas. I wanted to write the kind of composition in which the public would feel my unwritten program without an announcement. I wanted this work to express the Soviet people's joy and pride in their great and mighty country. . . . That's why I included so many trumpets, and the organ; I also wished to transfer the organ from its spiritual sphere to a social sphere.

Georgi Hubov points out that "it was capable of overwhelming the public by its sheer magnitude and of stunning them with its great volume of sound, but it touched neither the mind nor the heart."

As early as the 1930s Khachaturyan's compositions proclaimed that it was his position to extol Soviet reality. There was plenty of material for that purpose. Many writers, composers, and painters were enthusiastic about the events of those years. But though much Soviet art was coated with a layer of superficiality, Khachaturyan was no part of it. His music always remained a sincere ode to the Soviet way of life. "I have observed Khachaturyan's growth and development over a period of many years," comments Georgi Hubov, "and I have noticed that his blunders and mistakes were not the result of ideological misconceptions, but of passions that seized hold of his temperamental nature and led him away from the lofty goal he had set himself."

Khachaturyan spent some time in sanatoriums in Zheleznovodsk and Kislovodsk in the summer of 1948. He had ample time to ponder over events and his career. His mood changed often, swinging from one extreme to the other, ranging from complete indifference to musical affairs—"I have nothing to say about myself and am not interested in what is happening in Moscow"—to his usual thirst for any and all information, his desire to be at the center of musical events—"I knew about almost everything that you wrote me." It was, of course, not possible for him to ignore music and avoid meeting people in Kislovodsk, especially in summertime. "I live in the Grand Hotel in the center of town. It's unpleasant, like living on Stoleshnikov Street.* . . . My despondency is compensated by the kindness I receive here. It embarrasses me to write about this. I have been in Kislovodsk for a month now and every day several bouquets of flowers stand on my table."

He finally made up his mind, after toying for some time with the idea, to go to Armenia. "I will fly to Armenia," he decided, "and travel around the villages and farms, keeping my eyes and ears open."

Khachaturyan covered some two thousand kilometers in the republic, meeting old and young, workers and students, and people in the arts. Again he heard the improvisations of the *ashugs* and played his own compositions.

It was at this time that he decided Armenia needed popular songs. "I believe that Armenia needs that kind of song today," he wrote. "Not a single popular song has appeared in Armenia during the thirty years of Soviet government. I have traveled extensively throughout Armenia and not one Soviet song written by an Armenian did I hear in the rural areas."

Khachaturyan's collaboration with the Armenian poet Ashot Grashi produced the "Song of Erevan" and "The Armenian Drinking Song," among others. "I am writing what I half jokingly call street songs. . . . When I was in Zangezur [one of Armenia's high mountain regions] I promised to write songs

* A very busy sidestreet in the heart of Moscow.

that could be sung by the people. It is a worthy but difficult task, but I shall try to keep my promise."

And he did. His songs were sung everywhere, and Shara Talyan, whom the composer had admired in his youth, made a gramophone record of "The Armenian Drinking Song," performing it as a folk song.

Khachaturyan's love of Armenia is clearly seen in his letters. "Every time I drive up to an Armenian village," he writes,

> I am moved to tears by the aroma of Armenian smoke hugging the roofs of the houses. It awakens in me some very distant associations so familiar since childhood, a night spent in a village, a sad song heard at a distance, as though from beyond the mountains.
>
> I consider myself in debt to my people, who are so affectionate toward me. There can be no greater reward for an artist than the love I experienced in my homeland. . . . I am prepared to do everything in my power for my native Armenia. There is still so much I must write and write well to justify what my people give me.
>
> As for serving the Armenian people, my whole life, everything that I have created, belongs to them.
>
> I was overjoyed to learn that the song from the film *Pepo* is so popular. Some were even surprised to hear that the song had an author; they had considered it a folk song.
>
> What can be more gratifying to a composer than the realization that the people have made his song their very own!

Returning home in the 1950s after travel abroad, Khachaturyan liked to tell how at his concerts people would point him out and say, "That's the same Khachaturyan who was exiled to Siberia after 1948." Regarding this exaggeration, it seems appropriate to recall a few facts about him.

In March 1948, Mikhail Romm's film, *The Russian Question*, was released with music by Khachaturyan. In December 1948, his Ode to the Memory of Vladimir Ilych Lenin had its first performance, and a little later Romm's *Vladimir Ilych Lenin* appeared, also with music by Khachaturyan. In 1949 the two-part

*Battle of Stalingrad* with music by Khachaturyan, was released, for which the composer received his fourth State Prize. Sergei Mikhalkov's play *Ilya Golovin* had its opening night at the Moscow Art Theater on November 7, 1949. There was a great deal in common between the main role in the play—the composer Golovin—and Aram Khachaturyan. In a letter written at that time Khachaturyan says: "This play deals with musical events in our country in 1948."*

Khachaturyan finally started on his ballet *Spartacus* in 1950. He went to Italy, where he saw the famous monuments of ancient Rome and studied the music of modern Italy. In Moscow he headed the chamber and instrumental music section of the Composers Union and wrote articles for the press on the development of Soviet music. He also began to conduct at that time and, a little later, to teach.

The improved creative atmosphere and the reassessment of the cultural heritage of Soviet composers—for example, Shostakovich's opera, *Katerina Izmailov*, and his Fourth Symphony, and Prokofiev's Second, Third, and Fourth symphonies—the renunciation of hidebound interpretations of such concepts as realism and the national character, recognition of the possibility of broad, creative initiative and of varying forms and styles of musical composition within the bounds of socialist realism—all this resulted in the Party Resolution of 1958 on "Rectifying the mistakes in the assessment of the operas, *Great Friendship, Bogdan Khmelnitsky,* and *With All My Heart.*" Again, as ten years ago, it was not so much a question of specific operas as of the general situation in Soviet music and the prospects for its development. The Composers Union held its second congress in March 1957,

---

* The Moscow Art Theater directors Vasili Toporkov and Mikhail Yanshin expected Khachaturyan to compose Golovin's formalistic symphony, as called for in the plot. This was all but impossible for him; instead he composed music showing that Golovin's formalism was only apparent and that he was actually a gifted composer. According to the plot, one of Golovin's songs is overheard by some soldiers on maneuvers who like it and sing it. The song subsequently becomes popular and helps redeem the composer in the eyes of the public.

at which Aram Khachaturyan and Dmitri Shostakovich were elected to the Secretariat. Things were beginning to change.

# *The Conductor*

*I believe it is important to travel abroad. The concerts and the chance to meet people all help to popularize the Soviet principles of realistic art and to strengthen friendship with other countries. I am happy that I was able to win more friends for our country.*

ARAM KHACHATURYAN

For some time Khachaturyan had been dreaming of conducting an orchestra. He had rehearsed with small orchestras in theaters staging plays with his music. His dream finally came true in 1950, when he conducted a full orchestra. "What could be more exciting for a composer," he recalled,

> than to establish contact with the musicians, to lead them, and to hear the music played as you hear it in your heart. I had studied the difficult art of conducting several times but I was always so busy with my work and other duties that I could never really apply myself wholly to these studies. I was ready to forget my dream of conducting when, as luck would have it. . . .

Academician Sergei Vavilov, then President of the Academy of Sciences, was up for election to the USSR Supreme Soviet, our Parliament. An election meeting was to be followed by a concert.

> A telephone call informed me that a concert was being planned in honor of Vavilov. "We would like you to conduct the orchestra. Leonid Kogan will play the Finale of your Violin Concerto and the program also includes three dances from *Gayane*." This was so completely unexpected that I refused at first. "Come to the

196

rehearsals at least, the orchestra has already rehearsed and everything is ready," I was told. "The orchestra will play it correctly even if you conduct backwards."

Well, I was persuaded. I came to the rehearsal trying to remember what we were taught at solfeggio exercises: four-fourths is down, left, right, up, three-fourths is down, right and up, like drawing a triangle. On that principle I conducted the rehearsal. But the concert was scheduled for that same evening. I was very nervous all day long. I didn't know what to do with my hands, or how to stand. Eventually, everything turned out all right, the concert was a great success; Sergei Vavilov came backstage and thanked me.

Anyhow, on that evening I was smitten with the conducting bug. That summer I already had nine concerts on different open-air stages in Moscow. At first the newspapers carried long reviews of my conducting, but the better my conducting became, the less they wrote about me.

One of the first reviews was written by the composer Yuri Shaporin. He mentioned Khachaturyan's expressive hands, his ability to mold the composition, and his feeling of rhythm. "I think," wrote Shaporin, "that if he continues in this sphere, Khachaturyan may become an interesting conductor, capable of talented interpretations not only of his own works but of other composers as well."

Although Khachaturyan did say "I dream of conducting, it is the supreme delight . . . ," he had no intention of becoming a professional. He wished to conduct only his own compositions, to have contact with the public and the opportunity of interpreting his own works.

By the end of the summer he was already booked for fifteen concerts throughout the country.

He also had invitations to teach at the Gnessin School of Music and the Moscow Conservatory but was reluctant to cancel his engagements. He had invitations to conduct in Leningrad, Kiev, Kharkov, Odessa, Minsk, and Riga, and Tallin, Erevan, Tbilisi, Baku, and other cities. Khachaturyan preferred to appear in places "where concert orchestras had not yet appeared," as he put it. "My trips are not only concert tours," he would say, "they are more in the nature of popularizing performances."

On such tours he also met and talked with teachers and students of music schools, amateur performers, and the general public. In Armenia Khachaturyan gave eighteen concerts and held ten discussions on art in 1954 with local performers and teachers. He and Dmitri Kabalevsky traveled extensively through Siberia, the Kuznetsk Valley, and the Altai region in 1958. Here is how Kabalevsky described one concert held in the community center of a collective farm near the city of Barnaul.

> The huge barnlike building was altogether unsuitable for concert programs. There were about six hundred people sitting on long benches. The musicians had a difficult time arranging themselves on the primitive stage. Sitting in the front row was a young fellow in uniform with his wife, who was breast-feeding their child. During the first part of the program, when selections from *Gayane* were being played, the audience seemed to be trying to understand the music, and exchanged opinions quite freely. Then, following the puzzling sounds of the orchestral introduction, Viktor Pikaizen started playing the beautiful melody of the middle part of the Violin Concerto. The hall suddenly became absolutely quiet. I was watching the people in the front row. The young Russian boy in uniform discovered the magic of music, and there were tears in his wife's expressive eyes. Aram Khachaturyan could not see all this, of course. Later he told me that he had never been so nervous before nor had he experienced such complete satisfaction.

The more he conducted the more he improved. "It was very pleasant playing under his baton," recalled Viktor Pikaizen, "for he was able to inspire the musicians and the soloist; he knew exactly what he wanted and his conducting invariably impressed the public."

Although he no longer felt so tense on stage, he did not abandon the idea of perfecting his conducting. "I regret not having had the time to take a few lessons from you," he wrote to Konstantin Saradjev the conductor. "I intend to do that on my next visit to Erevan, which I think will be soon."

In 1950, when he was just beginning to experience the joys of conducting, Khachaturyan was in Rome with a Soviet delegation and was invited to conduct a program on the radio. "The Italian critics wrote warmly of my conducting," he recalled. "In their innocence they referred to me as 'an experienced maestro.' This gratifying flattery gave me courage. Ever since, I combine my trips abroad with performances."

Aram Khachaturyan once said in an interview that he had performed in forty-two countries, something not many professional musicians can boast of. He was applauded in the United States and Latin America, in Japan, Egypt, and Lebanon, Great Britain, France, and Australia, Italy, the Federal Republic of Germany, Belgium, The Netherlands, Finland, Norway, Poland, Bulgaria, Czechoslovakia, and the German Democratic Republic. When the first Soviet Sputnik went up into space the composer was in São Paulo, Brazil; he learned of Yuri Gagarin's space flight just before appearing on the stage of the *Staatsoper* in the German Democratic Republic. Khachaturyan was a true ambassador of Soviet art and culture; as one Japanese critic wrote, "If this is socialist art in content and national in form, then I vote for it with both my hands."

In Argentina he agreed to appear for members of the Argentina-USSR Society, thinking it would be a modest concert. What must have been his surprise then when he was brought to the Luna Park Stadium in Buenos Aires and found an audience of twenty-five thousand waiting for him. On his return to the USSR he helped found the Soviet Association of Friendship and Cultural Cooperation with Latin American Countries. His first trip to Latin America in 1957 was a real triumph. In Mexico he was made an honorary member of the Academy of Music and a member of the National Conservatory of Music. In Argentina he was mobbed by eager crowds, and in Brazil people threw their hats in front of his automobile. "It was worth all the time I spent learning to conduct," Khachaturyan must have been thinking when he was given a standing ovation in West Berlin after conducting his First Symphony, or when he saw the standing ovation he received in Iceland, or when he conducted the best American orchestras during a two-month tour of the country and was congratulated by Leopold Stokowski, Samuel Barber, Aaron Copland, Arthur Rubinstein, George Balanchine, and the then Secretary General of the United Nations, U Thant.

Aram Khachaturyan made his debut in the United States on January 22, 1968, in Constitution Hall in Washington, D.C. The music public was quite familiar with his work, but this was the first time they were to see him in person, and as one critic put it, American audiences were "becoming more and more Khachaturyan-conscious." His piano and violin concertos were already being played in the United States in the 1930s, and in 1940 the Cleveland Symphony Orchestra under Artur Radzinski performed the American premiere of the First Symphony. His music was played very often during the war. Jascha Heifetz performed the Saber Dance, which he himself transcribed for violin, and Josef Szigeti played his song-poem. Arthur Rubinstein created a sensation in Pittsburgh when he played the Piano Concerto. In the summer of 1942 Khachaturyan's piano and violin concertos, *Dance Suite,* and First Symphony were performed in the U.S.A. The *New York Times* wrote in July that Khachaturyan was becoming quite the fashion in the United States. In June 1945, the American critic Louis Biancolli wrote in the *New York World Telegram* that various orchestras would probably play the Saber Dance to death in a few months' time. It had the bite and beauty of the exotic, plus a tight rhythm. He suggested that everyone should visit Armenia, judging by what Aram Khachaturyan heard there.

Sergei Koussevitsky, who for many years conducted the Boston Symphony Orchestra, did a great deal to popularize Khachaturyan's music in the United States. Many American soloists and conductors were anxious to be the first to perform Khachaturyan's new works. His *Spartacus* was well received when the Bolshoi Ballet toured the States.

For his first appearance in the United States Khachaturyan chose to conduct his Second Symphony, which at that time was not too well known abroad. Besides Washington, he appeared in New York, Detroit, Chicago, Rochester, Kansas City, Indianapolis, and Hartford. He was enthusiastically applauded everywhere and, as one reporter said, "he did more to strengthen the friendship between the two countries than Soviet exports of vodka and caviar."

The magazine *America* arranged a meeting between Khachaturyan and America's outstanding composer, Aaron Copland. "I was both excited and happy to come to the United States," Khachaturyan said at the meeting.

> I was well aware that I was coming to a great country with a very high musical culture and that Americans have seen and heard all the best the world has to offer in music. I kept wondering how my music would be received. Well, I'm satisfied. The audiences are wonderful. All my concerts were played to full houses with tickets sold out long in advance. I was warmly greeted by the public and I usually played three encores, sometimes four and five. So I think I have established good contact with my audiences and have acquired a great many friends.

But the composer was beginning to feel the effects of his extended world tours. "I am tired of these trips," he complained. "I want to write, but it is becoming more and more difficult to do so. I would like to end my travels as soon as possible and start writing again. But I am afraid. I haven't written for so long that I have lost the feel of it. Will I be able to write something worthwhile?"

However, he continued to conduct unabated, since as a musician he found it very beneficial. "I probably would have arranged some of my compositions differently had I been conducting at the time. Khachaturyan the conductor sometimes criticizes Khachaturyan the composer, for one learns a great deal on the conductor's podium."

Nevertheless, his travels and appearances were quite suited to his temperament and his urge to associate with people. As a conductor he met many interesting people—Queen Elizabeth of Belgium, Pope John XXIII, Jean Sibelius, Arthur Bliss, Arthur Rubinstein, Arturo Benedetti Michelangeli, Ernest Ansermet, Nadia Boulanger, Charlie Chaplin, and Ernest Hemingway. Following are his observations on a few of these figures.

*Jean Sibelius.* I first met the composer not long before his ninetieth birthday, during my appearances in Finland in 1955. I was quite excited when I came to Ainola, the great musician's villa. Everything was so modest and simple. Sibelius himself was very vigorous, standing erect, not showing the burden of his years. He embraced me and looked deeply into my eyes. Then we started talking. He told me about his meetings with famous Russian musicians, and enumerated many works of Soviet composers he had heard on the radio. He also said he had once heard an unfamiliar violin concerto on the radio and had waited impatiently for the announcer to say who the composer was and who had played it so wonderfully. It turned out that he had heard Aram Khachaturyan's Violin Concerto played by David Oistrakh. I joined him in expressing admiration for Oistrakh's playing.

Sibelius had a surprisingly good memory; his age was evident only when he was autographing a book for me about his work, for he found it rather difficult to write. As I was leaving, Sibelius said to me, "Some write music with their heads, some with their feet, and some with their hearts." I hope he placed me in the last category. I am certain that Sibelius's own music always came from the heart of this great artist. It was this that enabled him to release Finnish music from the confines of his country and win it world acclaim. I invariably hear the work of a modern artist in his compositions because, to my mind, "contemporary" means the ability to embody the thoughts and feelings of your day, and your age, the ability to express it in a manner understood not by a handful of musical snobs but by the great majority of those who really love music.

*Nadia Boulanger.* Long before I had met Nadia I knew she was a great authority on music. Igor Stravinsky held her in high esteem and President John F. Kennedy presented her a gold medal for her work with American composers. Aaron Copland, Walter Piston, Roy Harris, and many others were among her students in Paris. I first met Nadia Boulanger in Bucharest on the jury of the George Enesco International Piano Competitions in 1964. My first impression was of a tall, gray-haired woman with a very Russian face. I was told she should be addressed as "Mademoiselle Boulanger." Sitting together with her on the jury I noticed that she followed the music as every contestant played, while her face expressed her every reaction and emotion. She was an excellent connoisseur of the classics and saw every contestant as though with X-ray vision.

In 1974, when I was appearing in Paris I attended her harpsichord class in Fontainebleau. Later, Nina Makarova and I were invited to her home in Paris. I shall never forget our meetings with this wonderful French musician, particularly since Nina Makarova risked playing her piano études for her, which to our delight she praised.

*Ernest Hemingway.* I made my first trip to Cuba in 1960, just about a year after the Cuban revolution, when the country was just starting to build a new life. Our two countries had not yet established diplomatic relations. Nina Makarova and I were accompanied on our tour of the country by Vladimir Kuzmishchev, a Vice President of the Soviet Association of Friendship and Cultural Cooperation with Latin American countries. In the Hilton Hotel he met a carelessly dressed unpretentious-looking man with a short, unkempt beard. But when this man raised his expressive, deep-blue, intelligent eyes, it was impossible not to recognize him. Yes, it was Ernest Hemingway, the world-famous author and legendary participant in two world wars and fighter for the Spanish people's freedom.

"When could I present you with a two-volume edition of your works published in the Soviet Union?" Kuzmishchev asked him.

"And what are you doing in Havana?" asked Hemingway.

"I'm accompanying the composer Aram Khachaturyan on his tour of the country," he answered.

"Then you must come and visit me at my home," he said.

We arrived at his modest place not far from Havana. Everywhere there were stuffed animals, trophies of his many hunts, for which both he and his wife Mary were famous.

"I shot that lion myself," Mary told us, "but he was pretty old."

We sat down to lunch. The mushroom soup which Mary had cooked was delicious and Nina praised it, knowing it would please her.

"Would you like some more?" Mary offered.

"With pleasure," answered Nina.

Suddenly Hemingway, quite unaffectedly, poured her the soup remaining in his plate.

Nina quickly ate Hemingway's soup without batting an eyelash. Later, knowing how fastidious my wife was, I asked her if she had done that to smooth over an embarrassing situation.

"I decided that one should forgive a great writer that kind of prank," she said. "I just imagined ourselves out in the ocean in a rowboat and the situation seemed to justify what he did."

Hemingway said he was familiar with my music and would have attended the concert with pleasure but, regrettably, could not, because he was pressed to finish one of his books. Most likely the book was *Dangerous Summer*. Once more I took in the author's home, where he had written his novels *For Whom the Bell Tolls, Across the River and into the Trees,* and *The Old Man and the Sea,* and his Paris memoirs, *A Moveable Feast.*

We brought Hemingway a bottle of our Stolichnaya vodka but he didn't open it. We learned later that Anastas Mikoyan and his son Sergei were his guests next day and were quite surprised to see the bottle.

Mary came to my concert. She sent me a note afterward saying she had admired both the music and the unusual skill with which the Havana Symphony Orchestra played. "It was like two miracles," she wrote.

*Charlie Chaplin.* I saw Chaplin's film *Modern Times* in Moscow, just before the war. Now, I am rather a somber person and not easily amused; I don't like it when others laugh a lot without reason. But as soon as the film started I found myself laughing fit to burst; later, recalling some of the scenes, I laughed again and again.

Many years later, in 1965, I was on the jury of an International Violin Competition in Geneva, and Nina Makarova was on the jury of a piano competition. Andre Marescotti, Chairman of the Geneva Competition, who today is President of the International Society for Contemporary Music, was kind enough to accompany us on a sightseeing tour of Geneva's outskirts.

Seeing the name Charlie Chaplin on the gate of a villa, we stopped the car and rang the bell. We were told that Mr. Chaplin was not receiving anyone, as he was preparing to leave for London. This, we learned, was just a device to turn away curious tourists. Later, however, we recognized Chaplin in a passing car. We asked Marescotti to find out Chaplin's telephone, something not so easily done, and call him. When Chaplin learned that Soviet musicians would like to meet him, he invited us to his home.

The old house was shrouded in greenery and grapevines, with a well-kept front lawn. Chaplin came out to greet us. I wanted to talk with him about composition for I knew that he had written much of the music for his films. The conversation was not very satisfactory. My Russian had to be translated into French, which Nina and Chaplin's wife Oona spoke, and Oona then translated into English. But Chaplin did understand what I was driving at. He got up and went to the piano as though to play something, but, either too embarrassed or hesitant, he excused himself and went into the adjoining room. He returned with a recording of Oistrakh playing the Violin Concerto and myself conducting. He asked me to autograph the record. And I asked him to autograph a photograph for me.

I was taken ill soon after and found myself in a Geneva hospital. The newspapers and radio reported this, hinting that I had suffered a heart attack. Luckily it was not true, it was a simple heart disturbance. I received telegrams and messages from many countries wishing me a speedy recovery. The French newspaper *L'Aurore* even wrote something to the effect that "Moscow was mourning the death of Aram Khachaturyan." Friends consoled me, saying that such an obituary was a good omen and that I would now live to be a hundred.

One morning the nurse brought a large box of red roses and a note from Charlie Chaplin. I was touched to the bottom of my heart. Soon I was out of the hospital and Nina and I left for Moscow, taking Chaplin's flowers with us. For a long time, the roses, though dry and brittle, remained standing in our apartment, a reminder of this great artist's big heart.

# Spartacus

*The courageous and heroic figure of Spartacus has for long been beckoning and inspiring me to write a ballet. I believe that the theme of Spartacus and the slave uprising in ancient Rome has great importance and appeal toay.*

ARAM KHACHATURYAN

On July 9, 1950, Khachaturyan wrote on the first page of the score of *Spartacus*, "I am beginning with a feeling of great creative excitement." And on the last page, "Work on *Spartacus* took over three and a half years. I worked mostly in the summertime, so actually it took me eight months. I completed *Spartacus* on February 22, 1954. All the music was written in the Composers Union retreat at Staraya Ruza. Aram Khachaturyan."

The idea for the ballet really belongs to Nikolai Volkov, a prominent critic and author of the books for Boris Asafiev's ballet, *The Fountain of Bakhchisarai*, and Sergei Prokofiev's *Cinderella*. Volkov turned to *Spartacus* in 1938, after completing work with Asafiev on the ballet, *The Flames of Paris*. *Spartacus* was to be a continuation of the historical-revolutionary theme in the Soviet ballet.

"Volkov lived on Arbat Street in a large old apartment," Khachaturyan recalled. "I was astonished by the great number of books that filled all the rooms and spilled out into the corridor. And they were not gathering dust on the shelves. I wish I could read half the books that Volkov did."

Khachaturyan wanted to write the ballet, but something in the very idea seemed to frighten him. "To tell the truth, this theme, which is so far from our day, frightened me. What could our turbulent age have in common with ancient Rome? Nikolai Volkov and I often met and argued a good deal. He finally dispelled my doubts, however, and convinced me that the theme of the slave uprising was just the thing for me."

Nikolai Volkov remembered that Aram Ilych did not start the ballet right away. "I visited him at the Composers Retreat in Ruza where he was living at that time. Seeing his hesitation, I wrote in a corner of the score, 'With this you shall succeed,' and he did."

The composer's fears were concerned mainly with the subject of the ballet, a story of far-off antiquity. After all, the plots of *Happiness* and *Gayane* were placed in modern times, and Khachaturyan was quite proud of what he had achieved. Many musicians, even those close to him, had misgivings. They thought that his music might not be dramatic enough to convey the tension and tragedy of the rise and fall of this remarkable hero of the ancient world. Nevertheless, Khachaturyan did start working on the ballet.

*December 29, 1940.* The newspaper, *Sovetskoe Iskusstvo,* reports Khachaturyan as saying that he intends to write the music to the ballet *Spartacus,* with choreography by Igor Moiseyev.

*March 31, 1941.* "Am starting *Spartacus* this summer. To be completed in the winter of 1942."

*December 29, 1941.* "I see *Spartacus* as a monumental tale of the ancient uprising of slaves, a mighty avalanche in defense of the freedom of the individual, to which I as a Soviet artist wish to pay tribute and express my deep respect and admiration."

*August 23, 1942.* "I must write so much this year. Immediately after the symphony [the Second] I shall start the Concerto for Cello and Orchestra and after that will immediately start on a ballet for the Bolshoi Theater."

*June 1947.* Igor Moiseyev informs the Leningrad Kirov Theater that he agrees to stage Khachaturyan's *Spartacus.*

*February 2, 1948.* Nikolai Volkov and Igor Moiseyev outline their scenario for the ballet during a meeting in the Kirov Theater. Pyotr Gusev, artistic manager of the ballet, Ivan Shlepyanov, director, Boris Haikin, conductor, and critics Valerian Bogdanov-Berezovsky, and Nikolai Tsiganov agree that the scenario is interesting though difficult. The premiere is scheduled for 1949. There is as yet no music.

*February 13, 1949.* "Am gathering material. Most likely will start work by the end of December."

*September 13, 1949.* Nikolai Volkov writes in a letter to a friend: "If it doesn't rain it pours. I met Moiseyev in a bookstore and then Khachaturyan in the Moscow Art Theater. Both swore that feverish work would begin in December on both the music and the structure of the ballet."

*October 5, 1949.* "Dear Aram Ilych. Awaiting your new work as manna from the heavens. Pyotr Gusev"

*January 28, 1950.* "Started the ballet *Spartacus*. Wrote the prologue. *Spartacus* will be my main work this year."

*January 30, 1950.* "Had a serious meeting with Volkov and met with Moiseyev yesterday. Both meetings helped me in my work. Completed the draft of the prologue, six to seven minutes of music. Don't know whether to go on or to orchestrate the prologue. Most important though, I think I have found the character music for *Spartacus*. The prologue starts off with trumpets followed by a ponderous but splendid march portraying the conquerors, the prisoners, the priests, the people, and so on. In a few days will start on the slave market. Moiseyev liked the prologue."

*March 8, 1950.* Nikolai Volkov writes: "Spoke with Khachaturyan twice—on January 12 and just recently, on March 6. Since his copy of the book is annotated by Moiseyev, he is composing without my notes. I shall keep the sacred fire going in him and I believe this time the music will be just what the doctor ordered. If things go well the production should be ready a year from now in March."

*March 16, 1950.* "Dear Pyotr Andreyevich. Why is it your letters affect me so? Whenever I talk with you I have the feeling that I've done something very wrong or unethical. I should like to get rid of that feeling. However, I think it is because I should have completed *Spartacus* long ago and I have not only not done so, but am beginning to break all deadlines. According to the agreement I should give the first act on April 2, but I cannot do it because I was laid up again for a whole month. I'm better now and able to work. I have a great deal composed in my fingers but, regrettably, not much written down. I am starting on the score now. All of 1950 will be taken up with *Spartacus.* Will I finish the music this year? I think so, but I may spill over into 1951.

"My conclusion: It is possible to start planning *Spartacus* and report about it in listings for 1950–1951. I am certain I shall write the music this year (unless something happens to me again). You may not have time enough to stage it.

"I am not certain my letter will satisfy you, but I hope that I will soon be able to satisfy you not only with letters but with music, too."

*July 8, 1950.* "*Spartacus* is already in production," writes Volkov. "Moiseyev went through all the choreography with Khachaturyan. For my part, every time I meet Aram Ilych, I go deeply into every dramatic situation that presents difficulties for him. I think he has made such good progress that he now speaks of November as a possible deadline for completing the score. We'll wait and see."

*December 1950.* Khachaturyan is in Italy with a Soviet cultural delegation: "I saw the structures of ancient Rome, the triumphal arches built by the slaves, I saw the barracks of the gladiators and the coliseum. . . . Often strolled through the places where the gladiator Spartacus walked with his comrades."

*October 30, 1952.* The Central Office on Theaters under the Committee on the Arts informs the Kirov Theater in Leningrad of its decision regarding the book of *Spartacus.* It points out that the slave uprising is not portrayed vividly enough, that the figure of Spartacus is incomplete, and that the tragic theme predominates in the Finale of the ballet.

*April 11, 1953.* Khachaturyan plays the first two acts of *Spartacus* in the Composers Union.

*December 16, 1953.* Khachaturyan attends a session of the Kirov Theater arts council for an audition of the two acts of the ballet played on two pianos.

*May 5, 1954.* "*Spartacus* is sapping my strength. There will be a broad discussion at the Union at the end of May. The music played on two pianos has been recorded for the convenience of the critics and anyone else who wishes to hear it in preparation for the discussion."

*June 3, 1954.* There is great interest in the music to *Spartacus.* Dmitri Shostakovich notes that the single line of symphonic development in *Spartacus* constitutes a great achievement for Khachaturyan.

*Autumn 1954.* Because Igor Moiseyev is on an extended foreign tour with his dance company, the Kirov Theater chooses to invite another choreographer for *Spartacus,* not wishing to postpone the production. The Committee on the Arts appoints Moiseyev to stage *Spartacus* in the Bolshoi Theater.

*December 1, 1954.* Khachaturyan plays the music of *Spartacus* for the Bolshoi Theater.

*December 1954.* Khachaturyan plays the music for Leningrad composers and critics.

*March 16–18, 1955.* Khachaturyan plays fragments from *Spartacus* for the Board of the Composers Union. "It is difficult to judge the entire ballet from what we have heard," writes Yuri Shaporin. "However, to those who heard the entire score played on two pianos for four hands—and I am among them—it is clear that *Spartacus* will become a milestone in the development of the Soviet ballet."

*August 20, 1955.* Shostakovich publishes a long article on *Spartacus.*

*October 16, 1955.* "The production [in Moscow] has been discontinued because Moiseyev has left for Paris and London. The production will be ready no earlier than November or December 1956. I am terribly disappointed."

*November 1955.* Feodor Lopukhov the choreographer suggests that Leonid Yakobson stage *Spartacus.*

*December 14, 1955.* The Kirov Theater approves Yakobson's choreography for *Spartacus* and asks Khachaturyan to make some modifications in the score to tie in with Yakobson's stage version.

*March 1956.* Khachaturyan attends a showing by the Kirov Theater in Leningrad of Yakobson's excerpts from *Spartacus.* "All the dances received thunderous applause," writes Yakobson. After the preview Khachaturyan writes to Lopukhov, "Allow me to express my gratitude to you personally, and through you to the splendid dancers headed by the talented choreographer Yakobson for the exceptionally artistic excerpts from *Spartacus.*"

*March 20, 1956.* Khachaturyan writes about the Bolshoi production in Moscow: "Things are bad for *Spartacus.* Moiseyev went abroad six times during rehearsals and is now going to America. So *Spartacus* is dead. It is dead because everything should be ready in its own time."

*July 4, 1956.* "The Kirov Theater's showing of all that was staged of *Spartacus* was a triumph," Yakobson writes.

*December 27, 1956.* The premiere of *Spartacus* takes place in the Kirov Theater, staged by Leonid Yakobson. Conductor, Pavel Feldt, sets by Valentin Khodasevich. The dancers: Askold Makarov as Spartacus; Nina Zubkovskaya as Phrygia; Alla Shelest as Aegina.

As may be seen, it was not an easy birth, or, as Khachaturyan said, "Writing a ballet is difficult, staging it is ten times worse."

Volkov's book had provided excellent material for the composer's imagination. Volkov rejected the idea of a melodrama;

he was more interested in the heroism of the plot. "The theme of Spartacus's struggle for freedom," he wrote, "the theme of an uprising against the chains of slavery, a desire to bring freedom and independence to the oppressed peoples, was considered the main theme of the ballet."

He based his version on the works of two ancient historians, Plutarch and Appian. Although Plutarch was hostile to the Spartacus movement, his works contained a great deal of interesting factual material. Appian, by contrast, wrote favorably of Spartacus, describing him as a courageous and physically strong person, highly intelligent and kind.

The actual facts of the uprising—the time (74–71 B.C.), the number of slaves who followed Spartacus (up to 120,000), and the cruelty of the Romans (the crucifixion of 6,000 slaves)—were embellished by Volkov with the characters of the sly Aegina and the treacherous Harmodius, characters which neither dominate nor overshadow the epic style and heroic pathos of the central theme that so attracted Khachaturyan. Though the book's shortcomings did find reflection in the score, Khachaturyan and Volkov saw eye to eye; this was the key to the success of the ballet. "I don't think any other composer could have succeeded in expressing the theme as Khachaturyan did," wrote Dmitri Kabalevsky. "The vividly dynamic events, the brilliantly luxuriant scenes of Roman life, and the tremendous impact of the uprising are all very much in keeping with Khachaturyan's individuality."

Once again, as in the case of the ballet *Gayane,* Khachaturyan faced the question of just what a ballet should be. Ideas had not changed. When he started *Spartacus* he already had behind him the experience of his stage music for *Macbeth* and his screen music for *Othello,* and was well aware of the importance of musical dramaturgy for the success of a ballet. For this reason he was equally demanding of Volkov and of himself. "I wanted the score to clearly express the drama of the music," said Khachaturyan. "That is what the classics of Russian ballet music teach us."

The main conflict in *Spartacus* hinges on a sharp musical

delineation of all the roles and the irreconcilable clash of two worlds—Spartacus, the gladiators, and Phrygia in one; Marcus Crassus, the Ruler of Rome, sly Aegina, and Harmodius the traitor, in the other. One world dreaming of freedom, the other representing blind power and slavery. In one world the high ideals of comradeship and love, in the other, inhuman brutality and unrestrained sensuality.

All the portraits in *Spartacus* are well molded and equally convincing. The composer was lavish in his portrayal of *la dolce vita* in ancient Rome; he deliberately did not play down its seductive charm, just as Mikhail Glinka did not in the Polish scenes in *Ivan Susanin,* Moussorgsky in the Polish act in *Boris Godunov,* and Borodin in the Polovtsian dances in *Prince Igor. Spartacus,* as portrayed by Khachaturyan, is not the tragedy of one historical individual; it is rather the tragedy of the ideals of the uprising he led. This is a social conflict of morals and ethics, a tragedy of human ideals of justice, ideals which, throughout man's history, not excluding this century, have too often been helpless in the face of obtuse power and violence no matter how it is disguised. That is why for a quarter of a century Khachaturyan's *Spartacus* has invariably excited the imagination of choreographers, dancers, musicians, and audiences.

It is clear that only exceptionally expressive music could give life to the ideas of the ballet's authors. And again, as Dmitri Shostakovich put it, "We see Aram Khachaturyan's wonderful ability to endow each of his characters with a complete musical portrait."

Crassus, so smugly self-satisfied in the blind conviction of his infallibility, cold and empty-hearted, a living personification of Rome; his music based on the empty intervals of fourths and fifths, the cold voices of two trumpets and the general forms of the movements depicting the extravagant side of life in Rome, its false facade behind which are hidden deceit, cold-heartedness, and cruelty.

The clarion calls of the trumpets introduce the leitmotiv of Spartacus, fearless leader of the slaves. The singing melody of the second theme suggests the supple intonations of Phrygia in the following scene. This is the leitmotiv not only of Spartacus but of the troops he leads. It expresses the greatness of the people, their dignity and suffering, and a foreboding of the uprising.

The voluptuous, convulsive movements of Aegina the temptress are heard more often in the score than she herself is seen on stage. She seems to echo the themes of Crassus; they are pervaded by a sense of treachery and evil.

Phrygia, the hero's wife, is the incarnation of femininity, spiritual purity, and ethical ideals. Khachaturyan molded her portrait in the warmest tones of the violins in a flowing, seemingly endless melody. Phrygia's idealism, converging with Spartacus's dreams of freedom for his country, is especially eloquent in the Ode to Freedom.

A large part of the ballet revolves around such broad dramatic scenes as the parting of Spartacus and Phrygia, Spartacus challenging Rome, the call to an uprising, Spartacus's troops appearing at Crassus's villa, the dissension among the gladiators, and the death of Spartacus. And Khachaturyan, in addition to three *Spartacus* suites, also published Symphonic Pictures from *Spartacus,* which includes the fourth scene (Barracks of the Gladiators), the fifth (Appian Way), and the ninth (Death of Spartacus), exactly as heard in the ballet.

There are, of course, many dances in the ballet not directly expressive of the main roles, such as the Slave Market, the Dance of the Greek Slave, and the Egyptian Dancing Girl. These are not just divertissements but integral parts of the general theme.

In the third scene, The Circus, we hear refrains of Crassus and Aegina, for this is their world of cruelty and brutality. In the fight to the death between gladiators and lions, Spartacus emerges victorious not only because he is the strongest, but also because he is depicted as the most humane of all those present.

In the sixth scene, The Feast at Crassus's Villa, Khachaturyan gave free rein to his imagination, creating such excellent numbers as the Dance of the Nymphs, the Dance of the Gaditanian Maidens, and the Dance with Swords. How naturally they blend with the classical pas de deux of Harmodius and Aegina and their variations, which lead to the concluding bacchanalia and the arrival of the gladiators.

A few of the numbers are purely interludes—the Wolf and the Lamb in the fifth scene, the Appian Way, the Dance of the Nymphs, and the Dance with Swords.

All these are not just random numbers; they are introduced to relax the tension and then lead up to the culmination of the second act, where Spartacus is proclaimed emperor.

Khachaturyan's *Spartacus* differs from his other ballets in that every act ends on a note of great emotional intensity: the second scene ends in the tragic parting of Phrygia and Spartacus; the third scene and the first act end with the victory of Spartacus; the fifth scene ends in the uprising, while Spartacus is proclaimed emperor at the end of the sixth. And many more examples could be cited.

The impact of the ballet is strong in its contrasts right from the very beginning of the lavish march which introduces the main characters on a huge stage filled with crowds seething with passions, and our attention is directed from one group to another. Khachaturyan is a master at creating such turbulent crowd scenes for the ballet. In painting a picture of Rome on a sunny day, with all the merchants, peddlers, housewives, pickpockets, stately matrons, and gay maidens, Khachaturyan could not but draw on his recollections of market scenes in Tbilisi. Then there are the scenes of the circus, the slave market, the feast, the gladiators' camp . . . each rich in vivid contrasts. No less contrasting are the adagios of Harmodius and Aegina and of Spartacus and Phrygia, the contradictory harmony and pathos of the love theme which hint at their illusory happiness, the Ode to Liberty proclaimed by Spartacus and the tragic sense that the uprising is doomed. And finally, probably the strongest dramatic contrast is achieved when Spartacus's troops break into Crassus's villa at the height of the orgy. The entire ballet seems to sweep across the stage in a single breathtaking leap.

In molding the musical portraits of the main roles, Khachaturyan came close to the model of the ideal ballet he had in mind when speaking of Prokofiev's *Romeo and Juliet*. Khachaturyan had no intention of building his ballet around folk melodies, as he had in *Gayane*. Here is what he had to say about his visit to Italy: "My many impressions were a great help. I must say, however, that I had no intention of stylizing the music to fit the epoch, for this would have been wrong in principle, and, besides, almost no musical documents from those ancient times have come down to us. I composed as I felt."

Khachaturyan could not have written otherwise, and those critics who claimed that the score was not rooted in folk music were wrong. Khachaturyan wrote "as he felt"; this meant he never strayed far from his native Armenian music, the strains of which are felt everywhere in *Spartacus:* for example, the theme of Phrygia is close to Armenian laments; the introduction to the fourth act is clearly influenced by the traditions of Armenian bards; and in the sixth scene one of the dances of the gladiators is very reminiscent of *Kochari*, the Armenian folk dance.

"The vivid coloring and atmosphere of the music," wrote Shostakovich, "are so strong that at times one fears that the main theme of the ballet, the revolutionary struggle of the slaves against their oppressors, could lose its impact. I hope Khachaturyan can avoid this." His fears were quite justified, for the scene depicting the capture of Crassus's villa, rather than the scene of the uprising, became the climax of the ballet; and the death of Spartacus was obviously lacking in symphonic development. Khachaturyan was also criticized for having put in too many culminations, for a certain monotony in the musical development, and for a lack of balance between the music and the choreography—for example, the unusual length of some of the dances. Said Khachaturyan, "Aegina's dance lasted two minutes and twelve seconds at first, instead of the two minutes required by the theater. I had to agree to shorten it."

Still, no one doubted that *Spartacus* was an outstanding work and Khachaturyan was awarded the 1954 Lenin Prize; he was the third composer to receive this award, after Prokofiev and Shostakovich.

Khachaturyan's music was astonishingly theatrical and "so easy to dance to," said the Bolshoi Theater choreographer Yuri Grigorovich, "immediately giving birth to a multitude of plastic images." *Spartacus* provided choreographers a wealth of opportunities, for the heroics of the ballet were on a scale never before seen on the ballet stage. They had to create a dance to fit the monumental portrait of Spartacus and find a dance language to suit Khachaturyan's musical language.

*Spartacus* was first staged by Leonid Yakobson, a highly original choreographer who started out on his career in the early 1920s with the intention of modernizing the dance. He staged Shostakovich's *Golden Age* and created gems of dance miniatures which were performed after the Second World War by a dance group he founded. "Even in his earlier years," wrote Dmitri Shostakovich, "his fine ear for music was astonishing."

Yakobson was convinced that the traditional classical ballet could not produce what Khachaturyan's music demanded. He studied ancient Roman vases and the friezes of the famous Pergamon Altar. And he was successful in creating movements quite in harmony with the music, movements so free in their plasticity, though precisely worked out in every detail, that they gave the impression of a spontaneous expression of emotion.

Nevertheless, *Spartacus*, acknowledged as an innovative, inspiring, and exciting ballet, was the subject of long debates and heated discussions revolving mainly around two basic questions: Did the choreographer have the right to abandon the language of classical choreography? And was it right to use Khachaturyan's score only as material to be fitted into a ballet, instead of leaving it unchanged?

The polarity of views on the first question is seen in what the critics wrote. Some claimed that Yakobson faithfully recreated the atmosphere of ancient Rome, just as Leonid Lavrovsky mirrored the epoch of the Italian Renaissance in Prokofiev's *Romeo and Juliet;* others insisted that the spirit of antiquity was conveyed by the dancers not using classical ballet slippers and strict positions for their feet; still others refused to accept the idea of the classical dance being replaced by pantomime, which is so harmful to the ballet.

Yakobson passed away, leaving unfinished an interesting and subjective autobiographical manuscript. This was something of a confession from the artist to his great predecessor, the eighteenth-century French choreographer Jean George Naverre. The three-volume manuscript is headed "Letters to Naverre, or the Stage Life of Spartacus and a Criticism of the Critics." The manuscript sheds light on many of Yakobson's views on art, which did not always find a sympathetic response. Reading between the lines, one sees that the discussion around the choreographic language of *Spartacus* merges with the much broader question of what, finally, dance is all about.

"Many in the theater," wrote Yakobson, "demanded that I apply classical ballet technique, the toe basis of choreography, in this production. I should like to tell those who accuse me of rejecting classical ballet that I have never rejected it, I have always admired it. But I do reject dogmatic classicism."

If by the ballet we mean the unchanging language of movements and stances, then Yakobson's language in *Spartacus* is pantomime. However, if the concept includes the entire range of human feelings and emotions expressed in plastic movement, then his language is undoubtedly the language of the ballet.

There was much to learn from Yakobson, but for such a massive production as *Spartacus* he could not compete with the language of true classical ballet, which had absorbed the experience of ages. And this was the focus of all criticism, shared even by such a supporter of his production as Askold Makarov, who danced the main role. There was not enough of the dance in his choreography, with the result that *Spartacus* lacked a certain heroism, while the theme of the uprising was somewhat diffused from the social viewpoint. Yakobson, a sensitive artist, was well aware of his shortcomings and therefore called the production "Scenes from Roman Life."

The history of art knows many instances when the experimental and innovative emerge only in the process of development, when the "extreme radical" merges with the "extreme traditional," enriching and renewing it.

While Yakobson's choreography in *Spartacus* was at least

debated, his treatment of Khachaturyan's music was unanimously criticized. But here, too, Yakobson was innovative, for he molded a new choreographic approach to the musical material.

Tempestuous arguments between choreographer and composer are not uncommon. Musicians usually consider their viewpoint absolutely logical and infallible, since the composer brings a complete and perfect score to the theater. But, irrespective of the quality of the score, the essence of the choreographer's work remains the same: he must interpret it in dance and this, too, follows its own laws. Consequently the choreographer regards his own logic as equally infallible.

Yakobson understandably made quite a few changes in the ballet. For instance, in the second scene—the Slave Market—all that he left was the Dance of the Egyptian Girl; the Appian Way—the entire fifth scene—was removed. The author's plans and ideas were turned upside-down, with "Scenes from Roman Life" taking over the entire ballet, while the slave uprising became only a vehicle for the plot.

The losses in music could not but result in losses of the ballet's ideological basis. "Few people in the theater will forget the heated debates between Yakobson and Khachaturyan," Askold Makarov recalled. And Yakobson remembered, "The battle started because each considered his own material, i.e., the script and the music, infallible, monolithic, and not permitting of any changes."

Khachaturyan oscillated between indignation and admiration, from thunderous disagreement to submissiveness. "I believe Yakobson to be exceptionally talented," he remarked, "and his miniatures are the work of a genius. He was criticized for being excessively sensual, but isn't the age-old history of art, sculpture, and choreography based on sensuality?"

The fragments of *Spartacus* that Yakobson showed Khachaturyan during rehearsals were more convincing for him than the finished production; he seemed to feel that a production of such scope was too much for Yakobson. Many agreed that although his miniatures and individual scenes were beautifully done, the entire structure was too loosely strung together.

With the passage of time Khachaturyan became more sober in appraising the production, although his general impression had not changed:

The entire ballet should not have been staged on half toes. The toes are to the ballerina what the bow is to the violinist, so why deprive the performer of his best means of expression? Time and again Yakobson would ask for new changes in the score, or else I would learn of changes post facto. I think I was too easily swayed at the time and agreed to certain changes and cuts too hastily. I doubt if I was right. A composer must be firmer and stand on his principles when his stage creations are being produced. I now believe that the short life of the Leningrad production of *Spartacus* was logically predetermined.

The performers in Yakobson's *Spartacus* were excellent. Askold Makarov prepared carefully and seriously for his role. Having read somewhere that when Spartacus first came to Rome he was surprised to see that the men all shaved, he started the tradition of Spartacus wearing a beard, a tradition continued by Vladimir Vasiliev. Aware that his hero figure was weak, Makarov tried to strengthen it but found it difficult to do so because of the shortage of dance material.

Alla Shelest's Aegina was psychologically convincing. "It is not easy to portray a courtesan on stage," she said,

and much more so in the ballet. You must constantly keep in mind that overplaying the role could neutralize it. However, Yakobson's choreography left little opportunity for the performers to improvise. Nevertheless, I was able to snatch a bit of flight from the producers for the scene of the feast, where Aegina makes the only high jump in the entire production.

One of the unparalleled scenes in the production is the concluding Adagio of Spartacus and Phrygia, danced by Inna Zubkovskaya. Phrygia is gentle, plastic, and highly impressive. If Yakobson allowed Aegina one high jump, Phrygia had but one upper support. Phrygia's expressiveness allowed the choreographer to do without the chorus of mourners in the concluding scene.

"When Phrygia, after her burst of despair, rises from her knees," Makarov wrote of the final Adagio,

and stands next to him [Spartacus] like a monument to grief, the theme flares up in the orchestra, bursting into flame and spreading like wildfire from one group of instruments to the other. The grieving violins are followed by the pathetic and vibrating voices of the cellos; the theme grows, embracing the entire orchestra. And I—this may sound naive—I want to rise. I know that my hero is dead, but the very notion that Spartacus may still be alive gives me no peace when I hear the anthem to immortality.

Irrespective of the differences of opinion on Yakobson's production, it was an outstanding event in the theatrical life of Leningrad and of the Soviet ballet as a whole.

Maris Liepa, who later danced the part of Marcus Crassus in the Bolshoi Theater, once remarked that every production of *Spartacus* in the Soviet Union marked a new stage in Soviet choreography; the very possibility of so many interpretations of this score, he said, is proof of its rich artistic content.

Igor Moiseyev produced *Spartacus* in the Bolshoi Theater in 1958. He had no intention of portraying Roman life; his plan was to make the dance stronger and stress man's perpetual striving for freedom, but, most important, to stay with the original score as far as possible, to give the audience the opportunity of "seeing what we hear with such feeling in this passionate musical composition." It was his intention to create a dance which would be the emotional equivalent of the music. He dreamed of a monumental simplicity, of a well-molded, well-developed dance.

But it often happens in art that the final product does not live up to expectations. So it was with *Spartacus*. During a rehearsal for the theater's art council in March 1958, Moiseyev was criticized for using operatic methods of directing, thereby creating the impression that the production was undanceable, and also for the lack of continuity in style; others said there were too few dances for Spartacus and his colleagues and that there was no Spartacus figure as such, although all the action revolved around him. There was no evidence that the Spartacus movement was growing, the entire production was eclectic, and so on.

Choreographer Leonid Lavrovsky voiced extreme dissatisfaction with the production. He also felt that the choice of performers for the main roles was unjustified. Though Khachaturyan was quoted in the theater program as saying that he was satisfied on the whole with the Bolshoi Theater production because his musical continuity was followed, he was not quite happy upon seeing the first rehearsals. "It is too bad that the roles of Spartacus and Phrygia have been played down, something I mentioned to Igor Moiseyev a long time ago," he recalled. "The hero, Spartacus, is deprived of dances and emotions. I imagined Phrygia as a true friend and comrade of Spartacus, but she appears as an incidental figure."

After the Bolshoi premiere, the critics almost unanimously agreed with the opinion of the art council. They praised Maya Plisetskaya for her magnificent portrayal of Aegina and repeated the view that there was more pantomime than actual dancing in the production, and not enough heroism. The Bolshoi Theater production did not have a long run. Someone suggested that Yakobson should stage *Spartacus* in Moscow, but this production, too, was not a success for as Yakobson said later, "I could not get the purity of style that I wanted from the Moscow performers." It was the Moscow version of Yakobson's *Spartacus* that was shown during the Bolshoi Theater's tour of the United States in 1962.

When he was writing the score, Khachaturyan dreamed of producing *Spartacus* in Armenia. "It would make me happy," he wrote, "if my *Spartacus* were to be produced in Erevan immediately after Leningrad."

The ballet was produced there in 1961. The conductor, Aram Katanyan, was able to bring out the passion and dramatic contrasts of the score in bold relief. Yevgeni Changa introduced many interesting choreographic innovations, though Yakobson's version was discernible through it all. It is to Changa's credit that he was able to make Spartacus the hero of the production. The role was danced first by Vanush Hanamiryan and later by the young dancer Vilen Galstyan. The production had its shortcomings, of course. There was an overabundance of pantomime, dynamic effect was achieved not through the dance but by cutting the score, many of the episodes were very fragmentary, and the atmosphere of the entire production was rather grim.

Khachaturyan was irritated by the new changes in his score. His first reaction to the Erevan production was cool and reserved, and later he became openly hostile.

The Bolshoi Theater turned to *Spartacus* for the third time in 1968. "The theater persistently tried to achieve a good, viable production, believing that the failures could be overcome; this undoubtedly was a sign of a correct and creative approach to the problem," wrote Yuri Fayer, the prominent Bolshoi Theater conductor, in his memoirs.

To dare undertake a new production of *Spartacus* a little more than ten years after its Leningrad premiere, ten years during which no theater had been able to create a full-blooded production of this ballet, required a choreographer capable of crossing something of a psychological barrier, one who had implicit faith in the composer's music. Only a very daring choreographer could risk a new production in the Bolshoi, where two previous productions had failed to satisfy the composer. Yuri Grigorovich, the Bolshoi's chief choreographer, was the man for the job.

Grigorovich had studied at the Leningrad School of the Ballet and danced with the Kirov Theater. He was in the cast of Yakobson's production, where he danced one of the gladiators and as a slave was slain night after night. But in Moscow he won the battle, the battle for Khachaturyan's music, which he had always liked. His production was highly successful.

Grigorovich was no newcomer to the Bolshoi. He had already staged these ballets there—*The Legend of Love* by the

Azerbaijanian composer Arif Melikov, Prokofiev's *The Stone Flower*, and Tchaikovsky's *The Nutcracker*. He was familiar with Khachaturyan's music from the war years, when the Leningrad Theater was evacuated to Perm, and was present during the birth of *Gayane*. Later, in Leningrad, he was present on that unforgettable day when Khachaturyan played *Spartacus* for the ballet group of the Theater. "That first impression of the music was colossal," he wrote later.

> It had overwhelming emotional impact; it seemed as though an ancient fresco were being unveiled before our very eyes. Its Armenian coloring gave it a particularly romantic sound. Everything was large, three-dimensional and striking. However, it was already apparent that this would be a difficult ballet to stage. Not because of the music, which seemed to blend naturally with the dance. It was the script, which was overburdened with events and with details that lacked a unified line of development.

The music suggested to Grigorovich that the ballet should be built on classical choreography, by means of "the developed classical dance," he wrote, "not in the traditional style of Petipas but in forms evolving from the experience of the contemporary ballet theater and from life itself." The new book was to place Spartacus and the theme of the uprising at the center of the plot. "Building the new composition was not an easy task," explained Grigorovich, "for we had to drop several roles and be strict in selecting the dramatic situations. In other words, we had to add a great deal which the earlier book had not included."

And so, like his predecessors, Grigorovich adapted Khachaturyan's music to his own ideas about the ballet. "Khachaturyan's music," he wrote, "did not fully coincide with my principles of drama." This may explain the skeptical attitude of many musicians, the conductor Boris Haikin among them, to his ideas. "Frankly, I was among the many who doubted the success of this venture," Haikin later admitted.

For Grigorovich, the backbone of his production was not the score itself, but Khachaturyan's work in general. This brought him closer to the heart of the composer's works than any of his predecessors, and despite his insisting on more radical changes in the original score than even Yakobson or Changa, he did not move farther from Khachaturyan but actually came closer to him. He thus won a strong ally—Khachaturyan himself.

"It was impossible, of course, to make all the changes without the composer's cooperation," wrote Grigorovich.

> The most difficult stage of the work was nearing, for it was necessary to convince Aram Ilych that my ideas were correct and thereby win his support. The "battle for the notes," as we jokingly called it, was about to start. Every request to cut something caused bewilderment, a raising of eyebrows, and a hurt expression; then he would slowly start pulling at his suspenders—a sign of extreme annoyance. Funny misunderstandings occurred. When I showed Khachaturyan the dance of the mutinous slaves and explained the place of the dance in the ballet, he asked, "But where are the women?" I explained that these were gladiators, slaves who had revolted. He thought a few seconds and again asked, "Yes, but where are the women?"*

The press unanimously acclaimed Grigorovich's production. "The strength of this latest production of *Spartacus*," wrote Maris Liepa,

> is in the unbroken continuity of the ballet drama and the music as the starting point of all the choreography. In comments on earlier productions, some critics claimed that the music lacked a single dramatic line of development. This erroneous point of view was brilliantly disproved by Yuri Grigorovich, for it turned out that the complex drama of the ballet lay in the music.

"The choreography of *Spartacus* is built on the laws of a symphonic composition," wrote choreographer Oleg Vinogradov. "The interaction of the different voices, of the many shift-

---

* In earlier productions there were women in this scene.

ing themes, at times confronting each other or blending in harmony, create a dance polyphony, one of the most important characteristics of modern ballet." And Galina Ulanova exclaimed, "If the essence of the new *Spartacus* had to be expressed in one word, I would choose the word 'contemporary.' "

"A performance for four soloists and a corps de ballet," was how Grigorovich characterized his production. Spartacus was brilliantly danced by Vladimir Vasiliev and Mikhail Lavrovsky. Each introduced something of his own, for Grigorovich always left room for improvisation. Prime ballerina Natalia Bessmertnova said of Grigorovich's choreography, "Every movement of his roles is meticulously planned, but every performer can remain himself." His Spartacus was courageous and heroic but capable of lyrical emotions. His romantic soul was expressed in the astonishing flight of his dance. "He reminds me of a soaring falcon—radiant, strong, and reaching for the sky," said Galina Ulanova.

Maris Liepa's Crassus was particularly impressive, for in earlier versions the role was hardly danceable or was played by an extra. "Grigorovich understood (and this was a discovery not only for this production but for the art of the ballet in general)," wrote Liepa, "that the logical truth is to be found in the fact that the strong-willed, courageous, and determined Spartacus could be defeated only by a worthy opponent." One critic wrote of Liepa's performance, "In his dance he embodied what to this day has not been destroyed, and still threatens the world—the cursed desire to trample, crush, and destroy all that is living, all that is free, all that is radiant."

The tragic Phrygia, as interpreted by Ekaterina Maximova and Natalia Bessmertnova, seemed to exude a sea of light, of *joie de vivre*, touching femininity, and selfless love. Nina Timofeyeva's Aegina was surprising in the contrast between her sensual inner world and the faultless lines of her classical dancing. Like Crassus, Aegina seemed to bring the audience back to the present day; as one critic noted, "When she dances her Adagio to something akin to European salon music [a saxophone is heard in the orchestra], one immediately feels that the roots of today's *la dolce vita* reach far back into the past."

And, of course, Suliko Virsaladze's wonderful sets, which immersed the stage in shades of gray and black with splashes of red and yellow, symbolizing blood and gold, added to the dramatic tension.

Gennadi Rozhdestvensky, who conducted, was able to bring out the single musical line in the ballet's development, highlight the contrasts in the emotionally moving scenes between Phrygia and Spartacus, the battle scenes, and the tragic finale. Under his baton Khachaturyan's music became very tragic. No wonder Aram Khachaturyan's works came to be seen in an entirely different light following the third Moscow production of *Spartacus*. However, no matter how strong the tragic or the dramatic element in Khachaturyan's music, the essence of his work remained unchanged. This essence "was always to be found in the composer's outlook, founded on a profoundly optimistic and life-asserting interpretation of our reality," wrote Dmitri Shostakovich.

# The Pedagogue

*Educating a composer is a responsible undertaking from the professional, moral and ethical viewpoints; after all, we must bring up artists, citizens, and future educators.*

ARAM KHACHATURYAN

Khachaturyan began teaching in 1950.

> Sveshnikov, Director of the Conservatory, and Shaporin, the Dean, said it was time I passed on my experience to the youth, in other words, it was time I started teaching. This was said both officially and unofficially. At the same time the Gnessins were urging me to come to them. Since I was a Gnessin graduate, they said, I should be attentive and devoted to them.

The Conservatory had a small enrollment in the composition department that year, not enough to form a class for Khachaturyan. Meanwhile Elena Gnessin, artistic director of the Gnessin School, was insisting that Khachaturyan should start work immediately, especially since Mikhail Gnessin, who taught composition, was retiring. Khachaturyan consented. Not long after, he started teaching at the Conservatory as well.

Khachaturyan was a mature musician by this time, with many excellent works to his credit, and highly respected by musicians, particularly the younger generation. He liked young people and believed in them. "Youth is always forging ahead," he said, "it is so interesting, so tempestuous and spirited. I am always glad to talk with young people, and to teach them."

Khachaturyan was very fond of his students, many of whom became well-known composers. He had in his class such prom-

229

inent contemporary composers as Andrei Eshpai, Edgar Oga-nesyan, Lev Laputin, Mikael Tariverdiev, the Rumanian Anatole Vieru, the Cuban Lopez Jorje, the Japanese Nabuo Terahara, and many others. "It is not the teaching I like so much as the results," he said. "It is a joy to see that my advice can help the student composer find himself, express his musical identity, and cope with the difficulties that arise."

Aram Ilych taught on the fourth floor of the Moscow Conservatory, in the same classroom where Myaskovsky taught in his time. Possibly twice in Khachaturyan's lifetime did opening the door to that classroom evoke such strong emotions: when he first entered Myaskovsky's class in 1930, and in 1950, when he entered the room as the teacher. "It is not possible to 'make' a composer," Khachaturyan would say.

> It would be strange, indeed, if, asked where I worked and what I did, I were to answer, "I teach young composers to compose music." It is impossible to teach someone to compose music. It is only possible to help him learn the secrets of the art. I often tell my students, "Never forget that I am your colleague, your friend and consultant. I will give you advice and talk with you, but it is you who must create, seek, experiment, and choose."

Khachaturyan believed that the teacher of composition was responsible for the formation of both an artist and a citizen, that he must shape the student's world view and his understanding of the meaning of art, as well as encouraging a mastery of musical technique. When he insisted that teachers should be involved in the entire complex of teaching and should check each other continually, he was thinking of the noticeable gaps in polyphony, harmony, and voice theory that he had noticed in young composers. "The practical side is very important in teaching polyphony," he said; "the more a composer composes, the better. The theoretical part is taught in the course of practical work. Only a composer can teach polyphony."

Khachaturyan preferred to work with musicians who were already familiar with the basics. Of Armenian composers who came to Moscow to study, he said they should be coming to "perfect themselves and not to learn the ABC's."

His students were free to consult with other musicians, for he insisted that they be familiar with various schools, trends, and methods. "It is necessary," he said, "to know the opinions of such musicians as Shostakovich, Myaskovsky, Shaporin, Kabalevsky. One or two remarks by any one of them could be more valuable than hours spent with a mediocre teacher. Beginning composers should write a great deal, for that is the age when the imagination is most active," he insisted.

> Young people should reach out for something big and difficult; they should learn to be fanatical about their work, to be patient. A true work of art, like good wine, must be seasoned. A composition should not be made public too soon; it requires a good deal of work before it is made public. Dedication, the ability to patiently and quietly overcome difficulties and swallow one's disappointments are what allow a composer to continue experimenting and aim for success.

Khachaturyan started teaching at a time when Soviet music was shackled by numerous directives and resolutions, a time when the absence of experimentation was most strongly felt, both in the Composers Union and the music schools, especially in the composing departments. Khachaturyan kept insisting that young composers have the right to experiment and make mistakes.

> It is both interesting and gratifying to see how our creative young people are developing. I fully understand their desire to seek new forms, new ways of expressing their individuality, their desire to deal independently with the complex problems of contemporary musical language. I see nothing terrible in a young composer being "too far out." It is much worse when his bubbling young spirit is channeled into producing anything new, so long as it is new.
> Young people naturally tend to reach for the new; they try to find their own way as they grow and they should not be hindered. There can be no art without experimentation; it cannot develop without its ups and downs, without the "cost of production." We teachers must not allow ourselves to become irritated when something doesn't turn out as we wish.

We must be tolerant with young people's creative quest and patiently wait for young talent to succeed.

Khachaturyan followed all these tenets in his work with students, both in the Conservatory and in the Gnessin School. He always respected a student who was able to defend his own music. "I often had to argue with him about my music," Anatole Vieru recalls. "We did not always agree, but he was tolerant of my viewpoint. At that time my artistic evolution provoked frequent arguments in the department of composition, and I recall with affection how intelligently Aram Ilych defended me without relinquishing his own tastes, which did not always coincide with mine."

Khachaturyan also prized intuition and perseverance. Here is what he had to say about the young Soviet postgraduate student Andrei Eshpai, now a recognized composer:

I was particularly attracted by a trait, which I called composer's willpower. I remember him showing me his diploma work—a piano concerto in one movement. I said I thought it was incomplete and suggested that he add at least two more movements. Composers know very well how difficult it is to add to an old composition or rewrite it; it is sometimes easier to write something entirely new. But Eshpai, without a word, quickly composed a second and third movement.

Khachaturyan was always ready to talk or write about former students and postgraduates and usually kept them in his field of vision. For example, his correspondence with Edgar Oganesyan shows how he helped, advised, and encouraged him. He spoke highly of the young composer's Symphony and ballet *Antuni*. "Oganesyan's score is very original," he said, referring to *Antuni*. "It possesses depth, supple beauty, and inspired musical portraits. He is in love with the art of his people, that is why his work is always marked by truly national coloring."

However, it was not only praise that Oganesyan found in these letters, for Khachaturyan was a sincere, professionally exacting, and solicitous teacher. As he wrote Oganesyan,

I am worried about your postgraduate work, or rather the new stage in your creative—and not only creative—biography, a stage which began when you moved to Moscow. I want you to be a first-class composer. I prize your exceptional gifts, but I am not satisfied with your work nowadays. I want to see more depth, more skill, and a very high degree of culture in your work. This also applies to other Armenian composers, myself included.

Khachaturyan prompted Oganesyan on how a composer should behave with musical theaters. "Don't be too bashful or unnecessarily soft. Demand what you will, but choose the correct form, one that is acceptable and reasonable in each specific situation. The composer's will should be felt. Remember, you are not there to ask for favors, you are there to ensure the best possible production of your 'brainchild.' "

Khachaturyan warned Oganesyan of the difficulties he would probably encounter and the opponents he might have to deal with. "Learn by my mistakes," he said. "When everyone was busy writing music I was in despair, grew angry, and so on. I was the only one to suffer from that."

Edgar Oganesyan, now one of the most prominent Armenian composers, author of such well-known works as the ballet *David Sasunsky,* a piano quintet, a cello sonata commemorating Minas Avetisyan, the Armenian painter, and the popular Armenian song "Erebuni," wrote in a letter to a friend, "Aram Khachaturyan played a major and decisive role in my career."

Commenting on the work of the Rumanian composer Anatole Vieru, Khachaturyan said,

He is a wonderful professional; all his works are balanced, there is nothing accidental in them. He is always searching for something and seems to be in a constant state of experimentation. Vieru is one of Rumania's leading composers today. His wonderful Cello Concerto won first prize at an international competition in Switzerland. I always found it interesting to argue and discuss the composer's art with him. Later, too, whenever we met, I rejoiced at the opportunity to associate with Anatole and discuss news of the music world.

For his part, Vieru recalled:

Khachaturyan's relationship with his students reminded me of a doctor and his patients. A student who wouldn't trouble himself to look for something new in form, who preferred banalities, would be advised to "be a formalist." By contrast, Khachaturyan would advise others to be "more banal." "They won't compose banalities anyway," he would say, "but it may soften their rigid style."

Khachaturyan was once asked if the conditions of today's budding composers were any different from those of his own generation. He replied,

Quite different. Budding composers now receive much more; everything comes easier to them, whether it be conditions for work, or getting a new composition performed or published. We were not pampered by national congresses and plenums and special reviews of our work. An ordinary performance of my work in the Small Hall of the Conservatory was a tremendous event for me, and for any other young composer, for that matter.

This is good of course, but sometimes young composers tend to become complacent, mercenary, and overly practical. Khachaturyan could not stand this. "I think the main shortcoming in today's creative youth," he would say, "is that they are excessively practical. They think too soon about what they stand to gain. I think this is belittling; it introduces a touch of utilitarianism in their work and sometimes results in hastily written work."

He cautioned young composers against

lapsing into philistine well-being. It's very bad when a young man, not yet thoroughly familiar with the ways of his chosen field, is already beating a path to the cashier's office.

One should never sit down to compose in the certainty that he will produce good music. The element of doubt should always be present. I remember one Moscow Conservatory student who played my Cello Concerto at an open-air concert. When I came backstage to thank him he said, "Well, now I can record the Concerto!" Such musicians will not go far, no matter how nimble their fingers or how spryly they jog down the roads adjoining art.

I sometimes detect conceit in students who are intent on gaining popularity even at the cost of using in their works cheap gimmicks that appeal to the tastes of the undiscriminating public.

I cannot understand the psychology of these double-faced, even triple-faced composers. They write one kind of music for themselves, another for their teacher, and a third for the films or radio. I consider this immoral— one cannot pray simultaneously to different gods. Myaskovsky, Prokofiev, and Shostakovich gave us many examples of a dignified approach to their work, no matter what genre they were composing in.

Neither could Khachaturyan tolerate insincerity in young people:

People who make mistakes are not hopeless. They can be corrected and success is still possible. But the insincere person is hopeless; the future has nothing in store for him, for he will never understand anything. So if you believe you are unlucky or misunderstood, take a better look at yourself and see if you have done everything possible to be understood. Are you not posing?

Though Khachaturyan did say that today's young composers have it better than his generation, he was aware that they too had serious problems and that it was not easy for them to study.

I sometimes think that ours is a rather callous century. I cannot say whether this is due to the widespread use of machinery or because people are daily subjected to an avalanche of information; I do not know. When I wake up in the morning I never know what to start the day with and involuntarily become grouchier than I really am. There seems to be a need to glorify simple human communication between people and their desire to understand each other's moods, desires, and concerns. I sometimes notice in the Conservatory that a student suddenly becomes an introvert. Later I learn that he is troubled by problems of his own. Being a man of the older generation, this worries me. I think we should all seriously consider instilling in youth a feeling of sociability and mutual trust.

Khachaturyan believed that teaching music, especially composition, was a very special field of human relationships.

Whatever ideas the composer-teacher invests in his student's work are forever lost to him, for he will never be able to use these ideas in his own work. We share our composer's ore, and sometimes even more, with our students. We empty ourselves and—this is no exaggeration—part of our personal wealth goes into the students. But we do not regret it; on the contrary, the more we give them, the prouder we are of their success.

Aram Khachaturyan gave generously of himself; this, in large measure, ensured his success as a teacher and his popularity with students. The atmosphere in his classes was always friendly and relaxed; he liked to joke and could easily establish contact with his students. "Respect," he liked to say, "must be sincere and not based on hierarchy."

His music was often played in class, not as a model of how to compose, but to hear the opinions of his younger colleagues, to argue with them and to tell them about the difficulties he had encountered. And he never failed to hold his students spellbound with stories of his travels abroad.

Whatever his reason for going abroad—as a tourist, as a member of delegations of the Soviet Peace Committee, as President of the Soviet Association for Friendship and Cultural Relations with Latin American Countries, or on a conducting tour, he was always a guest of the conservatory or academy of music of the given country, and he was always pleased to note that musical education in the Soviet Union was on a very high level. "Everywhere I heard enthusiastic comments, everywhere I was told that if a musician had studied in the Soviet Union it meant he was an excellent professional."

In 1978 Khachaturyan headed a panel of judges at the National Competition of Student Composers. During the seven days of the contest they heard over a hundred compositions. He called this competition a "national chair of composition"; he had been dreaming of it for more than twenty years since his first mentioning the idea at the Moscow Conservatory. Now, in the twilight of his career, he was truly happy to see the achievements of the young generation, its spiritual maturity and skill, its desire to produce large compositions, to reflect key events in the country's life, and to develop national folklore. Writing on the results of the competition (his last article for the press), he enthusiastically supported the idea of such events. "Music is dead without live contact with the public. Whether or not a composition will live is a particularly acute problem for the younger generation of composers. Only by testing his work on the public can a young author progress, perfect himself, continue his quest and mature, as both artist and citizen."

At the end of the 1960s, Khachaturyan spoke of the need to sum up the wealth of experience accumulated by the Soviet school of music, particularly as concerns the education of composers. At that time he said this should include such educators as Nikolai Myaskovsky, Reinhold Gliere, Anatoli Alexandrov, Maximilian Steinberg, Vladimir Shcherbachev, Pyotr Ryazanov, and Vissarion Shebalin. Many others could now be added to this list, not the least of them Dmitri Shostakovich and Aram Khachaturyan.

# The 1960s and 1970s

*Aram Ilych is sixty years old. It is difficult to believe it when you hear and play his recent works. His talent is as young and fresh as ever.*

LEONID KOGAN

"Modern and Classical," "The Pride of Soviet Music," "Perpetually Young," "Magician of Sounds"—these are but a few of the articles marking Khachaturyan's sixtieth and seventieth birthdays. The country paid homage to its famous maestro, composer, pedagogue, and public figure.

Khachaturyan was always attracted to the piano. In 1926 he composed the poetic "Andantino," which he later included in both his *Children's Album* and in the 1958 Rhapsody for Piano and Orchestra. His many compositions for piano—the two notebooks of his *Children's Album*, Seven Recitatives and Fugues, a Sonatina and Sonata, the Concerto and the Concerto-Rhapsody"—all marked stages in the evolution of his style.

His fugues showed that it was possible to write polyphonic compositions based on Eastern music. His Sonatina, written after an extended tour of Siberia and the Altai in 1958 with Dmitri Kabalevsky, is dedicated to the children of a music school in the town of Prokopievsk.

Many times, for various reasons, Khachaturyan had been called "a big child," and in the *Children's Album* he showed himself a sensitive psychologist capable of experiencing the joys, sorrows, and curiosity of a child. The collection rates among the finest Soviet compositions for children.

In his recollections of Sergei Prokofiev's compositions for

the young, Khachaturyan discusses the question of children's responses to his music, which is rather difficult to understand. "I am sure they do understand it," he said later. "Their love for this music, its popularity with children all over the world, proves it. Undoubtedly Prokofiev remains Prokofiev without relaxing any of his demands on himself."

In 1944 Emil Gilels, addressing a plenum of the Composers Union, chided Soviet composers for not giving enough attention to enriching the piano repertoire. Fifteen years later, in 1959, Gilels brilliantly premiered Khachaturyan's Piano Sonata. "I recall with great pleasure how Emil Gilels and I worked on my Piano Sonata," Khachaturyan said. "It was very interesting. I would come to his apartment and we would discuss it page by page. He made several excellent suggestions, and I agreed to rewrite some sections."

The opening chords of the Sonata captivate the audience with a sensation of soaring flight; the music seems intent on overcoming all obstacles placed in its way by the changing rhythms. Then follow the beautiful, lyrical slow movement and the fiery Finale, an ecstatic dance reminiscent of the Saber Dance.

In the 1960s Khachaturyan composed his second instrumental trilogy, comprising the concerto-rhapsodies for violin (1961), cello (1963), and piano (1968). Fifteen years after completing his concerto trilogy, the composer turned to the concerto-rhapsody form, for which his talent had a definite affinity; it also corresponded rather closely to the direction in which his national music seemed to develop. "All three rhapsodies," noted Khachaturyan, "are composed in the following form: introduction, cadenza of the solo instrument, the slow theme and its homophonic development, the fast theme and its polyphonic development, and the coda, where both themes merge, enriching each other emotionally and achieving extreme virtuosity."

One Soviet music critic, V. Vlasov wrote, "We are accustomed to festive, dancelike rhapsodies abounding in technical brilliance and virtuoso effects. Khachaturyan's Violin Rhapsody is more of a concerto, a poem, a meditative improvisation."

These words could be applied equally well to the entire trilogy, for which Khachaturyan received the USSR State Prize in 1971. The music of the rhapsodies is variegated, and they all require great technical skill in the performer. "Khachaturyan's music has never left me indifferent," wrote Leonid Kogan. "Its emotion, melodiousness, and originality have always been close to my heart."

Khachaturyan and Leonid Kogan first met when the violinist was just a boy called Lenny. "Some of our photographs evoke heart-warming recollections," Khachaturyan said in later years.

One is a snapshot taken in 1936 of the outstanding German conductor, Otto Klemperer, with Leonid Kogan and myself. It would be more appropriate to call him Lenny, for next to the very tall Klemperer stands a little twelve-year-old boy. Heinrich Neuhaus, then Director of the Moscow Conservatory, was introducing Klemperer to teachers and students. I was already a postgraduate student and was put on display together with my First Symphony. The famed conductor was also shown some very young students from the Conservatory's Central Music School, among them the violinist Leonid Kogan. That was when we first met, and I was astonished by this little musician's phenomenal talent, in whose hands the violin became an enchanting instrument.

I was particularly impressed by how naturally Kogan seemed to play and become one with the instrument, its sound and the music he was playing. This was no pupil playing; it was genuine musicianship. It was difficult to believe that such perfection was possible at such an early age.

I remember Lenny in my house during the war, playing the violin concertos of Mendelssohn, Tchaikovsky, and my own, accompanied on the piano by Naum Walter. The brilliance of his playing was astonishing, the tempos breathtaking, everything sparkled. . . .

We were often brought together under various circumstances in the postwar years. We appeared together in Moscow, in Erevan, and in Latin America. I was able to observe how zealously he practiced—he could go on all day. One could only wonder what he was working at, when everything seemed to come to him so effortlessly and naturally. . . .

Khachaturyan dedicated his Concerto-Rhapsody for Violin and Orchestra to Leonid Kogan: "While writing this composition, I kept thinking of his mighty talent, his interpretation of the music, his amazingly rich sound and technical perfection."

Karene Georgian, a young cellist, was one of the first to play Khachaturyan's Cello Rhapsody. Together they had a highly successful tour of the United States in 1967. With Nikolai Petrov, who premiered the Piano Rhapsody, and Kogan's son Pavel, who like his father performed the Violin Rhapsody, Georgian later toured Moscow and other Soviet cities playing the entire second trilogy. Other interpreters of the rhapsodies were violinist Victor Pikaisen, cellist Natalia Shakhovskaya, and pianist Vladimir Krainev.

Khachaturyan maintained a very warm relationship with the many outstanding performers of his compositions. Having himself started out as a cellist and having turned to conducting in his later years, he was well aware how difficult life was for the musician on tour; he was also thoroughly convinced of the educative mission of the performer.

Aram Khachaturyan would often attend concerts by his favorite musicians—David Oistrakh, Lev Oborin, Svyatoslav Knushevitsky, Leonid Kogan, Emil Gilels, and Svyatoslav Richter—and the ballet whenever Galina Ulanova or Maya Plisetskaya were dancing.

He was extremely demanding of anyone performing his compositions. "It is astonishing how Khachaturyan remembers every note of his score. He can bring every line to life just by talking about it and explaining the precise functions of one or another voice and which of them should be accented," wrote the conductor Boris Haikin.

When you are conducting, the entire musical texture is within his field of vision; if a voice is not brought out sufficiently you can be sure he will comment on it, but always kindly. Every meeting with Khachaturyan and his compositions is something of a challenge for me to improve my skill as a conductor. While his music was a source of great satisfaction to me, I was at the same time learning to interpret a score as the author would want it interpreted.

Khachaturyan did not straitjacket performer or conductor. On the contrary, he applauded those able to "breathe easily" in the pulsating rhythm of his music. David Oistrakh, Lev Oborin, Alexander Gauk, Nikolai Anosov, and Daniil Shafran all confirm this side of Khachaturyan's relationship with performers. Khachaturyan wrote,

> The knowledge that a performer is interested in your work gives you inspiration and a feeling of assurance. It is always pleasant to feel you are appreciated; for a composer it is especially gratifying to be "in demand" by a conductor. Many times, while I was still in the agony of creating, Alexander Gauk would say to me, "Don't forget, your new work has already been included in next season's concert program."

Khachaturyan turned to instrumental composing in the 1930s, when the Soviet performing school was at its best, and his work was to greatly influence Soviet performers of today. "Apart from the beauty of their themes and brilliant exposition," wrote David Oistrakh, "Prokofiev's and Khachaturyan's concertos show signs of innovative daring which furthered the development of the art of violin playing."

Several generations of instrumentalists and dancers were brought up on Khachaturyan's compositions. "Khachaturyan's Cello Concerto has become something of a milestone in my career," Daniil Shafran has stated, "especially in improving my skill and my ability to perform in broad, sustained sequences filled with emotion and strokes of colorful sound." As for the ballet, Maris Liepa has testified that "dancers today owe a great deal to Aram Khachaturyan; the ballets *Gayane* and *Spartacus* have played a tremendous role in my career."

Future generations will no doubt continue to study his music, not only through his scores and monographs on his work, but, even more so, through the masterful interpretations recorded by such eminent conductors as Alexander Gauk and Evgeni Mravinsky, Leopold Stokowski and Serge Koussevitzky, Herbert von Karajan and Paul Kletzki, George Georgescu and Gennady Rozhdestvensky, and by the pianists Lev Oborin, Emil

Gilels, Arthur Rubinstein, and Yakov Fliere, the violinists David Oistrakh, Leonid Kogan, George Enesco, Mikhail Elman, and Henryk Szeryng, the cellists Svyatoslav Knushevitsky, Daniil Shafran, and Andre Navarra, and the vocalists Zara Doluk-hanova and Eva Bandrowska-Turska.

The list of Khachaturyan's works ends with his third instrumental trilogy—sonatas for unaccompanied cello (1974), violin (1975), and viola (1976). In a discussion of these pieces he made the following remarks:

> There are not many compositions of this genre in the world library of music; however, the world-famous solo sonatas of Bach, Paganini, Ysaye, and Hindemith are truly works of genius. So any composer who decides to work in this genre is taking a great responsibility upon himself. I attempted to penetrate as deeply as possible into the essence of my beloved string instruments and to draw from their secret hiding-places as many tonal, dynamic, and emotional qualities as possible. I wanted my musical thoughts, which I attempted to express in modern language, to be spoken by the instruments as vividly as possible, to sing my music in vibrant, living voices.

His love of strings was not the only reason Khachaturyan composed his final trilogy. More important was the general direction of his searchings in the latter years of his life. The cello concerto of his first trilogy already showed signs of his desire for emotional stability, a simple, melodious style; upon its premiere, by Natalia Shakhovskaya, one critic called it the "emotional and dramatic monologue of a contemporary." This desire led him to compose his second trilogy in the concerto-rhapsody form, and when he sat down to write his third, his style had already undergone considerable changes.

"The composer played his violin sonata for me in June 1975, although the manuscript was not yet completed," the violinist Victor Pikaizen recalls.

He was carried away with his own playing and even hummed

to himself. I listened very carefully, trying to feel not only the notes but Khachaturyan's inimitable expressiveness when playing his own music. The many concerts I had played with Khachaturyan conducting had convinced me that any composition studied together with the author invariably sounds different; the opportunity of learning to understand how the composer himself hears his music is invaluable.

I was instantly attracted by the Sonata. In many ways this was a new and somehow unfamiliar Khachaturyan. The music seemed to me very personal, sincere, and highly dramatic. As I seemed to hear a hint of confession in it, it gave me the idea of suggesting to Aram Ilych that he should give it the subtitle Sonata-Monologue; he agreed. I was elated to be entrusted with the first performance of this new work.

Khachaturyan gave me the notes of the Sonata in August 1975, and I played it for him in September. It won unanimous public acclaim at the premiere and the many concerts that followed, here in the Soviet Union and in Bulgaria, Italy, the German Democratic Republic, and other countries. I played in the Sailors Club at the port of Nakhodka [USSR] in 1979, and my program included the Sonata. I was thrilled to see how raptly the audience listened to the music.

Like his three rhapsodies, each of Khachaturyan's solo sonatas is different; this is apparent even in the subtitles he gave them—Sonata-Fantasy for Cello, Sonata-Monologue for Violin, and Song-Sonata for Viola. However, their similarities are greater than their differences, and one feels Khachaturyan knows exactly what each instrument is capable of.

"Khachaturyan's three solo sonatas," commented the contemporary Armenian composer, Tigran Mansuryan,

are something new from the maestro. This is music with exceptionally profound content. Khachaturyan showed that he could compose graphically, sparingly. I was lucky enough to visit Martiros Saryan's studio not long before he passed away, and found him painting . . . potatoes! This was the same Saryan who was always up in the clouds. But here he wanted to delve deeper into the earth, to see it not from above, but close up, in detail. Osip

Mandelstam once said, "A poet is like our memory." I think Khachaturyan's solo sonatas were motivated by the same desire that led Saryan to paint potatoes. We see Mandelstam's "memory" in these sonatas—a huge slice of memory starting with childhood, making the music so surprisingly many-faceted, for it spans memories of the past plus the "I" of today.

So it was that two such prominent composers of our time—Dmitri Shostakovich and Aram Khachaturyan—played their swan songs on the viola: Shostakovich in his Sonata for Viola and Piano, and Khachaturyan in his Sonata for Unaccompanied Viola. Is this a coincidence? Possibly, but there is also something more significant in it. Shostakovich chose the viola because its tone is closest to the sound of the human voice; it expresses the typical chanting and declamatory style of Russian music so brilliantly embodied in his viola sonata. Khachaturyan chose the viola for the tonal qualities that had always intrigued him—the violas play the main theme in the first movement of his Second Symphony and the solo part in one of the dances in *Gayane*. He chose the viola as an instrument best suited to sing of his love for his country, to sing a farewell melody that seems to fade into complete silence. . . .

Khachaturyan composed in almost all musical genres except the opera. He had been fascinated for many years by the idea of writing an opera about the life and work of the Armenian poet-musician Sayat-Nova, one of his favorite poets. Valery Briusov, who translated Sayat-Nova into Russian, wrote, "A nation that has given the world two such talents as Naapet-Kuch and Sayat-Nova has already placed itself forever in the ranks of the cultured nations which create art in conjunction with all of humanity."

In March 1941, Khachaturyan wrote in a letter, "I am writing the ballet *Spartacus* this summer which I will complete in the winter of 1942; I will then write my *Lenin* Symphony dedicated to the twenty-fifth anniversary of the October Revolution, and that same autumn I will start on the opera *Sayat-Nova*."

The war, however, interfered with many of his plans. He

returned to the idea of writing an opera only after the war, and then with many misgivings. Apparently he found it difficult to combine his own music with the songs of Sayat-Nova, and to decide whether to include the original songs or to use them as a basis. He discussed the problem with the Armenian composer Alexander Arutunyan, who later recalled:

> For many years I had nurtured the idea of Sayat-Nova as an opera. I never started work on it because I knew that Khachaturyan, too, was interested in this theme and that he planned to start work immediately after completing *Spartacus*. However, time went on, and Sayat-Nova remained only an idea. When I met Khachaturyan in Erevan in 1963 he told me that he no longer intended writing the opera and advised me to do it. "This opera should be written," he said, "written so that it would be staged in Erevan and in Moscow, in Milan and in Paris." In a letter I received from him later, he wrote, "I envy you your youth, I envy you because you are writing the opera *Sayat-Nova*. You must write it, you can do it. I am certain of this and will wait impatiently for the day when I will hear it."

The fact that Khachaturyan really planned to write the opera is seen in an interview for the Soviet literary journal *Literaturnaya Gazeta,* in which he quotes a letter he received from the writer Alexander Fadeyev. Fadeyev had written,

> If I were a composer I would never really be satisfied with myself (if this were possible in general) if I had not tested myself by writing an opera. I am often embarrassed when our playwrights are criticized in my presence, for I myself have not written a single play and feel that I have not quite done my best. I think you have everything it takes to write a good opera.

It is doubtful he would have quoted this letter had he not intended to write the opera. "Strange as it may seem," Khachaturyan continued in the same interview, "almost ten years have gone by and I have not yet written an opera. There is as yet no literary foundation for the future structure. The minute such a project is mentioned many prominent writers say they are too busy. This doesn't make things any easier for us composers."

Three years later, in a letter to Edward Mirzoyan, he wrote, "The idea of writing an opera continues to haunt me. I am afraid of producing something trite, I am afraid of the Bolshoi Theater. I have some daring ideas but would like to enlist someone, a writer, a director, or just a friend, to help me commit this 'crime'—it would make things easier." The reference to the Bolshoi was, of course, an allusion to its productions of *Gayane* and *Spartacus*, so unsatisfactory to the composer.

As for *Sayat-Nova*, Arutunyan did write the opera and Khachaturyan saw it at the Bolshoi in 1969, when the Spendiarov Opera and Ballet Theater was in Moscow. "Talented music," said Khachaturyan in a letter to the composer, "very sincere and skillfully written. You have immortalized yourself with *Sayat-Nova*. . . . Congratulations and I am glad for our music."

Khachaturyan was always pleased to see any new contribution to the musical culture of Armenia; he viewed his own success as a part of that contribution. This was not vanity, but pride in his Armenia and its culture.

Asked once in an interview what qualities he prized most in a person, Khachaturyan listed tolerance, diligence, and kindness, in that order. He had won wide acclaim and prominence, but he always remained a very ordinary human being with all the faults and merits of any of us. He was demanding of himself and of those he taught; he had his difficulties, doubts, and torments.

Here is how he described his work habits.

*Pioneer*, the children's magazine, once asked me to write about how I work. I agreed, wrote a page, and then stopped to think. Every composition is carried in the mind for some time, long before we start putting it down on paper. You think, plan, check yourself, and watch how, somewhere inside, your future music starts growing like a snowball.

I have already said somewhere that the presence of anyone in the room interferes with my work. I think this is true of most composers. Ours is the kind of profession where we do not like to open our secret laboratories to anyone. Not because we are afraid of being robbed. It is rather the psychology of creating. I can work next to someone not versed in the essence of my profession, say a carpenter or cabinetmaker. But a musician —absolutely not. I have been told many times, and I hope sincerely, that I am a very natural person. If it's true, then the presence of a musician in the room while I am composing induces me to strike a pose internally; I can no longer be natural and the final result is that all inspiration evaporates.

I have noticed that I am more imaginative in the evening and at night. However, I think the time of day is not important. Peace of mind is most important to the composer. The excitement that accompanies the urge to create music is something entirely different. What I mean is the need to put everyday worries and concerns out of your head. I usually work outside of Moscow at the country place in Snegiri. In the past I often worked at our composers retreat near Ivanovo or Staraya Ruza. The season doesn't affect my work, although the fall months with their generous palette of autumn colors seem to put me in a working mood.

The composer composes all the time, not only at the piano. It is a continuous process, whether just walking, resting, or even sleeping. Because this requires concentration, he may seem to be moody, irritable, and not inclined to communicate; this is how he protects the profoundly intimate process of his musical thinking against possible intrusions from outside.

I hear music everywhere, at home and in the streets. My surroundings rarely have any effect on me. I can be composing music mentally while riding in a car, whereas I may return empty-handed from our retreat, where conditions are ideal for composing.

To compose music I do not necessarily need a piano . . . but I do like to have a keyboard, even if only on paper, in front of me. I'm used to that and it's too late to change. It's like having medicine by your bedside; you may not need it, but you feel better just knowing that it's there. . . . Sergei Prokofiev always composed at the piano and was never confined by the instrument, so it is purely an individual matter.

When I was young I improvised more than I do now, and it always stimulated the creative process. Ideas, harmony, passages, all spring to mind from improvisation; you sometimes don't even know how to make use of them. They remain in your mind, to surface when you most need them.

I am sorry to say that I do not make many changes once it's down on paper, although I teach others to do so. I'm always sorry to take apart what has already been assembled, since it is so difficult to compose anew, or to rewrite.

Of all the different stages of composing, I would say that orchestration is my favorite. I enjoy the very process, since one feels a certain peace of mind. The music has already been composed and is no longer eluding you. Still, even here, there is that sense of anxiety.

I do not like to discuss material I am working on, for you never know when it will be completed or what it will be like.

When writing for the stage and screen I like to have a detailed plan of the play, the director's ideas. The stage, the plot, scenes, the actor himself—all help to shape my thoughts.

Nikolai Volkov, who wrote the book for *Spartacus,* was associated closely with Khachaturyan through all the stages of the ballet's production. "You have to know how to communicate with him," he wrote. "I think I learned how. He needs to be told something emotional, he must be prodded all the time. . . . As far as I know he needs to be talked to. It helps him. He immediately goes to the piano and starts singing in his composer's voice."

"I have a mental picture of the orchestra, the conductor, and the audience filling the hall, and it stimulates me," Khachaturyan once said. "It is a very special feeling but I think it is the strongest motive force in a composer's work. There seems to be no end to your ability to create in this state; fatigue becomes a pleasure."

That is how Khachaturyan worked—quickly, energetically, with inspiration, changing little after the first draft was completed. "Nothing can compare with creative inspiration," he said. "It is wonderful both physically and morally. Thoughts and feelings are laid bare and the work is exhausting."

Khachaturyan was once asked what he thought of his own compositions. He replied,

To tell you the truth I like them. But, to be absolutely sincere, I would rewrite many of them if I had the time and the willpower. Some themes I would replace, others I would orchestrate differently, and still others I would rewrite. You know, whenever I hear applause in a hall where a work of mine has just been played, I feel acutely at that exact moment that I could have done better.

This is not the false modesty of a great artist, for in one of his very personal letters written in 1945 he complained, "I regret that I have not yet been able to write a composition that fully satisfies me. What appears on paper is not quite what I hear in my head." And in another letter that same year he wrote, "Fate, fate, it does not allow me the opportunity to fulfill myself. So little has been written, and not quite the way I would have wanted it."

However, it would be wrong to say that he lacked vanity. He was easily hurt, perhaps even offended by criticism. He eagerly accepted endless invitations to attend banquets, anniversaries, and other functions. Yes, he liked the theatrical side of life. But he paid for it, as it took too much of his time, and time, as he said on many occasions, was what he lacked most.

He heard the rumors, of course, that he was resting on his laurels. He said in one interview, "Some think that Khachaturyan has settled down and is now basking in his glory. This is not so and I hope it never happens to me."

He continued to compose profusely while basking in the glow of his fame.

In letters to friends Khachaturyan often complained of his health. This was not just hypochondria. As far back as the 1930s he wrote in letters that he had plenty of energy, strength, and imagination, but added, "I fear only for my physical condition. My health has worsened in recent years."

He had heart trouble and rheumatism, but most of all he suffered from a duodenal ulcer for which he underwent several operations in the postwar years. "I am frightened for the first time in my life," he wrote in 1945. "When I saw the deathly pallor of my face, when my pulse rate went up to 140 and 150, when I was so weak and dizzy I could not stand—I realized I was afflicted with a terrible illness."

Four years later he wrote to Gevork Ovanesyan, "After you saw me in bed I was taken to the hospital [he was there for two months], and then I spent a month and a half at the Academy of Sciences sanatorium. All told, I have been ailing for close to four months. Since it took me only six months to write the ballet *Happiness,* you can imagine what my illness has taken from me."

His health caused sharp changes in his moods, sometimes even to the point of depression.

> Life is like a merry-go-round. At first you start to rise, and then you descend, or, to be more precise, you are dropped. You are dropped because someone else wants to take your place on the merry-go-round. Intellectually speaking, this is dialectics.
>
> My thoughts are black, indeed. I realize that the old should make way for the young, that's only natural. But the young, for their part, should not forget the old.
>
> Tomorrow I will be taken to the hospital for an operation. A serious operation, I hear. How will it go? Will I live through it? I have in mind various postoperative complications.

When he was in such a mood his friends did their best to cheer him up. "Come now," wrote Dmitri Kabalevsky, "no ulcers or other such rubbish can drive artistic ideas out of the mind or heart."

And Khachaturyan went on composing, teaching, and conducting.

He retained his love of life to the very end, although his last ten or fifteen years were difficult. He loved everything about life—its beautiful landscapes, beautiful women, turbulent activity, and the sweet taste of success.

"Nina and I visited the famous and astonishing conductor, Ernest Ansermet," Khachaturyan wrote soon after returning from Switzerland. "He is eighty-four but he moves quickly, smokes, and drinks cognac."

Khachaturyan loved company, liked inviting friends for meals, and was ecstatic when his favorite dish, *dolmas*—minced meat with rice wrapped in tender grape leaves and boiled —appeared on the table. When visiting the Adjemyanov family in Erevan, he loved to telephone Nina in Moscow and tell her about the *dolmas* he ate and the wonderful farina prepared for him at breakfast.

Aram Ilych was always ready to help anyone who came to him for advice or support. One of his last students—Pyotr Bely—still remembers the letter he received from Khachaturyan, so touching in its sincerity, wise advice, and fatherly concern, though written not long after he had lost his wife, Nina Makarova.

Khachaturyan had his idiosyncrasies, his vanity, his shortcomings, but they never overshadowed his outgoing nature, kindness, and soft-spoken manner.

Vasgen, the Catholicos of Armenia, recalls,

I happened to be in Karlovy Vary [Carlsbad], Czechoslovakia with Aram Ilych in the 1960s. We spent a great deal of time together, and took the waters together at the spa. And as before, I was charmed by his fine qualities. But more than anything else, I was impressed by his uninhibited, natural manner. I remember going to the movies with him one evening. It was not a pornographic film but there was an abundance of outspoken sex, so I left the theater. The next day Khachaturyan asked me why I had left. "I felt it to be my duty," I answered. And Aram Ilych, with his characteristic temperament, said, "Well, I think you were wrong to leave; after all, everything on the screen was so natural and then it makes you feel so good!"

Khachaturyan's apartment in Moscow was a good mirror of the man himself. Located in the center of town in an apartment building where many other composers live, it resembled a museum storage room. In the living room stood a beautiful piano, groaning under piles of notes and scores; expensive carpets on the floors, shelves lining almost all the walls holding more notes, books, bric-a-brac and photographs of himself as a boy with his parents, with Nina Makarova and their son, with Yuri Gagarin, with Pope John XXIII, with Queen Elizabeth of Belgium, with Charlie Chaplin; snapshots of Prokofiev, Shostakovich, and many young Armenian composers. In his study the ornate desk was always piled high with letters, answered and unanswered, newspapers, magazines, and a calendar listing appointments and telephone calls for that day; on a chair in the corner lay a flat can containing a documentary film featuring himself, and on the table a huge dish with fruit from Erevan. Vases of flowers filled all the rooms, and everywhere were posters announcing his concerts in Moscow, and many, many souvenirs and mementos of tours, concerts, friends, and foreign countries.

Khachaturyan's seventieth birthday, June 6, 1973, was widely observed. Booklets on his life and work were published in Moscow and in Erevan. There were photographs of him in all the newspapers, as well as articles submitted by the most prominent names in the Soviet art world. Jubilee concerts of his music were held in the Grand Hall of the Moscow Conservatory, the Tchaikovsky Concert Hall, and the Hall of Columns; there was a large exhibition of photographs in the lobby of the Conservatory, and the Bolshoi Theater gave a special anniversary performance of *Spartacus*.

The celebrations continued in Erevan when the composer arrived there at the end of the year, and the Soviet government conferred the title of Hero of Socialist Labor on him for his contributions to the development of Soviet musical art.

Aram Khachaturyan was full of energy at that time, attending concerts of his music, meeting with people from all walks of life in Moscow, visiting music schools for gifted children, etc. It is difficult to imagine where he found the time for it all. He was on the executive committee of the Soviet Composers Union, the Soviet Peace Committee, the Society for Friendship and Cultural Relations with Foreign Countries. He was president of the USSR–Latin America Friendship Society, a member of the art councils of several publishing houses, the radio, and the Melodiya recording company, and lectured on Soviet music.

Add to this his busy conducting schedule, his concerts in the Soviet Union and abroad, and his teaching schedule at the Moscow Conservatory and the Gnessin School of Music.

But Khachaturyan was not getting any younger; also, his health was failing. In a letter to the composer Victor Bely, he wrote that they both should have written at least another ten symphonies each. This was not an expression of regret at having devoted too much of his time to public activities; it was a hint, rather, of his realization that too many public activities hindered composing. Apparently Khachaturyan was aware of this, for earlier he had written to Edward Mirzoyan, who headed the Composers Union of Armenia, "I want you to understand that you are a great talent, that you must compose. You should continue to compose, even if you are appointed Minister of Culture."

Khachaturyan's wife, Nina Makarova, died unexpectedly in 1976. To a friend, he wrote,

> I cannot reconcile myself to Nina's death. They say, "We don't prize what we have until we lose it." This has been a sad and unfortunate year for me. Tomorrow I will complete my postoperative treatment and rest and go home. I am terribly worried that I may not be able to compose. How can I go back to my apartment? I left everything untouched after Nina's death.

Khachaturyan's health was failing rapidly; he was often in hospital. But he never lost his love of life, his bubbling optimism and urge to compose. He had no intention of surrendering to his maladies and even talked of starting a Fourth Symphony and composing an Ode for the one hundred fiftieth anniversary of Eastern Armenia's union with Russia. The British Broadcasting Company planned to make a film about Khachaturyan's life and work in mid-1978.

Five years earlier, on the eve of his seventieth birthday, Aram Ilych had started writing his memoirs. He went to Tbilisi, revisiting places he had lived with his parents and brothers, talking to people who had known his parents, and hearing the sounds of his childhood as he strolled through the narrow, crooked streets of old Tbilisi. "I have taken upon myself the unenviable task of writing my memoirs, because I am urged to share with readers my long experience in helping to build our country's musical culture, to tell of my meetings with the most prominent musicians of our times, and also to touch on some of the problems of art facing Soviet music and myself as a composer and public figure."

Apparently it was this same urge that prompted Aram Ilych to collaborate on a book with this author. It was to be called *With and About Khachaturyan.* We would meet and discuss the various chapters whenever he was well enough and felt up to talking and remembering. He was an animated conversationalist, often jumping from one subject to another as though he sensed that he had little time left and wanted to remember so much. "After I have answered all your questions," he told me, "we must search among my papers for letters from Myaskovsky, Prokofiev, Romain Rolland, and Shostakovich. Since you intend to write a book about me, you must read them."

Khachaturyan was often in bed when I visited him. Talking quietly, he would answer all my questions; as he did so, he would become more and more animated, forgetting his illness. Sometimes we would talk for several hours; at other times he would tire quickly and I would leave.

Despite his worsening illness, Khachaturyan remained active during the last months of his life. In February 1978 he sent warm congratulations to the seventy-five-year-old Matvei Blanter, author of the legendary song, "Katyusha." "In his letter to me," Blanter recalled, "Aram Ilych wrote with feeling about my contribution to Soviet music. The tone of his letter left no doubt that he was aware of the gravity of his illness, but that he passionately wanted to live and was waiting impatiently for June to come, when he too would be celebrating his seventy-fifth birthday."

In February Khachaturyan was worried about the production of *Spartacus* in Erevan. In March he spoke at a meeting commemorating Sergei Prokofiev and in April he checked the notes of his biography taken down in shorthand by the correspondent of a Moscow newspaper. In one of his last letters to Armenia he expressed pleasure at the successes of the Armenian Violin Ensemble.

Aram Ilych Khachaturyan died on May 1, 1978, just one month and five days before his birthday.

Thousands filed by his body as it lay in state in the Grand Hall of the Moscow Conservatory, and, later, in the Opera and Ballet Theater in Erevan.

Khachaturyan had often expressed the wish to be buried in Armenia. After his brother's funeral in 1957, however, he said that the grief of losing his brother had not drowned out the flat notes of the brass band at the funeral, and added, "Bury me in Erevan but bring the orchestra from Moscow."

In seemed that all of Armenia came to Erevan for the funeral. He was buried in the Pantheon next to other great names of Armenian culture—Komitas, Avetik Isaakyan, and Martiros Saryan. As his coffin was being lowered into the grave the orchestra played "Garuna" by Komitas.

Seeing his grave brought to mind these words from a poem by Isaakyan:

> Sleep peacefully, you will be covered with glory.
> New heroes will follow in your wake.
> Armenia will flourish again,
> Your mound will be covered with roses.

# Artistic Principles

*I believe Khachaturyan's music has an invaluable quality, and that is its individual style. You will recognize the composer after the first few bars.*
DMITRI SHOSTAKOVICH

For ages artists have wondered, what is talent? So far there is no satisfactory explanation. To Khachaturyan it meant "technique, world view, personality, honesty, sensitivity, love for and dedication to one's country, and much more."

Among the many questions that arise when studying Khachaturyan's music is the issue of national traits. "The artist and the people. This is a comparison that comes to mind the moment one thinks of the work of Aram Khachaturyan," wrote Dmitri Shostakovich. "He is an artist truly and deeply bound to his people, their musical and poetic heritage, an artist gifted with the ability to see and understand the world, life, and modern history as they are seen and understood by the mind, heart, and soul of the people."

Is Khachaturyan an Armenian composer? He often asked himself this question. "Isn't it the supreme duty of every true artist to feel that he is part and parcel of his people, to draw on the inexhaustible sources of their art and to express their vital interests? I am happy to be an Armenian and a citizen of the great Soviet Union." However, he invariably stressed, "I am not an Armenian composer; I am a Soviet composer."

There is no contradiction here, for he would add, "No matter how I may waver between various musical languages, I remain an Armenian, but a European Armenian, not an Asian Armenian; together with others we will make all of Europe and the whole world listen to our music. And when they hear our music people are certain to say, 'Tell us about that people and show us the country that produces such art.' "

Khachaturyan spoke on many occasions of his great respect for non-European and Asian cultures. The composer was intent on bringing the music of his people to the world and, through this music, to proclaim the virtues of his people, who for centuries had been oppressed.* However, he was vehemently opposed to any lowering of artistic standards when interpreting national art. "Grieg, Verdi, Moussorgsky, and Tchaikovsky were deeply national," he always insisted,

> just as all great music is deeply national. By that I mean art deeply rooted in the people, in the history of the nation, its way of thinking, its customs, the character of the people. The Russian expresses joy in music differently than the Georgian; the Frenchman expresses his nostalgia differently than, say, the Black.
>
> A composition may be national though absolutely void of folklore and, conversely—national melodies inserted in the score do not always signify that the music is national in the best sense of the word.
>
> When I was working on *Spartacus* I tried to make the music general, so to say. And I failed, for it was evident that it had been written by an Armenian. A composer lays his own national "I" at the foundation of any composition—on any theme.

These convictions explain why Khachaturyan could never agree with Mikhail Glinka, who claimed that it was the people who created music while the composer only arranged it. Khachaturyan said,

> We must learn from the people and not merely photograph the styles they create. The composer is master of all that comes from the people and therefore must not look upon national music as a scholar does; he must carry it in his heart, his blood, and his

---

* As early as 1928 Khachaturyan wrote, "The goal of my music is to produce Armenian music, with its wealth of melodies and rhythms, through the prism of European methods of composing, of European musical art, and to make our music the property of all nations."

conscience. The composer must win the right to draw on this source; he must win it by tireless efforts, his love for art, and his knowledge of it.

The painter Martiros Saryan once said, "I am five thousand years old and Aram Khachaturyan is just as old. Artists are made of the biography and history of their people."

The roots of Armenian folk music reach far into the past; they are as ancient and yet as fresh as the roots of Armenian literature, theater, and painting. Khachaturyan was influenced by the art of the *gusans* and *ashugs*, with their own interpretation of old peasant songs and the less ancient urban folklore. The *gusans* were professional singers and storytellers in ancient, pre-feudal Armenia, preceding the *ashugs*. The latter sang and played various instruments, performed in pantomime, recited, and danced. They survived despite persecution by the church, despite centuries of oppression by foreign conquerers. Their art was charged with optimism.

No less important an influence in Khachaturyan's work is the Armenian landscape—the sharp winds of Zangezur that have carved so many manlike figures in the stone cliffs; Sevan Valley with its burning sunshine on the banks of the huge lake, whose ice-cold water reflects the snow-capped mountains. He heard the songs of Armenia and saw its spirited folk dances. However, Armenian culture was not the only influence. "There can be no true development of the national musical culture in any of our republics without studying the musical culture of the Russian people," he said, a conclusion based on his own experience. "It is from the Russian masters," he wrote, "from the perfect creations of Glinka, Borodin, Moussorgsky, Tchaikovsky, and Rimsky-Korsakov that I learned to put my love of country into sound, to apply the musical treasures of the people in my work, and to create truly national compositions. From them I learned to see life's truths and to be humane and truthful in art."

Khachaturyan was, of course, aware of the interest in Eastern music among Russian composers. He always spoke highly of the use of Eastern music in the Russian classics, for example, the *lezginka* in Glinka's opera *Ruslan and Ludmila,* the Polovtsian Dances in Borodin's *Prince Igor,* Balakirev's Fantasy for Piano, *Islamei,* and the Persian Dances from Moussorgsky's opera *Khovanshchina.* "The Russian classics," he said, "were able to portray the Eastern peoples in music with a great deal of respect for them."

In the 1930s, however, when the "Eastern" scores by Mikhail Ippolitov-Ivanov, Maximilian Steinberg, Lev Knipper, and Boris Shekhter were being heatedly discussed, and when Reinhold Gliere, Evgeni Brusilovsky, Alexei Kozlovsky, Vladimir Vlasov, and many other Russian composers were helping the Soviet Union's Eastern republics to develop their national music, Khachaturyan was already able to discriminate between genuine and stylized Eastern music, no matter how talented the latter. He was aware that it was time for national composers to appear who would compose genuine Eastern music. Mikhail Glinka had found a brilliant solution to a similar problem more than a century ago. It was now the job of Aram Khachaturyan and many other Soviet composers.

In the early years of Khachaturyan's career, it was generally conceded that Eastern music had its limitations and was incapable of assimilating anything European.

"At that time," said Khachaturyan, "no one even imagined that the *ashug* themes could ever provide material for symphonic music or that the Azerbaijan epic *mugams* would become the basis of symphonies and concertos." His own compositions, his original music, revolutionized the musical culture of the East.

He always defended the artist's right to be innovative and individual, his right to experiment on the basis of firm ideological and esthetic convictions. "I am for innovation, originality, freshness, and inventiveness. Everyone should strive for his own style and manner," he said. "A real artist should always respect those of his colleagues who do not mark time, who are pathfinders (even if they are not always successful); he should be thoroughly familiar with all the latest trends—even the most unorthodox."

These comments reflect the convictions of a great artist; Khachaturyan invariably acted on his convictions when judging the works of his colleagues, even "way out" composers who had been severely criticized by professionals. This was the case with Shchedrin's *Poetorio*. Khachaturyan offered several suggestions but on the whole spoke highly of this work. He also applied these convictions in his own works. Because Armenian music is basically monophonic, both Komitas and Spendiarov believed it would be difficult to harmonize Armenian folk music, that it was more susceptible to polyphonic arrangement. Though Khachaturyan used various forms of polyphonic composition, he preferred those that best accented the possibilities of Armenian melodies. It was from them that the composer borrowed the manner of developing variations both in the main melody and the accompanying instruments. "A study of Khachaturyan's work has shown," wrote the critic Chebotaryan, "that his wealth of melodic gifts is seen not only in his ability to create a vivid, inspired theme with a deep content, but in his ability to discover numerous opposing lines no less expressive than the theme itself."

Khachaturyan's musical thinking is polymelodic, and in his scores we often hear an excellent blend of two or even three melodic layers, for this is his basic polyphonic manner, the very essence of his polyphony. In the first movement of his Second Symphony we simultaneously hear the secondary voice and a counterpoint of the main voice, which in the third movement combines the theme of the Lament and the Dies Irae.

The same ideas are behind Khachaturyan's discoveries in harmony, also based on national music. He took the classical European harmony based on thirds and enriched it with the seconds so common in Armenian music. When Khachaturyan was still a student Myaskovsky noticed his inclination to develop the aspects of Armenian harmonic organization, the manner of playing and even of tuning national instruments, which he found to have something in common with the experiments of progressive composers of his day.

Khachaturyan's music offered visual proof that Eastern

music was highly responsive to symphonic development, even predisposed to it. "Khachaturyan has done a great service to the musical culture of the Armenian people," said Dmitri Shostakovich. "His contribution to the musical culture of the entire Soviet Union is just as great, for he was the first of our composers who irrefutably and convincingly showed the many ways of symphonizing the music of the Soviet East to express strong and dramatic emotions, great patriotic ideas, and profoundly sincere sentiments."

Khachaturyan's instrumental compositions were likewise innovative. We know from the history of medieval Armenian music that the itinerant bards and minstrels of many Eastern countries originally came from Armenia. The professional works of composers from Armenia and all the Transcaucasus, for that matter, were mainly operas and vocal compositions. Armenian music became known through the songs of Komitas and the operas of Tigranyan and Spendiarov; Azerbaijanian music through the operas of Gadjibekov, and Georgian music through the operas of Paliashvili. Spendiarov's *Erevan Sketches* and the orchestral selections from his opera *Almast* are almost the sole exceptions. It was Khachaturyan who blazed a trail in the symphonies and instrumental music of the Soviet East by writing the first compositions that transcended the national framework.

In order to create the Armenian symphonic style he was aiming for, Khachaturyan had first to adapt the classical European forms to the specific demands of Armenian music:

I wanted to interpret the vast variety of folk music, its sounds, rhythms, and images, in order to create something new. I probably would not have succeeded had I attempted to squeeze the characteristic sounds and rhythms of folk music into the Procrustean bed of European forms, for instance of the classical sonata form. With folk sources as a starting point, I sought to create my own form, something of a new alloy.

He was not always successful in this, for he wrote in 1974,

When I turn to some of my earlier compositions I now see their shortcomings, especially as concerns form. The point is that my musical language contradicted the classical European schemes. I felt I could not fit into the procrustean bed [one of Khachaturyan's favorite expressions] of the canons and reluctantly obeyed them. That is why one has the impression of a certain awkwardness of form. Perhaps I should have diverged more from the models and been more resolute in molding my own form.

From the traditional Eastern music Khachaturyan borrowed improvisation. "Improvisation is acceptable," he noted, "when you know exactly what you are after. Only then does it spur the imagination, urge you to work and create a well-balanced structure of the whole."

Khachaturyan often complained that the Saber Dance had become his emblem. "I would prefer some of my other compositions to be as popular as the Saber Dance," he said. "When I was visiting Sibelius in Finland and Arthur Bliss in London, we agreed that a composition sometimes becomes famous unexpectedly. When the name Khachaturyan is mentioned the Saber Dance immediately comes to mind. This may be pleasant, but it hurts a little, too."

But it was not all as simple as Khachaturyan would have us believe. Though only a short orchestral piece, the Saber Dance tells us a great deal about the composer's love of rhythms and their various combinations, a love from his childhood days. Take any of his scores and you will immediately find the rhythms so typical of him. Rhythms are his paints, his images, his means of dramatic development. "Even in the most acutely hypnotizing episodes," wrote Shakhnazarov, a critic,

the barbaric and primitive that one hears in the rhythms of Stravinsky, Prokofiev, and Bartok are not characteristic of Khachaturyan. His rhythms are frenzied, a sweeping temperament, an overbearing force, but it is the frenzy of the temperamental and fiery folk dance. Apparently the dominating factor of this sensation is the presence of a lively and expressive tonal quality, always present in Khachaturyan's music, even in those episodes (such as the Saber Dance) where the entire structure is determined by the rhythm and dynamics.

"The human heart is the source of all creativeness," said the Armenian writer, Ovanes Tumanyan. This is very true of Armenian music, music created by the people, by Komitas, Tigranyan, Spendiarov, and Khachaturyan. For Aram Ilych the lyrical is not just a means of expression, it is his way of looking at the world and expressing what he sees in sound. "The lyrical plays a big role in my music," he said. "It reflects a very important side of my work."

One of the best expressions of Khachaturyan's emotional generosity is his treatment of the orchestra. His splurging of orchestral colors led the critic Boris Asafiev to call him "a Rubens of music. It is a musical feast. There is something of Rubens in the splendor of the melody delighting in life and in the uninhibited exuberance of the orchestra." And Dmitri Shostakovich said, "Few modern Soviet composers have such a command of the resources of a symphony orchestra as Khachaturyan."

In all these comments on Khachaturyan's work one comes upon the opinion that the brilliantly colorful, gigantic musical carpet which the composer presented to Armenia does not coincide with the rather harsh landscape of that country, where the rocky soil makes life so difficult for the farmer. But what about the Armenian painter Martiros Saryan, whose canvases are just as colorful, if not more so?

That chance meeting on the road between Khachaturyan and Saryan in 1921, mentioned above, led to a strong and lasting friendship. "Saryan has always been very kind to me," Khachaturyan said once. There were many reasons for their mutual attraction. Both were educated in Moscow. The outstanding Russian masters Valentin Serov and Konstantin Korovin were among Saryan's teachers. "He was a man of great intellect, with a big heart, a wonderful soul, and boundless charm," said Khachaturyan of Saryan. Of his paintings he said, "Whether he was painting landscapes [Armenian], or in-depth psychological portraits, he always remained a national painter.

One is always captivated by that surprising combination of severity, restraint, and remarkable emotional generosity one feels in the Armenian landscape and the people."

Saryan spoke of Khachaturyan in almost identical words.

When I think of Khachaturyan's works I imagine a mighty, beautiful tree whose strong roots go deep into the land, absorbing the best it has to offer. The strength of the land lives in the beauty of its fruit, its leaves, and its majestic crown. Khachaturyan's compositions embody the best feelings and thoughts of his people, their deep internationalism. The fact that the composer brought to his palette the treasures of national music is not the only precious thing about his works. It is not uncommon in art, particularly in the field of music. For me his greatest achievement is his generalized reconstruction of the people, his inspired picture of his native landscape and the spirit of the people.

What brought these two artists even closer together was the pure musicality of Khachaturyan's works. "You ask if I like music?" wrote Saryan. "What a strange question! It is not possible to live without music." Saryan loved Armenian folk music, the plaintive sound of the *zurna,* the *kemancha,* and other instruments; he often hummed his favorite operatic arias while working in his studio.

Saryan first painted the composer in Moscow in 1944, showing him at the peak of his career, soon after the premiere of the Second Symphony. The dominating color is red, with an intricate Armenian design in the background.

"His paintings are like music," said Khachaturyan. "You feel the urge to compose when you look at his paintings. His landscapes are like symphonies."

In 1963, when Khachaturyan was sixty years old, Saryan painted a second portrait, this time in his Erevan studio. Speaking at the birthday celebrations, the painter said, "I was told that Aram Khachaturyan had turned gray. That's not true. When I painted you the first time your hair was black; now I see you have turned blue-black. I say this as a painter. But if I have the luck to see you turn gray, I shall paint your third portrait."

The painter did a third portrait sooner than he expected. This was while Khachaturyan and Saryan were staying at the Armenian retreat for composers in Dilijan. As Khachaturyan recalled,

> Besides just being friends, Martiros and I were bound by our concern for his son Lazar, who before the war had studied at the Gnessin School of Music under Vissarion Shebalin. After the war, in which he fought, he studied at the Moscow Conservatory under Dmitri Kabalevsky, Dmitri Shostakovich, and Anatoli Alexandrov. He is a talented composer; I especially like his symphony, *Armenia,* which was inspired by four of his father's paintings.

When Martiros Saryan died in 1972, Aram Ilych attended the funeral together with his wife Nina and their son. "Armenia's sun has set," he said then. "Saryan's death is a great loss for the entire nation and all of Soviet art. His was a great life. His great heritage will be a guiding star for painters, for Soviet painters, especially Armenian painters."

Some people contended at one time that Saryan's genius weighed on other Armenian painters, particularly those of the younger generation, hindering the development of their original art. "I can only say," Khachaturyan commented,

> that some people love to create idols. This is terrible. I know, for instance, that though Saryan is half a century older than Minas Avetisyan, he takes a fatherly interest in him; he thinks highly of his individual manner, and his entire attitude to him is that of one artist to another, to an equal. I have heard that the same has been said about me. Only the makers of idols could believe that traits lacking in the style of their idols have no artistic value.

As far back as the 1950s Saryan himself said, "My true followers will create canvases which do not resemble my own." That is what happened in Armenian painting, and in music.

Aram Ilych loved bright colors, flowers, and fruits. "I think

I would have been very happy if I had become a botanist or a gardener instead of a musician," he once said. "These professions are closely associated in my mind with the profession of a musician, which also involves colors and aromas."

Khachaturyan greatly influenced his contemporaries. This is especially true of the younger generation of Armenian composers. Two tendencies may be discerned in his attitude toward them—one, close attention to their work and interest in each new composition, and two, his own determination not to lag behind the younger generation, its ambitions, and the level of their work. "Any artist who believes that there is nothing to learn from one who has not yet attained fame, or someone less experienced, is neither wise nor will he achieve much, no matter how talented he may be."

Khachaturyan learned from Arno Babajanyan's Trio, Edward Mirzoyan's Symphony, Alexander Arutunyan's opera *Sayat-Nova,* and the works of many other Armenian composers. His views on music were objective and he could be critical of Armenian composers, and of himself as well. "I want to see compositions of greater depth, skill, and culture. We Armenians," he said, "have been too direct. Our music now has such a strong foundation that it is time we pursued philosophical ideas, and tried for a monumental and refined manner of expressing our thoughts. . . . [T]his applies to all Armenian composers, myself included."

Khachaturyan was not indifferent to what the younger generation thought of his work. He greatly desired that whatever he had pioneered in his art be recognized as his contribution. After all, the experience had too rapidly become accessible to many composers, not only in Armenia. "I want the little that I have discovered to be recognized as mine. I want my colleagues, particularly my Armenian colleagues, to accept this and never be embarrassed to speak about it. Recognizing the priorities of others means striving to be a trailblazer yourself."

Khachaturyan yearned for genuine cooperation with the younger Armenian composers.

I am pleased to see that the young composers understand my

relationship with them, that we are working together in a common cause and that while learning from me, they are teaching me at the same time. We older composers can learn from Babajanyan's Trio, although it is possible that he had developed something in it already expressed by an older colleague before him. Therein lies the strength of Soviet music. We supplement each other. The Armenian national school of music is being developed. Many volumes will be written about our epoch. I consider myself an active participant in the building of the new Armenian musical culture.

In the post-Khachaturyan period, Armenian music experienced a certain synthesis of the traditions emanating from two of its giants—Komitas and Khachaturyan. Two outstanding artists, so similar and yet so different. Komitas, who relied mainly on Armenian peasant folklore, Khachaturyan—on urban folklore; Komitas, who believed in the self-evident value of folk melodies; Khachaturyan, who considered them material from which to draw inspiration; Komitas, who epitomized extreme emotional restraint, Khachaturyan—a feast of emotions and colors. And yet, both had a common goal—to create a national, professional musical culture. So it is not at all surprising that a Komitas and a Khachaturyan tradition may be seen in the work of Armenia's composers today. These two traditions do not clash in the works of such modern Armenian composers as Edgar Oganesyan, Avet Terteryan, and Tigran Mansuryan. That is how it has always been in the history of music; time is more tolerant than the human mind; it irons out the differences and brings out the similarities. We have forgotten the heated debates among the contemporaries of Brahms and Wagner, each group defending their idol; the imagined incompatibility of the St. Petersburg and Moscow schools of Russian music in the nineteenth century; the differences between the Big Five and Tchaikovsky which Sergei Rachmaninov dispelled so brilliantly—all are now forgotten.

The national basis of Khachaturyan's music gave it international significance; it provided a key to the discovery of various forms of national art and afforded an opportunity to judge the balance between the national and the international, for in his art Aram Khachaturyan always remained a convinced internationalist.

There are still critics today who insist that non-European cultures must protect their "innocence" and should consider themselves fortunate if they are successful in remaining "virginal." Khachaturyan objected strongly to this view. "I believe," he once said,

> that not only the republics of the Soviet East, but the ancient musical cultures of Asia, Latin America, and Africa as well are confirmation of the fact that art lives in movement, in its improvement by modern progressive social and artistic tendencies and in the influence of related composing schools on each other. Isolation is a false road; it artificially retards the development of all musical cultures, irrespective of ethnological background.

The musical culture of the many nationalities inhabiting the Soviet Union confirms this. Take for example the composing school of Azerbaijan, formed on the one hand by the national classic *Uzeir Gadjibekov* and on the other by the works of Dmitri Shostakovich, who taught the prominent Soviet composer Kara Karaev, author of such well-known ballets as *The Seven Beauties* and *The Path of Thunder*. Kara Karaev taught several generations of Azerbaijanian composers and musicians. "Aram Khachaturyan," he said, "carried on the work of his predecessors—the older generation of Transcaucasian composers—and opened a window into the wide world of musical culture for the music of the Soviet East; at the same time he started a new trend in Soviet music, thereby giving invaluable aid to many composers who started out much later."

The test of a great artist is his ability to interpret the realities of his day, to create original and inimitable reality in his works. It is also the extent to which the trends in his art remain a definite trend in the development of art generally. Finally, it is the extent to which his heritage remains a source of discoveries for new generations. Time, of course, is the best if not the sole judge. However, this does not mean that we cannot reach our own conclusions; some of them have already been expounded in preceding portions of this book.

In his book *The Psychology of Art,* the Soviet scholar Lev Vygotsky writes,

> Art would have a dull and ungrateful task if its only purpose were to infect one or many persons with feelings. If this were so, its significance would be very small, because there would be only a quantitative expansion and no qualitative expansion beyond an individual's feeling. The miracle of art would then be like the bleak miracle of the Gospel, when the five barley loaves and the two small fishes fed thousands of people, all of whom ate and were satisfied, and a dozen baskets were filled with the remaining food. This miracle is merely quantitative: thousands were fed and were satisfied, but each of them ate only fish and bread. But was this not their daily diet at home, without any miracles?
>
> ... The miracle of art reminds us much more of another miracle in the Gospel, the transformation of water into wine. Indeed, art's true nature is that of transubstantiation, something that transcends ordinary feelings; for the fear, pain, or excitement caused by art includes something above and beyond its normal, conventional content. This "something" overcomes feelings of fear and pain, changes water into wine, and thus fulfills the most important purpose of art. One of the great thinkers said once that art relates to life as wine relates to the grape. With this he meant to say that art takes its material from life, but gives in return something which its material did not contain.*

I believe that this quotation is quite appropriate when discussing Khachaturyan. Artists have always differed; some wish to reflect acute psychological conflicts, dramatic collisions, the tragic side of life, split personalities, and the ever-present need to choose between feelings and obligations, rights and duties, desires and opportunities. Others believe it to be their mission to glorify the universe and man's lofty thoughts and emotions.

* L.S. Vygotsky, *The Psychology of Art.* Cambridge, Mass.: M.I.T. Press, 1971, p. 243.

Naturally, this is extremely loose; it is highly doubtful that any artist has ever represented one or the other group in its "pure" form.

The dominating feature in Khachaturyan's art was undoubtedly his paean to the beauty of life, the joy of being, the pleasure of creating, and the purity of human feelings. It is clear that an artist of Khachaturyan's caliber certainly faced the problems of "overcoming," "transforming," "brightening"—in other words, the problem of "water" and "wine." This is most evident in his three instrumental trilogies, his Second Symphony, and his ballets. These works allow us to say that Khachaturyan is here to stay. "It is difficult to imagine Soviet and world musical culture without Khachaturyan," said Dmitri Shostakovich. "Khachaturyan's music, his rhythms, riot of colors, love of life and of country, love of our land and our people," said Rodion Shchedrin, "have made the life of every one of us richer and fuller." "Khachaturyan's music and his principles," explained Kara Karaev, "contain many still unutilized opportunities. Many elements of his style can be developed and I am certain that those who have taken the place of the older masters will do it." That outstanding figure in the Indian world of music, Narayan Menon, believes that Khachaturyan's works are like a beacon to Asia's young and ambitious musicians, who strive to compose music with European means of expression.

If, as some scholars claim, the twentieth century will go down in history as the age that ended the isolation of European and non-European artistic traditions, then it will go down in the history of music with such names as George Gershwin, Hector Villa-Lobos, and Aram Khachaturyan.

For Khachaturyan's eightieth birthday in June 1983, a Khachaturyan museum will be opened in Erevan; in Moscow the first volumes of his *Collected Works* will be published, together with recordings of his compositions.

Historians long believed that Erebuni, the ancient capital of Armenia, dated back to the tenth or eleventh century B.C. Recent archeological finds, however, have pushed that date back another fifty centuries at the very least.

In his *Joseph and His Brothers,* Thomas Mann wrote that paradise was located in Armenia, in the region of the Araks river. However, this paradise has too often turned into a hell on earth for its people. For thousands of years Armenians have been defending their freedom and independence from invaders, often having to leave their country to avoid physical extermination.

Suffering has made them strong but not bitter. The Armenians built and rebuilt, created and yearned for knowledge. "Know wisdom, fathom the words of genius," were the first words written sixteen centuries ago by Mesrop Mashtots, formulator of the Armenian alphabet.

Today the Matenadaran library in Erevan is a huge depository of ancient Armenian manuscripts. It is not just another library; it is a priceless collection of rarities, a symbol of Armenia, a pantheon of its thoughts, and a monument to its courage.

"Was it conceivable to enslave a people who learned from their mountains never to bend their backs, a people who assimilated the severe and well-proportioned beauty of their architectural monuments, who studied their cuneiforms and parchments and never forgot their source?" asked the Armenian writer Gevorg Emin. This was a nation which, after losing close to two million of its people in the genocidal slaughter at the turn of the century, started building a new life and drew up a master plan for its capital that would accommodate 200,000 inhabitants, although no more than 30,000 lived there at the time.

The years that have elapsed since then are excellent proof that the people's social optimism has been repaid a hundredfold. Not just because that master plan had to be revised three times to accommodate the city's present population of three million, but because Armenia has made a tremendous economic, industrial, and cultural progress; because in the twentieth century Armenia has given the country many outstanding names in engineering, medicine, astronomy, mathematics, architecture, literature, art, and music.

And among the many who have made Armenia known far beyond its borders is Aram Khachaturyan.

# Bibliography

## Speeches, Interviews, Articles, and Reviews by Aram Khachaturyan

Notes to the Association of Fellow Countrymen of Transcaucasian Students in Moscow, 1926. Manuscript. The Armenian Central State Archives of the October Revolution and Socialist Construction (CSAOR ArmSSR), Erevan.

Autobiography (1928–1929). Manuscript. The Charents Museum of Literature and Art of the Armenian SSR, Erevan.

Speech at the discussion of the concert given by student composers of the Moscow Conservatory, at the Chair of Composition, April 23, 1933. Manuscript. The USSR Central State Archives on Literature and Art (CSALA), Moscow.

Speech at the joint meeting of the Chair of Composition and Chair of History and Theory, the Moscow Conservatory, January 20, 1934. Manuscript. CSALA.

Thoughts and Impressions. *Sovetskaya Muzyka*, 1938, no. 4.

Feelings of a Citizen. *Sovetskoe Iskusstvo*, December 2, 1938.

How I Worked on the Ballet *Happiness*. In: *The Armenian Opera and Ballet Theatre*, Moscow, 1939.

The Ballet *Happiness*. *Izvestiya*, October 20, 1939.

Jubilee of R. M. Gliere. *Pravda*, February 8, 1940.

Our Creative Plans. . . . Aram Khachaturyan. *Sovetskoe Iskusstvo*, December 19, 1941.

Message to the Company of the Kirov Theatre. *Za Sovetskoe Iskusstvo*, January 4, 1943.

Composers' Contribution. *Vecherniaya Moskva*, February 25, 1943.

Symphony Number Two. *Literatura i Iskusstvo*, January 8, 1944.

Speech at the Plenary Session of the Organizational Committee of the USSR Union of Composers, 1944.

Symphonic Music. All-Union Radio program, October 25, 1945. CSALA.

Report at the Plenary Session of the Organizational Committee of the USSR Union of Composers, 1946. Shorthand record. CSAOR ArmSSR.

275

To the Motherland. Speech on the All-Union Radio. CSALA.

Three Arias. *Vecherniaya Moskva*, March 5, 1946.

Speech at the Conference of Soviet Musicians in the Central Committee of the All-Union Communist Party, January 1948. In: Conference of Soviet Musicians in the Central Committee of the All-Union Communist Party. Shorthand record. Moscow, 1948.

In Armenia. *Sovetskaya Muzyka*, 1949, no. 8.

Musical explication to the film *The Battle of Stalingrad* (second part), 1949. CSALA.

The Ballet *Spartacus*. *Sovetskoe Iskusstvo*, January 9, 1951.

My Concept of the National in Music. *Sovetskaya Muzyka* 1952, no. 5.

Review of the Creative Work of Soviet Composers. *Literaturnaya Gazeta*, February 14, 1953.

Composer's Complaint. *Iskusstvo Kino*, 1953, no. 8.

On Creative Endeavor and Inspiration. *Sovetskaya Muzyka*, 1953, no. 11.

Dmitri Shostakovich. *Sovetskaya Kultura*, June 1, 1954.

Exciting Problems. *Sovetskaya Muzyka*, 1955, no. 7.

Music for the Screen. *Iskusstvo Kino*, 1955, no. 11.

British Impressions. *Sovetskaya Kultura*, December 13, 1955.

From My Memoirs (N.Y. Myaskovsky). *Sovetskaya Muzyka*, 1956, no. 5.

Eminent Composer of Our Day. *Izvestiya*, September 26, 1956.

Before the First Night of *Spartacus*. *Vecherniy Leningrad*, December 16, 1956.

From My Memoirs (N. Y. Myaskovsky). In: *N. Y. Myaskovsky. Articles. Letters. Recollections*, ed. S. Shlifshtein, Vol. 1. Moscow, 1959.

How I Worked on the Ballet *Spartacus*. *Moskovskiy Komsomolets*, March 29, 1958.

In Pursuit of the Perfect. *Sovetskaya Kultura*, April 24, 1958.

Radiant Talent. *Literatura i Iskusstvo*, April 29, 1959.

For Creative Friendship, for Musical Progress. *Sovetskaya Muzyka*, 1960, no. 2.

My Republic's 40th Anniversary. *Literaturnaya Armenia*, 1960, no. 6.

Creative Work in the Soviet Union. *Nedelia*, November 5, 1960.

Some Thoughts about Prokofiev. In: *S. S. Prokofiev. Materials. Documents. Recollections*, ed. S. Shlifshtein. Moscow, 1961, 2nd rev. edition.

A Few Words about My Teacher. In: *M. F. Gnessin. Articles. Memoirs. Materials*, ed. R. Glezer. Moscow, 1961.

Inspiration, Temperament, Mastery. *Sovetskaya Kultura*, December 5, 1961.

N. Y. Myaskovsky. 80th Birthday Anniversary. *Sovetskaya Muzyka*, 1961, no. 4.

Brilliant Artist, Outstanding Personality. *Sovetskaya Muzyka*, 1961, no. 11.

Brilliant Musician. In: *K. S. Saradjev. Articles. Recollections*, ed. G. Tigranov. Moscow, 1962.

Melody Is the Soul of Music. *Sovetskaya Kultura*, March 17, 1962.

Feeling Proud of Our Motherland. *Sovetskaya Kultura,* November 6, 1962.

Says Aram Khachaturyan. *Sovetskaya Muzyka,* 1963, no. 6.

You Are Dearest of All to Me, My Country! *Literaturnaya Gazeta,* June 6, 1963.

Thoughts about Music. *Kommunist* (Erevan), November 17, 1963.

Greetings to the Young Enthusiasts. *Smena* (Leningrad), December 19, 1963.

A Man with a Heart of Gold. In: *Reinhold M. Gliere. Articles. Recollections. Materials,* ed. D. Person & V. Bogdanov-Berezovsky. Moscow & Leningrad, 1965.

Your Talent Does Not Wear Out with Time. Letter to D. D. Shostakovich. *Muzykalnaya Zhizn,* 1966, no. 17.

Dedicated to the October Revolution. *Sovetskaya Muzyka,* 1967, no. 11.

About Komitas. Armenian TV program. The Kevorkov family file, Erevan.

Talks with Masters. Aram Khachaturyan. *Muzykalnaya Zhizn,* 1970, no. 3.

Youth Is Our Future. *Muzykalnaya Zhizn,* 1971, no. 6.

Music and the People. *Kultura i Zhizn,* 1971, no. 6.

Sixth Feeling. *Ogonyok,* 1971, no. 43.

We Met in Arbat Street. On the 100th Birthday Anniversary of Zakharia Paliashvili. *Zaria Vostoka* (Tbilisi), October 12, 1971.

About Saryan. Interview to Radio Armenia. The Armenian State Archives of Cine-Photo-Phono Documents, Erevan.

The Sounds of Music. *Literaturnaya Gazeta,* May 1, 1973.

From My Memoirs. Literary version by G. Shneerson. *Sovetskaya Muzyka,* 1973, no. 6.

My Hero Is Spartacus. *Sovetskaya Rossia,* June 6, 1973.

Vital Traditions of the Socialist Arts. *Sovetskaya Muzyka,* 1974, no. 4.

A Life Dedicated to Art. *Izvestiya,* May 30, 1974.

Guest of the 13th Page. Aram Khachaturyan. *Nedelia,* 1975, no. 8.

In Harmony with the Time. *Sovetskaya Moldavia* (Kishinev), May 11, 1975.

Eternal Beauty Is Alive. *Kommunist* (Erevan), September 12, 1975.

My Party Task. *Sovetskaya Kultura,* November 4, 1975.

Friend of Soviet Music. In: *Alexander Vasilyevich Gauk. Memoirs. Selected Articles. Recollections of Contemporaries,* ed. L. Gauk, R. Glezer, & Y. Milshtein. Moscow, 1975.

His Name Has Gone Down in History. *Sovetskaya Muzyka,* 1976, no. 10.

Addressing the Youth. Speech at the 4th Plenary Session of the USSR Union of Composers, dedicated to the creative work of the youth. *Sovetskaya Muzyka,* 1977, no. 5.

Dialogue about Life, Profession, and Art. Aram Khachaturyan—Boris Petrovsky. *Moskva,* 1977, no. 11.

David Oistrakh. In: *D. F. Oistrakh. Memoirs. Articles. Interviews. Letters,* ed. V. Grigoryev. Moscow, 1978.

According to the Highest Criteria. *Sovetskaya Kultura,* January 24, 1978.

Nobody Can Live without Music. *Sovetskaya Panorama.* Vestnik APN, May 11, 1978.

Music Is Composed by the Heart. . . . *Smena*, 1978, no. 11.

## Books by Aram Khachaturyan

Khachaturyan, Aram Ilych. *Articles and Memoirs*, ed. I. E. Popov. Moscow, 1980.
Khachaturyan, Aram Ilych, *Collected Articles*, ed. G. Geodakyan. Erevan, 1972.
Khachaturyan, Aram Ilych, *Collected Articles*, ed. S. Rybakova. Moscow, 1975.
Khachaturyan, Aram Ilych. *On Music, Musicians and Myself*, ed. M. Ter-Simonyan & Y. Khachikyan. Erevan, 1980.

## Letters of Aram Khachaturyan (Listed by Recipient)

Adjemyan, G. V., Personal file, Erevan
Agbalyan, G.Y., The Charents Museum of Literature and Art of the Armenian SSR (MLA), Erevan
Altunyan, T. T., Personal file, Erevan
Arutunyan, A. G., Personal file, Erevan
Balasanyan, S. A., Personal File, Moscow
Bely, P. S., Personal file, Sochi
Bely, P. S., Personal file, Moscow
Bogdanov-Berezovsky, V. V., The Leningrad State Institute of the Theater, Music and Cinema (LSITMC)
Bondarenko, F. P., CSALA
Demirchyan, K. S., Personal file, Erevan
Derzhavin, K. N., The Saltykov-Shchedrin State Public Library (SPL), Leningrad
Enesco, G., Enesco archive, Bucharest
Fadeyev, A. A., MLA Atabekyan, personal file, Erevan
Gayamov, A. Y., CSALA
Gayamova, Z. A., CSALA
German, P. D., CSALA
Gevorkyan, Y. A., Personal file, Erevan
Gliere, R. M., CSALA
Gulakyan, A. K., MLA ArmSSR, Erevan
Kabalevsky, D. B., Personal file, Moscow
Karaev, K. A., Personal file, Baku
Kevorkovs, Family file, Erevan
The Kirov Opera and Ballet Theater, Leningrad, LSALA
Mendelson-Prokofyeva, M. A., CSALA
Menshikov, V. Y., CSALA

Mikoyan, A. I., CSALA
Mirzoyan, E. M., Personal file, Erevan
Myaskovsky. N. Y., CSALA
Oganesyan, E. S., Personal file, Erevan
Oistrakh, D. F., SCMMC
Orlov, G. N., The Leningrad State Archives on Literature and Art (LSALA)
Ovanesyan (Kimik), G. S., Personal file, Erevan
Pasternak, B. L., MLA Atabekyan's personal file, Erevan
Prokofiev, S. S., CSALA
Radin, E. M., LSALA
Repertory Board of the State Center of Sound Recording, CSALA
Saradjev, K. S., MLA ArmSSR, Erevan
Saryan, L. M., Personal file, Erevan
Shaporin, Y. A., CSALA
Shastin, N. P., LSALA
Shostakovich, D. D., CSALA
Svasyan, D. A., Personal file, Erevan
Tsyganov, N.A., LSALA Vinokur, L. I., The Glinka State Central Museum of Musical Culture (SCMMC), Moscow
Yesayan, Kh.A., MLA ArmSSR, Erevan
Zolotarev, V. A., SCMMC

## Books by Other Authors

Anisimov, N., *My Recollections About the First Production of the Ballet Gayane*. N. Anisimov, personal file, Leningrad.
*The Armenian Opera and Ballet Theater*. Moscow, 1939.
Asafiev, B., *Armenian Sketches*, ed. G. Tigranov. Moscow, 1958.
Asafiev, B., *Selected Works*, Vol. 5. Moscow, 1957.
Bek-Nazarov, A., *Memoirs of an Actor and Film Director*. Moscow, 1965.
Bitov, A., Armenian Lessons. In: *Seven Journeys*. Leningrad, 1976.
Chebotaryan, G., *Polyphony in A. Khachaturyan's Work*. Erevan, 1969.
Conference of Soviet Musicians in the Central Committee of the All-Union Communist Party, 1948. Shorthand record, Moscow, 1948.
Emin, G., *Seven Songs about Armenia*. Erevan, 1979.
Enesco, G., *Memoirs and Biographical Materials*. Moscow, 1966.
Entelis, L., *Silhouettes of Twentieth Century Composers*. Leningrad, 1975.
*Essays about Soviet Music*. Moscow & Leningrad, 1947.
Etkind, M., *Natan Altman*. Moscow, 1971.
Fayer, Y., *About Myself, Music and Ballet*. Literary version, ed. F. Roziner. Moscow, 1970.
The First Congress of Soviet Composers, 1948. Shorthand record, Moscow, 1948.

*Gauk, Alexander Vasilyevich. Memoirs. Selected Articles. Recollections of Contempo-*
*raries,* ed. L. Gauk, R. Glezer, & Y. Milshtein. Moscow, 1975.
*Gliere, R. M. Articles. Recollections. Materials,* ed. D. Person & V. Bogdanov-
Berezovsky. Moscow & Leningrad, 1965.
*Gliere, R. M. Articles and Recollections,* ed. V. Kiselev. Moscow, 1975.
Gnessin, M., *An Elementary Course in Practical Composition.* Moscow & Lenin-
grad, 1941.
*Gnessin, M. F. Articles, Recollections, Materials,* ed. R. Glezer. Moscow, 1961.
Grigoryev, V., *Leonid Kogan.* Moscow, 1975.
Ikonnikov, A., *N. Y. Myaskovsky.* Moscow, 1966.
Izrailevsky, B., *Music in the Productions of the Moscow Art Theater.* Moscow, 1965.
*History of Music of the Soviet Peoples,* Vol. 2. Moscow, 1970.
*History of Music of the Soviet Peoples,* Vol. 4. Moscow, 1973.
Hubov, G., *Aram Khachaturyan.* Moscow, 1962.
Kalantar, K., *Amo Bek-Nazarov: The Art of Film Directing.* Erevan, 1973.
Kamensky, A., *Etudes on the Artists of Armenia.* Erevan,, 1979.
Kharadjanayan, R., *The Piano Pieces of Aram Khachaturyan.* Erevan, 1973.
*Khachaturov, Suren. Articles. Recollections. Letters. Documents,* ed. A. Arutunyan.
Erevan, 1969.
Kushnarev, H., *Problems of History and Theory of Armenian Monodic Music,* Mos-
cow, 1958.
Kuznetsov, E., *Pirosmani.* Moscow, 1975.
Lenin, V. I., *Collected Works,* 5th edition, Vol. 29. Moscow, 1963.
Lopukhov, F., *Sixty Years in Ballet. Recollections and Notes of a Ballet-Master.*
Moscow & Leningrad, 1966.
*Marx and Engels on Art,* Vol. 1. Moscow, 1957.
*In Memory of I. I. Sollertinsky. Memoirs, Materials, Studies,* ed. Mikheyeva. Len-
ingrad & Moscow, 1974.
*Music of the Transcaucasian Republics,* ed. G. Ordjonikidze. Tbilisi, 1975.
Musical Life in Foreign Countries. 1944–1945. Bulletin of the All-Union
Society for Cultural Relations with Foreign Countries. Moscow, 1945.
*Myaskovsky, N. Y. Articles. Letters. Recollections,* ed. S. Slifshtein. Vols. 1, 2.
Moscow, 1959.
Nestyev, I. *The Life of Sergei Prokofiev.* Moscow, 1973.
*Oborin, L. N. Articles. Memoirs. 75th Birthday Anniversary,* ed. M. Sokolov. Mos-
kow, 1977.
*Oistrakh, D. F. Memoirs. Articles. Interviews. Letters,* ed. V. Grigoryev. Moscow,
1978.
Organizational Committee of the USSR Union of Composers. *Collected Ma-*
*terials,* No. 3-4, Moscow, 1943; Nos. 7-8, Moscow, 1945.
*Prokofiev, S. S. Materials. Documents. Recollections,* ed. S. Slifshtein. 2nd rev.
edition. Moscow, 1961.
*Prokofiev, S. S. and Myaskovsky, N. Y. Correspondence.* Preface by D. Kabalevsky,
ed. M. Kozlova & N. Yatsenko. Moscow, 1977.

Resolution of the Central Committee of the All-Union Communist Party "About the Opera Great Friendship" by V. Muradeli. Moscow, 1948.

Resolution of the Central Committee of the Communist Party of the Soviet Union. New Assessment of Muradeli's Operas *Great Friendship, Bogdan Khmelnitsky,* and *From the Bottom of the Heart.* Moscow, 1958.

Romm, M., *Talking about Cinema.* Moscow, 1964.

Rukhyan, M., *Armenian Symphony.* Erevan, 1980.

*Saradjev, K. S. Articles. Recollections,* ed. G. Tigranov. Moscow, 1962.

*Sayat-Nova in Briusov's Translations.* Erevan, 1963.

Schneerson, G., *Aram Khachaturyan.* Moscow, 1958.

Shaginyan, M., *Armenian Literature and Arts.* Erevan, 1961.

*Skrebkov, S. S. Articles and Memoirs,* ed. D. Arutiunov. Moscow, 1979.

Sollertinsky, I., *Selected Articles about Music.* Leningrad & Moscow, 1946.

Tchaikovsky, P., *Articles and Notes.* Moscow, 1898.

Tigranov, G., *Spendiarov.* Erevan, 1953.

Tigranov, G., *Khachaturyan's Ballets.* Leningrad, 1974.

Tigranov, G., *Aram Ilych Khachaturyan. His Life and Work.* Leningrad, 1978.

Tigranov, I., *Lyrical Portraits in Khachaturyan's Work.* Erevan, 1973.

Yakobson, L., Letters to Noverre, or *Spartacus's* Stage History: Criticizing the Critics. Manuscript. CSALA.

Yuzefovich, V., *David Oistrakh. Conversations with Igor Oistrakh.* Moscow, 1978.

## Articles, Reviews, Other Materials

A. I. Khachaturyan. Obituary. *Pravda,* May 4, 1978.

Ambartsumyan, V., Letter to the Author, January 10, 1979, Erevan. Personal file.

Anisimova, N., *Gayane* (The ballet-master of the ballet's new production in the Leningrad Kirov Theater talks about her work). *Za Sovetskoe Izkusstvo* (Leningrad), February 22, 1945.

Anisimova, N., Our Creative Conception. *Kommunist* (Erevan), July 26, 1947.

Aram Khachaturyan and Aaron Copland. A Historical Meeting. *America,* (March, 1969), no. 149.

Aram Khachaturyan, A Guest of Tbilisi. *Zaria Vostoka* (Tbilisi), December 11, 1973.

Aramyan, R., With Our Country in the Heart. *Kommunist* (Erevan), May 6, 1978.

Arutunyan, A., Our Great Contemporary. Erevan (in Armenian), June 6, 1963.

Asafiev, B., Through the Past to the Future. *Sovetskaya Muzyka,* Collected Articles, Ser. 1. Moscow, 1943.

Asafiev, B. (Igor Glebov), Soviet Music: Ways of Development. In: *Essays about Soviet Music,* Moscow & Leningrad, 1947.

Atabekyan, M., Mastership. *Kommunist* (Erevan), October 14, 1954.

Atayan, R., Letter to the Author. January 23, 1979, Erevan. Personal file.

Author of the Ballets *Spartacus* and *Gayane*. *Kurortnaya Gazeta* (Yalta), April 17, 1960.

Bandrowska-Turska, E., Letter to the Author of September 25, 1978. Personal file.

Bek-Nazarov, A., My Work on the Film *Pepo*. Kino, October 4, 1934.

Berko, M., A Piano Concerto by Aram Khachaturyan. Notes to a radio program. CSAOR ArmSSR, Erevan.

Bogdanov-Berezovsky, V., A Heroic Ballet. *Izvestiya*, January 5, 1957.

Bondarchuk, S., A Bard of Harmony. In: *Aram Ilych Khachaturyan. Collected Articles*, ed. S. Rybakova. Moscow, 1975.

Discussing R. Shchedrin's Poetoria. *Sovetskaya Muzyka*, 1969, no. 11

Discussion about Soviet Symphonic Music. February 4–6, 1935. Moscow, *Sovetskaya Muzyka*, 1935, no. 5.

Discussion about the Production of *Spartacus* at the Repertory Board of the Bolshoi Theater, March 7, 1958. Shorthand record. CSALA.

Dobrynina, E., For the Fourth Time in Moscow. *Sovetskaya Muzyka*, 1977, no. 2.

Fourth Festival of Soviet Music in Moscow. *Sovetskaya Muzyka*, 1941, no. 2.

Geodakyan, G. Komitas, In: *Music of the Transcaucasian Republics*, ed. G. Ordjonikidze. Tbilisi, 1975.

Giatsintova, S., Music Is the Actor's Friend. *Sovetskaya Muzyka*, 1966, no. 7.

Ginzburg, L., Profound Ideas. *Sovetskaya Muzyka*, 1976, no. 8.

Gliere R., All-Union Review of Talents. *Sovetskoe Iskusstvo*, December 2, 1938.

Gnessin, M., My Meetings with Armenian Musicians. Manuscript. MLA ArmSSR, Erevan.

Gnessin, M., & Gnessin, E., Notes to the Association of Transcaucasian Students in Moscow. CSAOR ArmSSR, Erevan, April 6, 1926.

Goleizovsky, K., The Artist's Style. *Teatr*, 1968, no. 7.

Gorky, M., *Travels in the USSR*. Collected Works in 30 vol., vol. 17, Moscow, 1952.

Haikin, B., About an Artist. *Muzykalnaya Zhizn*, 1973, no. 10.

Hubov, G., Aram Khachaturyan. *Sovetskaya Muzyka*, 1939, nos. 9–10.

The Informbureau's Combat Task. Publication by S. Krasilnikov. *Voprosy Literatury*, 1980, no. 5.

Kabalevsky, D., A Composer's Impressions. *Muzyka*, 1937, no. 30.

Kabalevsky, D., Yemelyan Pugachov and *Gayane*. *Sovetskaya Muzyka*, Collected Articles. Moscow, 1943, Ser. 1.

Kabalevsky, D., The Composer's Artistic Individuality. *Sovetskaya Muzyka*, 1955, no. 8.

Kabalevsky, D., Letter to A. I. Khachaturyan of June 6, 1973, Moscow. D. B. Kabalevsky's personal file, Moscow.

Kabalevsky, D., Thrice Rich: A short suite on the themes of Khachaturyan's music. *Sovetskaya Muzyka*, 1973, no. 6.

Kabalevsky, D., A Wonderful Friendship. Preface to the book: *S. S. Prokofiev and N. Y. Myaskovsky. Correspondence*, ed. M. Kozlova & N. Yatsenko. Moscow, 1977.

Kaputikyan, S., Let the World Hear. *Kommunist* (Erevan), November 27, 1960.

Karaev, K., A Truly Internationalist Artist. In: *Aram Ilych Khachaturyan. Collected Articles*. Moscow, 1975.

Katz, S., When I Was a Gnessin Student. *Sovetskaya Muzyka*, 1977, no. 8.

Khanbekyan, A., Khachaturyan's Great Work: Its Sources. In: *Problems of Musical Science*, Ser. 1. Moscow, 1972.

Kharadjanayan, R. A Paean to the Radiant and the Good. *Golos Rigi*, June 6, 1973.

Kogan, L., Evergreen Talent. *Vechernaya Moskva*, June 5, 1963.

Konen, V., The Contemporary Scene as History. *Sovetskaya Muzyka*, 1957, no. 5.

Konchalovskaya, N., The Road to Immortality. *Literaturnaya Gazeta*, April 17, 1968.

Korev, Y., Meeting Khachaturyan's Hero. *Sovetskaya Muzyka*, 1961, no. 10.

Korev, Y., The Great Mission of Music. *Sovetskaya Muzyka*, 1979, no. 9.

Legg, V., Recollections of David Oistrakh. Manuscript. Personal file.

Levina, A., A Tribute to a Friend. *Sovetskaya Muzyka*, 1973, no. 11.

Liepa, M., A Few Words about an Artist. *Muzykalnaya Zhizn*, 1973, no. 10.

Liepa, M., Yesterday and Today in Ballet. *Druzhba Narodov*, 1980, no. 12.

Lukin, Y., & Hubov, G., *Spartacus:* Khachaturyan's Ballet in the Leningrad Kirov Opera and Ballet Theater. *Pravda*, February 17, 1957.

Lvov-Anokhin, B., Maris Liepa. *Theatr*, 1970, no. 6.

Makarevich, I., Five Continents Listen to His Music. *Sovetskaya Panorama, Vestnik APN*, 1978, March 10.

Makarov, A., My Spartacus. *Sovetskaya Muzyka*, 1968, no. 11.

Makarova, N., Letter to Z. A. Gayamova, 1942 (no date), Sverdlovsk. CSALA.

Makarova, N., A Man and a Composer. (Recollections of N. Y. Myaskovsky.) Manuscript. CSALA.

Mar, N. Six Hours. *Sovetskaya Muzyka*, 1963, no. 6.

Materials to the production of Khachaturyan's ballet *Happiness (Gayane)* in the Leningrad Kirov Opera and Ballet Theater. LSALA.

Mazmanyan, M., Letter to the Author of September 19, 1980, Erevan. Personal file.

Medvedev, A., Music of Joy. *Komsomolskaya Pravda*, February 4, 1960.

Melik-Avakyan, G., A Generous Soul. *Kommunist* (Erevan), May 4, 1978.

Menon, N., A Lighthouse Beacon. *Sovetskaya Muzyka*, 1973, no. 6.

Meyer, K., Khachaturyan the Composer. *Ruch Muzychny* (Warsaw), 1978, no. 23.

Meyer, K., Khachaturyan the Man. *Ruch Muzychny* (Warsaw), 1978, no. 23.

Moiseyev, I., A Heroic Theme: Materials for the booklet *Spartacus* in the Bolshoi Theater, 1958. Manuscript. CSALA.

Moscow Conservatory entrance examinations report, 1929/1930. CSALA.

Moscow's Farewell to Khachaturyan. *Kommunist* (Erevan), May 6, 1978.

Myaskovsky, N., Character reference of the Moscow Conservatory postgraduates, 1935. Manuscript. CSALA.

Neuhaus, H., A New Piano Concerto. *Sovetskoe Iskusstvo*, December 29, 1936.

New Materials about Komitas. Publication by R. Atayan & M. Muradyan. *Sovetskaya Muzyka*, 1959, no. 10.

Oganesyan, E., Love of Life. *Sovetskaya Muzyka*, 1963, no. 6.

Oganesyan, E., Letter to the Author of May 26, 1981, Erevan. Personal file.

Oistrakh, D., Notes of a Musician. *Sovetskaya Muzyka*, 1954, no. 9.

Oistrakh, D., Heart-Warming Music. *Vechernaya Moskva*, April 23, 1959.

Oistrakh, D., About an Artist. *Muzykalnaya Zhizn*, 1973, no. 10.

Ordjonikidze, G., Certain Characteristics of the National Style in Music. In: *Muzykalny Sovremennik*, Ser. 1. Moscow, 1973.

Plenary Session of the Organizational Committee of the USSR Union of Composers, March-April 1944. Shorthand record. CSALA.

Prokofiev, S., Speech on the All-Union Radio. December 5, 1940. CSALA.

Prokofiev, S., Letter to A. I. Khachaturyan of May 9, 1943, Alma-Ata. CSALA.

Report of the Moscow Conservatory Qualification Commission, 1933/1934 Academic Year.

Reports of the Moscow Conservatory Chair of Composition, CSALA.

Reports of the Moscow Conservatory Professors for 1930/1931 Academic Year. CSALA.

Reports of the Sessions of the Chair of Composition of the Gnessin School of Music. CSALA.

Rolland, R., To Have a Clear Notion: Rolland's Letters to S. Bertolini Garieri-Gonzaga. *Inostrannaya Literatury*, 1963, no. 3.

Saryan, M., Music Lovers Speak. *Sovetskaya Muzyka*, 1961, no. 5.

Saryan, M., Thoughts about Music. *Kommunist* (Erevan), May 17, 1963.

Saryan, M., With Love and Interest. *Kommunist* (Erevan), June 6, 1973.

Shakhnazarova, N., Artist of the World. *Sovetskaya Muzyka*, 1963, no. 6.

Shakhnazarova, N., Aram Khachaturyan. In: *Music of the Transcaucasian Republics*. Tbilisi, 1975.

Shchedrin, R., A Musical Feast. *Sovetskaya Kultura*, April 29, 1962.

Shaporin, Y., Poem to Stalin. A. Khachaturyan. Manuscript (1938). CSALA.

Shaporin, Y., Khachaturyan's Application for Professor of Composition. Rough draft, June 22, 1951. CSALA.

Shaporin, Y., Concert Given by A. Khachaturyan. *Sovetskaya Muzyka*, 1953, no. 12.

Shaporin, Y., Speech at the 8th Plenary Session of the Union of Composers, 1955. Manuscript. CSALA.

Shorthand record of the discussion of the *Spartacus* production at the Repertory Board of the Bolshoi Theater on March 7, 1958. CSALA.

Shorthand record of the Session of the Musical Section of the USSR Committee on State Prizes, March 16, 1944. CSALA.

Simonov, K., Today and Long Ago. *Literature Obozrenie*, 1974, no. 8.

Shostakovich, D., About L. Yakobson. Manuscript. LSALA.

Shostakovich, D., Notes of a Composer. *Sovetskoe Iskusstvo*, December 2, 1938.

Shostakovich, D., An Original Artist. *Sovetskoe Iskusstvo*, June 10, 1953.

Shostakovich, D., Khachaturyan's Ballet *Spartacus. Sovetskaya Kultura*, August 20, 1955.

Shostakovich, D., Problems of Musical Creativity. Composer's notes. *Pravda*, June 17, 1956.

Shostakovich, D., Review of the Festival of Armenian literature and Art in Moscow, 1957. Manuscript. CSALA.

Shostakovich, D., A Brilliant Talent. *Sovetskaya Muzyka*, 1959, no. 6.

Shostakovich, D., True to National Character. *Kommunist* (Erevan), June 6, 1963.

Shostakovich, D., Radiant Art. *Sovetskaya Muzyka*, 1973, no. 6.

Shostakovich, D., Great Talent. *Kommunist* (Erevan), June 6, 1973.

Sixtieth Anniversary of A. I. Khachaturyan. Congratulations from Dmitri Shostakovich, David Oistrakh, Lev Oborin, Yuri Zavadsky, Vaclav Dobias, George Enesco, Alfred Mendelson, Samuel Barber, Raymond Laucheur, Renato Guttuso, Herbert von Karajan. *Sovetskaya Muzyka*, 1963, no. 6.

Tariverdiev, M., A. I. Khachaturyan's 60th Birthday. *Komsomolskaya Pravda*, June 6, 1963.

Tsitsikyan, A., Letter to the Author of March 28, 1981, Erevan. Personal file.

Ulanova, G., Spartacus. *Izvestiya*, April 10, 1968.

Vecheslova, T., Leonid Yakobson. Manuscript. LSALA.

Vieru, A., Foreign Musicians Speaking. . . . In: *Aram Ilych Khachaturyan, Collected Articles*, ed. S. Rybakova. Moscow, 1975.

Vinogradov, O., The Lyricism of the Heroic Dance. *Pravda*, April 14, 1968.

Vlasov, V., Khachaturyan's New Rhapsody. *Izvestiya*, November 10, 1962.

Volkov, N., A Tragedy about Spartacus. In: *Spartacus*. State Academic Bolshoi Theater booklet publ., Moscow, 1958.

lsky, V., On the Death of A. Khachaturyan. *Sovetskaya Muzyka*, 1978, no. 8.

Is New with the Muses? *Nedelia*, April 28, 1968.

ustovsky, B., Personal Style Plus Civic Spirit. *Sovetskaya Muzyka*, 1970, no. 10.

Yuzefovich, V., What Deep Feelings for His Native Land! *Sovetskaya Muzyka*, 1978, no. 7.

Yuzovsky, Y., Author and Actor. *Voprosy Literatury*, 1960, no. 8.

Zavadsky, Y., I Think We'll Be Working Together Again. In: *Aram Ilych Khachaturyan. Collected Articles*, ed. S. Rybakova. Moscow, 1975.

## Author's Conversations about Aram Khachaturyan

Anisimova, N. A.
Arutunyan, A. G.
Blanter, M. I.
Chalaev, Sh. R.
Kabalevsky, D. B.
Litinsky, H. I.
Mansuryan, T. E.
Musinyan, N. N.
Oganesyan, E. S.
Pikaizen, V. A.
Riauzov, S. N.
Sazandaryan, T. T.
Shafran, D. B.
Shelest, A. N.
Terian, M. N.
Vazgen, Cathlicos of Armenia

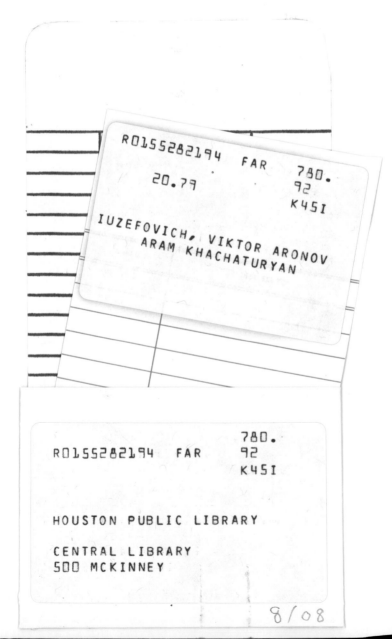

8/08